PRESIDENTIAL LEVERAGE

STUDIES IN THE MODERN PRESIDENCY

A series edited by Shirley Anne Warshaw

Studies in the Modern Presidency is an innovative book series that brings together established and emerging voices in modern presidential research, from the Nixon administration to the present. While works on the modern Congress abound, this series seeks to expand the literature available on the presidency and the executive branch.

Scholars and journalists alike are increasingly writing and reporting on issues such as presidential rhetoric, executive–legislative relations, executive privilege, signing statements, and so on. We are committed to publishing outstanding research and analysis that reaches beyond conventional approaches to provide scholars, students, and the general public with insightful investigations into presidential politics and power.

This series features short and incisive books that chart new territory, offer a range of perspectives, and frame the intellectual debate on the modern presidency.

A list of the books in this series can be found online at
http://www.sup.org/modernpresidency

PRESIDENTIAL LEVERAGE

PRESIDENTS, APPROVAL, AND THE AMERICAN STATE

Daniel E. Ponder

STANFORD UNIVERSITY PRESS

Stanford, California

Stanford University Press
Stanford, California

Printed in the United States of America on acid-free,
archival-quality paper

Library of Congress Cataloging-in-Publication Data

Names: Ponder, Daniel E., author.
Title: Presidential leverage : presidents, approval, and the American
state / Daniel E. Ponder.
Description: Stanford, California : Stanford University Press, 2018. |
Series: Studies in the modern presidency | Includes bibliographical
references and index.
Identifiers: LCCN 2017032093 (print) |
LCCN 2017035282 (ebook) | ISBN 9781503604070 (e-book) |
ISBN 9781503602830 (cloth : alk. paper) |
ISBN 9781503604063 (pbk. : alk. paper)
Subjects: LCSH: Presidents—United States. | Executive power—
United States. | Presidents—United States—Public opinion. | United
States—Politics and government—Public opinion. | Public opinion—
Political aspects—United States.
Classification: LCC JK516 (ebook) | LCC JK516 .P595 2017 (print) |
DDC 352.23/50973—dc23
LC record available at https://lccn.loc.gov/2017032093

Cover design: Preston Thomas

Typeset by Thompson Type in 10/15 Sabon

For Crystal, Shaylyn, Patrick, Noelle, and Elijah,
who make everything worth it.

Contents

Figures and Tables

Figures

Tables

Acknowledgments and Debts

THE ORIGINS OF THIS PROJECT ARE ROOTED in procrastination. In the fall of 1995, I hastily wrote up a proposal for the American Political Science Association conference and mailed it off barely in time to meet the deadline. That paper was an effort to understand how contextualizing presidential approval in the separation of powers might affect presidential action. I had meant it to be a conference paper and perhaps an article or two. Little did I know that the seeds of that proposal, written under pressure of meeting a deadline, would consume much of my working thoughts for the next two decades.

Fast forward a number of years, to January 2007, when I gave a paper at Jimmy Carter's 30th Inaugural Anniversary in Athens, Georgia. The paper was a longish attempt to place Carter in the context of other presidents, and it included a fair bit of presidential leverage. Over dinner one night during the conference, Erwin Hargrove suggested I should expand the idea into a book. I had recently moved from Colorado back to my hometown in Missouri and had begun teaching at a liberal arts college. Thus, by necessity, teaching became my focus for a few years. I had written a few conference papers and published a piece in an edited volume, and I thought I might be winding down on leverage. But by then, thanks to Erwin's suggestion, the idea began to turn over in my head, and soon a couple of articles no longer seemed adequate to say what I wanted to say. Still, time was not on my side, and another half decade passed.

When the opportunity for a sabbatical presented itself in the fall semester of 2012, I decided to focus exclusively on the project. My sabbatical proposal outlined a plan to do some more data collection and writing and try to turn these ideas that were more or less constantly percolating in my head into a book. What followed were opportunities for a little work here and there in subsequent semesters and relatively intense research summers.

The project began when I was a member of the faculty at the University of Colorado at Colorado Springs, where I spent thirteen years working with a smart and supportive group of scholars. In particular, Josh Dunn, David Moon, and Jim Null all provided valuable counsel. Jim, acting as director of the Center for Government and the Individual, provided early research funds and an opportunity to present preliminary findings. Scott Adler invited me to present very early results in the American Politics Colloquium at the University of Colorado at Boulder.

Since moving back to the Show-Me State to teach at Drury University and give our children the opportunity to get to know their grandparents, I have the great benefit of working at a liberal arts college that prioritizes teaching but also values research. Elizabeth Paddock and Jeff VanDenBerg have been exemplary chairs of the Department of Political Science and International Affairs, and they were instrumental in supporting and encouraging my research in a variety of ways. Dan Livesay managed to read parts of the manuscript with the keen eye of a historian. He has since moved on to California, so I am especially grateful that he took the time to read and comment on a couple of chapters before he left. Special thanks go to Peter Browning, Professor of Religion at Drury. Peter and I had our offices in the same building and commiserated on many a summer day about being "stuck" in the office working on our respective research projects. His encouragement and support was an enduring source of strength.

Karen Hult, Paul Quirk, and Chuck Walcott all provided much needed encouragement and insight at a very crucial point in this project's history. Several other friends and colleagues, many who are members of the Presidency and Executive Politics section of APSA, a collegial and stimulating community of scholars, contributed directly to my thinking through their comments and conversations. In particular, I have benefitted from comments and conversations with Julia Azari, Jon Bond, Lara Brown, Jeff Cohen, Mary Lenn Dixon, George Edwards, Matthew Eshbaugh-Soha, Victoria Farrar-Meyers, Charles Franklin, Daniel Franklin, Jim Giglio, Lori Cox Han, Erwin Hargrove, Diane Heith, Karen Hult, Dave Lewis, Mark Petracca, Paul Quirk, Russ Renka, Brandon Rottinghaus, Chuck Walcott, and the late, great Pat Fett. For methodological advice, I thank

Nathan Kelly, David Leblang, and especially George Krause. Justin Leinaweaver helped get the graphs in shape. Thanks to Matt Eshbaugh-Soha, Donna Hoffman, Alison Howard, Andy Rudalevige, Jose Villalobos, and Adam Warber, all of whom shared some of their data with me.

Several students helped collect some of the data used in this book. At UCCS, thanks go to Davin Montgomery, and at Drury my appreciation to students Lexi Brewer, Jordan Butcher, Max Byers, Kate Elam, Michael Means, Keely O'Sullivan, and especially Tyler Habiger. Thanks are due to the many students at UCCS and Drury who took my course on the American presidency over the years and allowed me to work through some of these ideas in class, many of whom provided interesting and useful comments and questions. Thanks to our departmental student worker Arieanna Bates, who saved me an enormous amount of time by helping put the final manuscript together, and to Debbie Goosey, who helped format the final product.

Shirley Anne Warshaw, who invited me to submit a proposal for inclusion in the Studies in the Modern Presidency series, is a quintessential editor. Her keen eye and insightful comments led me to sharpen and clarify the book at every turn. She championed the project for several years and waited patiently for the manuscript and its rewrites. Needless to say, I am in her debt. Thanks as well to the two anonymous reviewers for their excellent, thoughtful, and supportive critiques. I also thank Micah Siegel of Stanford University Press for her guidance and patient responses to my many questions as the manuscript moved toward publication, as well as Margaret Pinette, who made my writing readable. I am grateful to Dave Luljak for his skill in indexing. As the project evolved, I have had the good fortune to try out various parts of the argument in print, and I would like to acknowledge the book and journal editors who allowed me to publish early thoughts and results of the project as they emerged. These include "Presidential Leverage and the Politics of Policy Formulation" *Presidential Studies Quarterly* (June 2012), pages 300–323; "Presidents, Leverage, and Significant Public Policy." In *The Presidential Dilemma: Between the Constitution and Political Party*, edited by Lara Brown, Julia Azari, and Zim Nwokora. Albany: SUNY Press, 2012; "Leadership in a Fractured State: The Presidency and the Quest for Autonomy." *International*

Journal of Public Administration, 28 (2005): 531–546; and "Presidential Leverage and the Presidential Agenda." In *In the Public Domain: The Challenges of the Public Presidency*, edited by Lori Cox Han and Diane Heith. Albany: SUNY Press, 2012, pages 89–112.

Three scholars had a profound influence on this project. First, Andy Rudalevige generously shared his centralization data with me, read and reread several drafts of various chapters, and provided encouragement and prompted me to be ever bolder in the claims I make in this book. *Presidential Leverage* would literally not have been possible without his good cheer and friendship. He has even refused to gloat when I had to pay gambling debts of ballpark food when my Cardinals failed to defeat his Red Sox in the World Series, or when the Chiefs fell short trying to beat his Patriots in the AFC playoffs. I consider anything he writes to be a must-read, and I am fortunate to have had his input and support as I worked and reworked the manuscript.

Anyone who knows Ray Tatalovich can attest to his work ethic, his insight, and his capacity for tough criticism wrapped in warmth and pa-tronage. He read and reread the manuscript several times, and the manu-script is a better, clearer reflection of what I wanted to say as a result of thinking through and addressing his detailed critiques. I had the great privilege of doing research with Ray on another project, and all I can say is that if I had his work ethic, this book would have been done before it was started! He has my enduring admiration and appreciation.

Doug Lemke has been my closest friend in academia since our gradu-ate school days at Vanderbilt, and we have been in touch several times per week for more than a quarter century afterward. More than anyone, he has had to listen (well, read via e-mail) my trials and tribulations. He has been an adviser and encourager-in-chief over the entirety of this project, and he has read almost as many drafts as I have written. I owe him an immeasurable debt of gratitude, from giving advice on theory and method, to just listening to me lament the setbacks and celebrate the victories that accompany the long production of any piece of scholarship. He is an exemplar of the word *friend*, and I hope I can begin to pay the debt, though I know it will never be paid in full.

All I have mentioned above have contributed to the production of this book. Whatever merit there may be in the final product, the book is certainly better for their comments and suggestions. All remaining errors of omission and commission are my burden alone.

My mother Loretta Ponder has been a rock in my life, a constant supply of love and support and love. Ed, my father, would have loved to see this book in print. Not a day goes by that I don't think about him and wish he were still here. My in-laws Janice and Dennis Kurtz and Bert Ovitt have helped cheerlead this book to completion. And finally, my greatest debt is to my wife and children, who for years had to hear me talk about "finishing the book" and did so with good humor and grace. It is a joy to sit around the dinner table with these five unique and wonderful people and know that I am only the sixth smartest person at the table. My brilliant and beautiful wife Crystal displayed enormous patience while sharing her house with innumerable scraps of paper and incessant e-mails to myself with ideas to run down, and who put up with my sometimes distracted attention. She is an incredibly deep thinker, and I can only wistfully admire the connections and observations she makes as we strive to make sense of this life we navigate together. A couple of years ago, she bought me a banjo as a "carrot" to get the book done, urging me to learn to play once that day would come. Now that it's here, I fear she will come to regret that choice, but she has my heart and interminable love. Our children have grown up around this project and have provided much needed perspective as to what is important about living life. Shaylyn is tenacious and curious in seeking her path. Patrick, like the young George Bailey in *It's a Wonderful Life*, was "born older" and is wise and talented beyond his years. Someday I hope to see the world in the same way that philosophical Noelle does. And Elijah is a constant stream of insight, thought, and wit, and he shares Crystal's and my interest in politics, a common topic of conversation as we drive to school together. Did they contribute anything else to the completion of this book? Not really. In fact, if it had not been for date nights, long conversations, little league and high school baseball, Drury basketball, family getaways to Springfield Cardinals and St. Louis Cardinals baseball games, judging high school debate tournaments, fulfilling the duties as chauffeur to all manner of events, birthday parties, and sleepovers, attending competitive cheer competitions, orchestra concerts, band concerts, choir concerts, school plays, family vacations, trips to the gym, and on and on, this book would have been done *long* ago. So I can only thank God that I failed to finish it even one second sooner than I did.

PRESIDENTIAL LEVERAGE

CHAPTER 1

Introduction

Locating Presidents In the American Political System

BARACK OBAMA'S PRESIDENCY was one like few others in American political history. His presidential approval ratings were stubbornly mediocre despite the historic nature of his election and the considerable domestic and, to a lesser extent, foreign policy legacy he left. Rarely did his approval rise above 50 percent, and, with some exceptions on both the low and high end of the scale, it was generally in the mid-40 percent range throughout his presidency. But, despite this, his was an active and largely successful presidency. Most notably, he signed the Affordable Care Act in March 2010, even as his approval ratings stagnated at 50 percent at the time of the celebrated or castigated legislation, depending on the side of the political fence observers occupied. But although his approval ratings were barely average, public assessment of trust in government was nearing an all-time low. Presidential approval is arguably the most cited statistic in American politics. Presidents with high approval ratings are likely to be deemed powerful, particularly by the media, whereas presidents with low or middling opinion are seen as weak or ineffective. But presidential approval ratings are only part of the story. Obama's approval ratings, such as they were, far exceeded those of competing institutions such as Congress that would otherwise oppose his signature policy. In short, President Obama had leverage.

Webster's New World Dictionary defines leverage as "increased means of accomplishing some purpose" (1982: 812), and another source defines it as the "power to get things done," such as exerting power over people with an advantage that is not openly referred to (Microsoft Encarta 2002). This "advantage" comes with having something no one else has and reflects what is meant by presidential leverage in this book. Presidential approval considered in isolation is misleading as a matter of presidential "power" or influence. In this context, Elmer Cornwell's insight that "the leverage the President has acquired in the lawmaking process has been indirect, based on the arts of persuasion, and ultimately grounded in the popular support he can claim or mobilize" (Cornwell 1965, cited in Heith 2000: 380) is particularly appropriate to the analysis presented here.

To understand when presidents derive leverage from their standing with the public, estimates of presidential approval need to be contextualized relative to the public's judgment of the government as a whole. Understanding presidential leverage is to think of the relationship between the president and the public in terms of specific support (presidential approval) nested in diffuse regime support (public trust in government), to borrow David Easton's terminology. To be sure, high or low approval ratings are indicators of presidential standing with the public, but they cannot be quarantined from the public view of the government as a whole. Why would a president with high approval have any greater leverage with the public if that same public holds the rest of government in similarly high esteem? The public, presidential scholars, and presidents themselves can better understand how a president is situated in the American mind at any particular time by attending to the president's public standing (for example, via presidential approval). But, for it to be meaningful, that reading must be referenced in the context of public assessment of government in general. This relationship measures when presidents have something that others do not. In this book I empirically operationalize this as the ratio of presidential approval to trust in government, which generates an index revealing the degree of a president's public leverage.

Consider the experience of President Bill Clinton, which illustrates the various components of presidential leverage. Barely a year into his presidency, Clinton had no way of knowing that worse times would come—1994 was bad enough. Storm clouds gathered over his presidency late in 1993 when health care reform, his would-be signature policy priority, withered and died in agonizing fashion. Adding insult to a deeply injured president, Clinton suffered the humiliation of enduring the very public defections of forty-seven congressional Democrats on high-profile legislation such as the 1993 Omnibus Budget Reconciliation Act. Only the tie-breaking vote cast by Vice President Al Gore rescued the bill from defeat when forty-one Democrats in the House and six in the Senate rejected the president's position and voted with the Republicans. To top it off, the Democratic president had considerable trouble moving the Democratic Congress (particularly the House of Representatives) to pass a crime bill that included a ban on certain assault weapons. Though Democrats controlled 261 seats, the final bill passed with just 235 votes. No fewer than sixty-four Democrats abandoned the president by voting against the bill; indeed, it would have died outright but for forty-six Republicans who crossed the aisle to cast "yea" votes.[1]

Clinton's perceived ineffectiveness and low approval ratings, which had free-fallen fifteen percentage points in a year, contributed to his having to endure further public humiliation when many congressional Democrats running for reelection asked him *not* to campaign for them even as they clawed and scratched to keep their seats.[2] For those members of Congress (MCs), it seemed an appearance by the unpopular president would drag down their reelection prospects. Sure enough, the year culminated in a near-historic beat down for the president and his party. While Clinton's approval declined steadily in 1994, public confidence in the presidency declined 5 percent from 1993 levels, whereas confidence in Congress (never high to begin with) actually *increased* in 1994 and 1995. Against this backdrop, Democrats lost their majority in both chambers when fifty-four House members and ten senators went down in defeat. The loss of the House was particularly difficult to rationalize, as that chamber had not seen a Republican in the speaker's chair since Dwight D. Eisenhower lived in the White House.

After the election, Republicans, led by brilliant and bombastic Newt Gingrich (R-GA), dominated national politics. Clinton's presidency was at low ebb when, barely three months later, he was asked by a reporter if he thought his voice would be heard above the din of the new Republican majority. Clinton's answer was telling: "The president is relevant. The Constitution gives me relevance" (Harris 2005: 178).[3] It seemed that the president was, at least for a while, alone and adrift in the sea of the American state. Clinton weakly clung to the presidency's formal powers, most notably the veto. Clinton wrote in his memoir that he looked for ways to negotiate and compromise with Republicans but that he would freely wield the veto pen when he disagreed (Clinton 2004).[4] In the aftermath of 1994, his was a presidency in peril.

Soon, though, a convergence of tragedy and partisan politics reversed the president's fortunes. As it turned out, the day after Clinton was compelled to assert his "relevance," the nation was rocked by the horrific bombing of the Alfred P. Murrah Federal Building in Oklahoma City. Clinton's legendary political skills were on full blast when he took to national television and reassured a stunned, scared, and grieving nation. The inevitable rally effect reinvigorated his lagging approval ratings, and he hovered in the mid- to upper 40s and lower 50s for the remainder of the year. Add into the mix two government shutdowns at the end of 1995 that the public largely blamed on the Republicans,[5] and the president's political resurrection escalated to full throttle.

Like all presidents, Clinton could fall back on and employ constitutionally and statutorily derived institutional leverage such as the veto. What he lacked, though, was publicly generated political leverage, and many in his party abandoned him. Not only was he able to reclaim public leverage in 1995 and 1996, but the public's verdict conditioned his resurgence. Where *trust in government* was down steadily in 1995 and 1996, Clinton's stock grew both *personally and institutionally* when his approval ratings and public confidence in the office of the presidency increased. In short, Clinton had little leverage in 1994 and early 1995, but it increased dramatically in the latter part of that year and into the crucial reelection year following. Thus, in the larger context of American politics, President Clinton's leverage increased beyond what he could derive from the Constitution. Barely a year after his "still relevant" plea, his approval was a healthy 56 percent, and by the end of the year Clinton waltzed to reelection. The president's party gained seats in the House and lost only two in the Senate. Two years later, in the 1998 midterms, with the president under threat of impeachment, Republicans failed to capitalize and for only the second time in the twentieth century, the president's congressional copartisans did not lose any seats at all. And, in a stunning turn of events, Clinton's nemesis Newt Gingrich was widely blamed for the failure and was effectively drummed out of the speakership. Soon after, he resigned from the House altogether.

Throughout, President Clinton and Congress moved within the parameters of the American state. The actions of the framers some two centuries earlier were made concrete by the public via the ballot box, the maneuverings of Congress as the president's coequal branch, and the threat of constitutional leverage such as the veto. Clinton himself had little autonomy. His meager public opinion coupled with temporarily increased public trust in government made Clinton, however briefly, just another player in American politics. Or so it seemed. A president is almost never "just another player," nor is he ever really a "bit player." The pall of persistently dismal public attitudes toward Congress fed an overall decline in trust in government. At the same time, increasing presidential approval strengthened Clinton even when the system in which he operated was, by design, fractured (Ponder 2005a). The president regained his foothold via "presidential leverage," a measure of how presidents are situated in terms of popular approval and public trust in government. This leverage, more varied than the sources of influence derived from the Constitution and statute, places individual presidents in context of public judgment of the government they inhabit.

PRESIDENTS AND PRESIDENTIAL LEVERAGE

The Obama and Clinton examples illustrate the forces that presidents deal with, though not all are as varied as their experiences. Emphasizing the interplay between public and constitutional leverage animates the aspects of presidential action analyzed in this book. The main point developed across several different contexts is that presidents can gauge their place in the system as a form of political capital and either use it or push back against it, depending on the context. Whereas public activity often plays out as high-profile showdown politics that animates the political world of Washington, D.C., public presidential leverage acts as a sort of window that opens or closes, making certain kinds of activity more attractive at some times than others. The evidence presented in this book extends further than examining the impact of presidential approval measured in isolation. Although the analysis does not discard approval as an important concept, this book locates presidential approval ratings in the *context* of the overall trust the American public places in the federal government as a whole. The key insight derived from the analysis is that leverage is not a matter of merely including approval in an index of presidential leverage (IPL) but rather that *leverage is a new and more accurate way to measure a president's public political capital*. Presidential action moves in both public and institutional/statutory dimensions with public leverage conditioned on a variety of factors. Quite often, leverage in one dimension (for example, public) is related to leverage in another (such as constitutional) dimension. But it is the *public* context of presidential leverage that drives the analysis of this book.

So what is the nature of that context? I elaborate in Chapter 3, but here suffice it to note that the American state poses great obstacles and presents even greater opportunities for strategic presidents. Presidents occupy a unique place in the political system because, although the office they occupy is decidedly *not* the state, they are certainly part of the state and for many in the public they *are the face* of the state. As two presidential scholars put it, "The president is both the embodiment of the national government and the country's leading political figure . . . The architects of the Constitution created the need for such a figure" (Landy and Milkis 2014, 95).[6] In a 1978 interview with Bill Moyers, President Jimmy Carter observed that "as President, you are the personification of problems, and when you address a problem even successfully you become identified with it" (Carter 1982: 109).[7]

Where once it may have been an exaggeration to argue that the public sees the president as the embodiment of the state, expectations for presidential leadership began to form a complex web of opportunities and constraints that presidents have to bear more so than any other single player in American politics. The New Deal in the 1930s and the expansion of national responsibilities, growth in government, formulation of a legislative agenda, passage of policies that made presidents responsible for the economy,[8] and increasing public expectations of both government and the presidency weakened virtually any other interpretation. To be sure, high-profile congressional leaders such as the speaker of the House share responsibility for the direction, successes, and failures of politics and policy. But presidents are normally burdened by expectations, and, as Carter's observation suggests, they feel the pressures acutely and need other sources of leverage than "merely" constitutional or statutory from which to draw power or the appearance thereof and thus not to appear weak or ineffectual.

The fractured American state erects formidable barriers to action by political leaders. The high profile of the presidency makes decisive action even more difficult for presidents because public expectations focus largely on them. The separation of powers, which is the lynchpin of the American state, means that presidents have an opportunity to govern (Cronin and Genovese 2013). To govern or to set the terms of the debate requires bargaining position; in other words, leverage. The American state provides presidents with sources of leverage, constitutional and extraconstitutional, formal and informal, to get traction in American political life.

For the purposes of this book, then, *presidential leverage is operationalized as a president's popular approval nested within public trust in government as a whole.* This construction draws on Easton's distinction between specific and diffuse support. Specific support refers to support for an individual politician or government official, whereas diffuse support focuses on the political system as one (Easton 1965; 1975). The degree of presidential leverage confers or denies further legitimacy beyond the more formal sources of leverage presidents have at their disposal. But informally, like electoral margin or seats controlled by a president's co-partisans in Congress, presidential leverage is a measure of a president's political capital. Further, it is a measure of power and authority in the political system—when a president whose leverage with the public is high has a strong measure of authority with which to act. Sometimes, this publicly derived political capital affects other dimensions of political capital as leverage relates to a president's use of formal command authority and agenda setting, both of which are sources of leverage themselves. The question then is, how do informal and formal sources of presidential leverage interact? An underlying thesis of this book is that understanding the presidency's place in the political system and what those who occupy the office do with and in that place expands our understanding of the presidency writ large.

Public presidential leverage is part of the president's store of political capital, adding to power derived from constitutional and extraconstitutional sources of leverage. To put public leverage in context, these other bases of a president's overarching leverage are briefly explored and could be used in future research to examine possible effects of these contexts on presidential leverage, as well as how leverage may have an impact on the shape of those environments.

Constitutional

The American system and the politics it produces are breeding grounds for the use of both formal and informal sources of leverage to employ when trying to gain strategic, institutional, and political advantage. Indeed, as one Brookings Institution report put it, we "live in an age of leverage . . . There is no one way that leverage is always used to get things accomplished. But in the early 21st century new patterns have emerged for individuals, organizations, and countries to exert power, and leverage frequently plays a critical role in how power is used" (Anderson 2010: 1). Presidents are most likely to rely on a variety of leverage points in their quest for power and policy as they labor in a political system that has turned institutional advantage on its head. Here it is sufficient to note that a sort of "institutional inversion" has occurred wherein the constitutional system of congressional dominance has given way, publicly, in some instances legally via Supreme Court rulings, and statutorily, to one of *presidential dominance*, or at least public expectation of such dominance. All of this constitutional inversion has occurred with precious few words actually changed in the Constitution.

Thus, presidents must rely on the Constitution when they can, but it gives them only limited guidance on a day-to-day basis. The veto is clearly a source of constitutional leverage explicitly given to the president in Article I, Section 7, and is the most visible source of leverage for presidents. By threatening to use the veto, and then actually using it, presidents keep members of Congress (MCs), congressional parties, interest groups, and the public aware of the power of the presidency. The veto has evolved into a virtually unilateral power; of all the vetoes issued in American history and subject to override, approximately 94 percent have been sustained. The two-thirds requirement in each congressional chamber necessary for override has proven to be a daunting hurdle to overcome and allows presidents to wield great power. This percentage is even higher when we consider the policy implications of congressional shifts to avoid a veto in response to a veto threat (Cameron 2000). Still, a veto can be overridden and sometimes is, so presidents must consider their options carefully. Indeed, sometimes MCs will accept a veto even if they can override it because they calculate that they have the political upper hand and can win in the court of public opinion (Gilmour 1995).

Although the veto is the most visible form of constitutional leverage, there are other sources as well. For example, Article I, Section 7, of the Constitution requires that laws pass in identical form in both houses of Congress, allowing for leverage to be exerted over bargaining situations between the chambers, particularly in periods of split-chamber partisan control. Other sources of formal leverage, such as the plethora of unilateral powers that presidents derive from the "executive power" clause in Article II, including executive orders, proclamations, and directives, as well as the ability to negotiate executive agreements that bypass the treaty process, afford presidents considerable advantages but only from a policy perspective. Neustadt wrote that a president who has to resort to unilateral, or "command," powers has failed (Neustadt 1960). But other scholars see command authority as simply another opportunity for presidents to gain traction in the fractured state, which in turn provides capacity for asserting presidential autonomy (Howell 2003; Ponder 2005a).

Multiple access points in American politics clog the system given the myriad veto points available to competing institutions and public groups, creating a "structure-induced" lack of presidential autonomy. But presidents, acting as the face of the American state, can use this problem to their advantage, along with other built-in by-products of institutional structure, such as the collective action problem in Congress (Lewis and Moe 2010) along with public expectations to set the agenda and the prospect for large policies to pass. Many of the same access points that make

Congress a representative institution can hamper it when it tries to take action, and bifurcated chambers with myriad actors and personalities beholden to different constituencies create obstacles to achieving policy objectives. Although there has been a partial resurgence of congressional power in the postreform era of the mid- to late 1970s, the general pattern of institutional relations has been one of presidential "imperialism" (Rudalevige 2005; Schlesinger 1973; Sundquist 1981). Constitutional leverage, enhanced and clarified by Congress and the Supreme Court and expanded by the president's executive role as given in Article II, provides many resources for presidents. But that is often not enough. Presidents can go solo to good effect, but they need other signals and sources of power to legitimize what they have done. Public presidential leverage can signal when a president needs to build capacity, assert autonomy, or push large, ambitious policy agendas.

Extra-Constitutional Sources of Leverage

Presidents can also look to other avenues for leverage when the Constitution is not enough. The president as the face of the state can use the media to his or her advantage (Lim 2014; Cohen 2010). Indeed, the media may play a critical role in shaping a president's public leverage. The manner in which presidents use or are used by the media, how they frame an issue, the degree to which the media affect public perception of the president and/or the political system can all have an impact on approval, trust, or both and therefore affect a president's leverage. Positive coverage of foreign travel, domestic events, and others that show presidents as strong all help in terms of building robust approval, which likely increases his or her leverage. "Bad" news may affect the president's prestige, but mostly if that news comes from president's copartisans. Indeed, it can also strengthen or weaken trust in government, presidential approval, and all manner of evaluations of government officials. The changing perception of the media's role can contribute to how presidents and government are evaluated. For example, although members of the press have stated that they knew about John F. Kennedy's extramarital affairs, they did not report this issue because they did not see it as part of their job description. But by the time the country became mired in

Vietnam, particularly the Tet offensive in late January 1968 and then the slow unveiling of the Watergate scandal just four years later, the role of the media had changed. Outlets began to report the good, the bad, and the ugly of political life, and, as will be demonstrated in Chapter 4, the public's trust in government plummeted to a level from which it has not yet recovered.

Political opponents can use the media to efficiently cast aspersions on presidents, albeit with limited success. Opposition members of Congress, for example, may criticize the president and have that criticism covered in the media but not affect the president because such talk is expected from his or her opponents (Groeling 2010). Still, in a hypercompetitive media environment, the success with which presidents can reach citizens has declined. For example, the rise of cable television and targeted media has decreased the president's share of the television market, reaching fewer and fewer viewers (Baum and Kernell 1999). Yet, more recently, presidents have adjusted to that increasingly competitive context and moved toward a more narrowly focused audience, less worried about trying to move public opinion at the national level and building coalitions by adjusting their tone and tenor of public appeals at the local level (Cohen 2010). This raises or lowers their prestige, depending on the success of their efforts, and thus can affect presidential leverage. Although I do not explicitly incorporate the media component into the measure, the media context is present at virtually every stage, and further incorporation or measurement could be a focus for future research, a topic I return to in the final chapter.

A president's ability to negotiate the obstacle course of the American political system and, when possible, use powers of persuasion to convince fellow stakeholders of the rightness of his or her preferred course of action can leverage advantages in bargaining situations (Neustadt 1960; Dickinson 1997). Presidents can also use the policy process to advantage copartisans in Congress. For example, there is a burgeoning literature on presidential use of the pork barrel to strategically target funds for both policy (Berry, Burden, and Howell 2010) and electoral gain (Hudak 2014; Kriner and Reeves 2015). All of these can be used to supplement constitutional leverage and even to help form public leverage.

Public Presidential Leverage: Approval in Context

Presidential approval itself has been seen to be a source of leverage, though the literature surveyed later disputes its ability to move others in the political system toward presidential objectives. Presidential leverage is a source of power, not in a constitutional sense but as a source of *authority*. High leverage is a source of power that enables presidents to withstand political storms and move policy in the face of opposing political winds. Moreover, when presidents are weaker, they engage in strategies or activities that might shore up their public leverage.[9] The "popular support (a president) can claim or mobilize" (Cornwell 1965) must include more than leaning on the percentage of the public that approves of a president. For scholars to understand the real support presidents claim, it should be grounded in context of the rest of government. Although presidents may be the face of the American state, they coexist in an intricate web of institutions that compete for power and legitimacy.[10] When presidents and their approval by the public rise above those of competing institutions, they can more appropriately and forcefully lay claim to real popular support and can thus move and shape American politics. So, before proceeding, it is important to dig a little deeper and develop an idea of what public leverage is and how it offers insight to analyzing the American political system by understanding its place in our political system.

PRESIDENTIAL LEVERAGE AS POLITICAL CAPITAL

Thus far, this book has described presidential leverage and differentiated it from formal and informal sources of power. Here, I want to spell out what presidential leverage *is*, and doing so is best accomplished by an analogy. Presidential leverage as it is used in this book is akin to financial capital. An investor who is well financed has the flexibility to take risks when necessary, remain aloof when needed, and sometimes control the nature of the transaction. So at one level, when the IPL increases or decreases, the index itself measures and marks a president's public capital in a way that presidential approval does not and cannot. Because it contextualizes presidents relative to the government writ large, it measures the ratio of how well presidents are doing (however defined as measured by approval) relative to how highly the government they inhabit is trusted by the public. The higher the value of the index, the more "financial" (read: presidential) capital they have and can spend or hoard as the case may be. The greater their store of capital, the more they can use it to leverage themselves in pursuit of their political and policy goals. This store of capital presidents have affects how well they can translate that capital into leverage.

There are other resources that presidents can pull from, apart from the trappings of constitutional and legally defined sources of command, and comprise informal political capital that they can leverage to maximize their chances of achieving their goals. In his discussion of the presidential agenda, Paul Light writes that "the President's political capital rests on several external sources: party support in Congress, public approval, electoral margin, (and) patronage" (Light 1999: 15). Presidential copartisans in Congress, for example, or perceived "mandates" from the electorate are resources that, like financial capital in a business deal, are used to exploit and signal an intention to use it. The day after his reelection in 2004, George W. Bush famously declared, "I earned capital in the campaign—political capital—and now I intend to spend it" (Chen 2004).

Although the academic jury on the tangible effects of approval is still out, it is certainly true that popular presidents operate from a position of perceived strength, even though whether they actually do have increased strength is still widely debated. Whereas presidents often take the high road and claim they eschew public approval in favor of doing the "right thing," it is equally true that they invest in intricate and highly sophisticated polling organizations in the White House (Heith 2004). It is not a stretch to think that presidents would, on balance, prefer to be popular than unpopular. And, although we still do not know the full extent of when or how approval helps presidents (for example, success in Congress), it is likely the case that low and sinking approval makes life difficult for them.

Still, there is much variation in approval. Bill Clinton, for example, was popular even as he was being impeached and tried in the Senate. His overall approval in the Gallup poll was 67 percent as his Senate trial began on January 7, 1999, and was actually one point higher in February when he was acquitted. It never crept lower than 53 percent, where it stood in May 1999, and he rode out the last year of his presidency averaging in the upper 50s to lower 60s. On the other hand, Barack Obama was able to get things accomplished, such as Wall Street reform via Dodd-Frank and the Affordable Care Act, with approval ratings that usually measured at or below 50 percent. So the effects of approval are variable. But leverage as *approval in context* makes approval and its relative weight to trust in government stand out.

Thus, higher presidential leverage means more capital—the president "stands apart" in the same way that a financier might have more resources than her or his competitors and be able to influence the outcome or set the terms of debate. Presidential public leverage is a recognition that presidents exist in a separation of powers, *in* the state, as well as acting *as* the state. Approval is not measured merely in raw terms but in response to events, actions, and outcomes. It is doubtless true that trust may rise and fall with approval. But that correlation, although robust, is far from perfect.[11] Interestingly and perhaps counterintuitively, presidents after the Watergate era are not beleaguered but find themselves in an advantaged position largely because public trust in government is usually low. So like raw presidential support in the electorate, seats in Congress, and so forth, presidential leverage is capital that presidents can use to move their agenda. As demonstrated later, when presidents lack leverage, they can take action to increase or recover their political positions by increasing the politicization of the executive office of the president (EOP), centralizing policy making in the White House, proposing more on the public stage of the State of the Union address, and issuing more executive orders.

Yet another convenient way to think of presidential leverage is as a signal from the American public as to how well-situated the president is in the relation to competing institutions. Recall the formulation that presidential leverage is specific support for a president nested within diffuse system support. There is a crucial difference between signals derived from presidential leverage and more specific policy-related signals. Polling organizations and private polling in the White House measure public opinion on a variety of topics, seeking to understand how the public responds to proposed policy issues and possible strategies. Presidents respond by incorporating public sentiment into their policy agendas, modifying their proposals, and, on occasion, deleting proposed policies from their program.[12] The nature of the democratic process and political accountability dictate that presidents will not ignore these signals, though they may not always follow them to the letter. Presidents can on occasion manufacture movement in the priorities of the public through prolonged and systematic attention given to issue areas in high-profile settings, such as the State of the Union address.[13] Presidents can deal in whatever way they feel appropriate to these specific targeted opinions.

On the other hand, presidential leverage is a systemic signal. Because the IPL is the ratio of approval to trust, the usual issues of identifying the ingredients of approval apply. But that does no damage to the concept. At the end of the day, presidents are likely to interpret their approval as high or low. They may place great stock in shifts in approval, such as what caused approval go up or down, especially in the short term. So the signal is a general indication of strength (high leverage) or weakness (low leverage) from which presidents may respond by taking action, pursuing legislative or unilateral strategies, centralizing or decentralizing policy making, and the like.

Each of these signals has its strengths and weaknesses. Presidential leverage does not focus on a particular policy or strategy but rather provides a strong indication of when presidents are strong, weak, or middling in the political system. On the other hand, policy-specific signals are good for providing direct guidance for presidents who may wish to tailor their policy agendas to maximize political advantage.[14] Additionally, the public may hold short- or long-term consistent beliefs, but if they are not strongly held priorities, presidents can be taken down a wrong path. For example, the public may hold consistent and even well-formed views on Policy X, but Policy X may not be high on the public's list of priorities.

Having high approval ratings is a presidential aspiration, and presidents actively pursue them (though there is considerable variation as to what they do, if anything, once they have them) (Eisinger 2003; Heith 2004). It is not clear whether presidents can influence change in public opinion (Edwards 2003); where research shows they can, the issues and conditions are relatively narrow, such as on issues that have high salience and are highly technical (Canes-Wrone 2006). The president has even less ability to control public attitudes of trust in institutions of government.

Congress, for example, has consistently low public ratings (Hibbing and Theiss-Morse 1995) and trust varies with time (Hetherington 2005), mapping well with the state of the economy over which presidents exert relatively little direct influence (Stimson 2004).

Presidential leverage suggests that whether or not presidents can systematically affect their approval ratings in the short term, any assessment of presidential strength or preeminence should be balanced by a signal from the public. That is, presidential leverage is a relative measure of support; high approval in times of high trust affords the president no significant leverage over and above that of competing institutions. Similarly, a president may have relatively low approval, but, if trust is even lower, a president is in a more favorable strategic situation than might be expected by looking at approval ratings in isolation. Presidents who enjoy high degrees of presidential leverage may be emboldened to pursue ambitious policy. And when leverage is weak, they may battle from a position of retrenchment and rely more heavily on unilateral sources of presidential power, such as executive orders.

Presidents can use leverage strategically so as to maximize their power potential, thereby gaining a degree of autonomy in the American system. What does increased presidential leverage yield? At one level, presidential leverage can be conceived of as having a familial resemblance to Skowronek's "warrant" for power, by which he means a kind of license or authority to put political power into action that is contingent on the political time in which presidents serve (Skowronek 1993: chapters 2 and 3). Presidential leverage provides a degree of autonomy and is reflected in the systematic measurement of this position, identifying when a president truly does "stand preeminent" in American politics. However, unlike in Skowronek, who argues that presidential leadership opportunities follow more-or-less predictable patterns in the life cycles of "regimes," presidential leverage does not reject the notion of cyclical opportunism, nor does it depend on it. But drawing on the insight of "preeminence," the theory holds that such an advantage for a president obtains when leverage is high.[15]

Presidential leverage, broadly conceived, derives from and builds on these insights into presidential authority. The leverage a president has, which is largely outside his or her ability to control, adds a sense of autonomy and is not antagonistic to "warrants" or "leeway" but is part of a cumulative process that helps explain presidential action where presidents can assert leverage over the course of American politics and public policy. As such, the IPL is more than a tweak or even a correction on approval; more than that, it allows scholars to take a step outside the president to evaluate presidential choices and actions given the conditions found by the IPL.

DISTINGUISHING PRESIDENTS AND THE PRESIDENCY

Because much of this book locates presidential support in context of trust in the system, it is worth considering briefly if the public conceptualizes presidents as individuals and the presidency as an institution in the same way. One way to think about presidents generally is to trace the relationships between microlevel attitudes toward individual presidents and macrolevel systemic attitudes toward the presidency. Does the public see the presidency as an office and the individual president in the same way?

Figure 1.1 tracks the degree to which the public distinguishes between the presidency as an institution and the individual president. Notably, and perhaps surprisingly, the president is almost always held in greater esteem than the institution of the presidency. Although presidential approval and public *confidence* in the presidency generally track together, the fact that less than 23 percent of the variation between these variables is explained by their correlation ($r = 0.48$, $p = 0.001$, two-tailed test, $R^2 = 0.23$), and the remaining 77 percent is explained by other factors suggests that the public views the individual and the institution as distinct (see also Ponder 2005b). Indeed, if the institution and the individual were identical or nearly identical in the public mind, the correlation between the two series would likely be much higher. To be sure, confidence and approval track more closely after 2001, when President Bush was the face of the nation both domestically and in the world. Although the overarching correlation is reasonably strong, the two series are more loosely coupled through the early 1990s when President George H. W. Bush took the nation to war in Iraq. This relationship lends credence to the notion that,

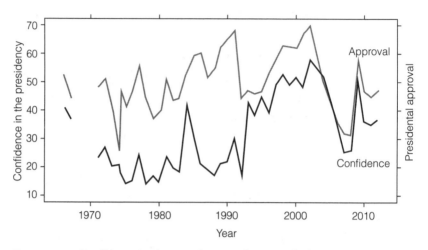

FIGURE 1.1. Confidence in the presidency and approval of presidents, 1966–2012. Breaks in White House confidence occur because no polls were taken in the years 1968, 1969, and 1970. Presidential approval is generated using WCALC (Stimson n.d.), and confidence in the White House is from Ragsdale (2014, Table 513, 332–333), as well as various polls to fill in the years from 1985 to 1990, collected by Opinion Piece and reported in Ponder 2005b.

although similar, the public distinguishes between the presidency and the institution, though less so since the dawn of the twenty-first century.

PLAN OF THE BOOK

The book proceeds as follows. Chapter 2 surveys how and why presidents pay such close attention to their approval ratings, why the inferences made about the strength of presidential approval are the source of much scholarly conflict, and how the signal conveyed by presidential leverage is superior to examining approval in isolation. Chapter 3 takes a step back to survey the broad terrain presidents must navigate. An overview of the American state, broadly conceived and characterized by the separation of powers, is provided. The presidency has been the victim or beneficiary (depending on one's perspective) of an institutional inversion. Presidents have become the face of the American state, and they have done so largely because the process of institutional inversion has flipped constitutional ordering of power on its head. Expectations accompanying the expansion of national responsibilities provide the glue that holds this inversion

TABLE I.I
Summary of theoretical predictions of the index of presidential leverage.

	Presidential action	As the index of presidential leverage (IPL) increases . . .
Macropolitical environment	Legacy policies	Increases
	Unilateral presidential action	Decreases
	Agenda size	Decreases
Micropolitical environment	Centralization of policy making in the White House/EOP	Decreases
	Politicizing the executive office of the president	Indeterminate

in place, relegating Congress to second fiddle, albeit a very powerful and often hostile second fiddle.

Chapter 4 begins the empirical part of the book and lays out the measurement of the index of presidential leverage (IPL) as well as macro- and micropatterns of presidencies from John F. Kennedy to Barack Obama. Chapters 5 and 6 test the IPL against a variety of dependent variables measuring various aspects of presidential activity in both macro- and micropolitical environments. Table 1.1 summarizes the predictions of the theoretical framework on various dimensions of each. Chapter 5 considers the macropolitical context and examines presidential success on legacy issues, such as major legislation that originated with the president, unilateral decision making via executive orders, and agenda size. The theoretical argument developed in that chapter predicts that presidents with high leverage will be more successful in securing large, important policy issues that help define their legacies. In that sense, a positive relationship between IPL and legacy issues is driven by strongly leveraged presidents. However, on issues such as unilateral action and agenda size, the theory predicts that these actions are driven by weaker, low-leveraged presidents. This should not be interpreted to mean that stronger presidents do not use unilateral action, nor that they pursue small legislative agendas, but rather that most of the variation is defensive in nature, with weak presidents resorting more to unilateral action and trying to appease constituencies by advocating for more expansive policy agendas. Again, this does not suggest that strong presidents do not have opportunity and incentive to use unilateral action or to mollify political constituencies but rather that most of the variation in those dimensions is driven by weaker presidents.

Chapter 6 tests hypotheses related to capacity (the growth of the EOP) and autonomy (centralization of policy making in the White House). Not unlike the dynamics tested in Chapter 5, the theory predicts that weaker presidents will be more likely to drive variation in the dependent variables. Weaker presidents centralize policy making in the White House so as to protect the integrity of the proposals and control the definition of their issues. The theoretical argument suggests that, although strong presidents will centralize from time to time, weaker presidents are much more likely to do so. Weaker presidents often find themselves in defensive postures as to the nature and direction of their policies, and thus they are more likely to centralize so as to protect the perceived integrity of their policy. The chapter also examines politicization of the presidential branch by measuring the size of the political staff in the executive office of the president (EOP). For reasons explicated there, the theory is indeterminate on the direction of the relationship. In the end, it is observed that there is a negative relationship, again suggesting that weaker presidents are more likely to add political staff but that the results are sensitive to model specification.

Chapter 7 concludes with some ideas for further theorizing about the relationship of presidential leverage to the political system. One suggestion is that prospect theory, a decision theory developed in psychology, can help explain why low-leveraged presidents will engage in more activity (as I have measured them here) than when presidents have higher, more stable leverage. I also provide an updated graph that traces the IPL through the end of President Obama's second term.

CHAPTER 2

Presidents, Approval, and Trust
Toward a Concept of Presidential Leverage

THE CONNECTION BETWEEN PRESIDENTS and the public goes back
nearly two hundred years, when Andrew Jackson pioneered a "new" understanding of the relationship. Where his six predecessors saw their role
as representing the government (and thus the interests of the country as
a whole), Jackson famously claimed to speak for the people. He took his
cue from the "message" of the electorate, especially in his second term
when he interpreted his reelection as a "mandate" to carry on his fight
against the national bank (see Ellis 2012, 90–91). Jackson derived legitimacy from the public and its intent that he should govern as expressed
through the ballot box, and he asserted that the presidency was a policy-
making institution in its own right rather than a mere executor of the
Congress's will (Milkis and Nelson 2016: 134–135). But it was Abraham
Lincoln who, nearly seven decades before the systematic measurement of
public opinion became possible during Franklin D. Roosevelt's second
term, observed, "With (public sentiment), nothing can fail. Without it,
nothing can succeed" (Zarefsky 1994: 128). Lincoln, building on Jackson's assertion, moved toward a deeper understanding of the ties binding
the public and the presidency.[1]

The influence of Lincoln's ghost notwithstanding, there is widespread
disagreement among presidency scholars as to how true Lincoln's observation is. The record shows that presidents view their prospects for success
in a variety of arenas to be directly related to their standing in the polls
(Brace and Hinckley 1992). Whether they actually derive success from
public opinion, or even do anything with it, presidents seem to *believe*
that public approbation is key to policy and political success and pay close
attention to their approval ratings and change in public opinion on their
policy priorities.[2] They see approval, for whatever reason, as part of their
legacy or how they stand at any one time with the public.

It is clear that presidents do track how they are doing with the public and seem to see public opinion as a resource. For example, John F. Kennedy was "an avid consumer of public opinion polls" and speculated that his approval would dip below 50 percent in wake of his civil rights fights in 1963, though in the end his ratings did not fall below 60 percent (Sorenson 1965: 333). H. R. Haldeman relates how Richard Nixon called him at Camp David early one morning in August 1969, "concerned about Harris poll, shows huge drop" (Haldeman 1994: 79). In his own memoir, commenting on his "silent majority" speech reaffirming the U.S. commitment in Vietnam, Nixon wrote that "Gallup telephone poll taken right after the speech showed 77% approval" (Nixon 1978: 410). He also recorded a low point in the Watergate saga. "We must face facts - - - analysis of trends from 38% in August 1973 to 32% and rise in Harris (poll) for resignation" (Nixon 1978: 928).

Gerald Ford was acutely aware of his own peculiar political position as the only person to serve as vice president and president having been elected to neither, and so he paid particularly close attention to his public position. A month after taking office, he pardoned Nixon for crimes committed in the Watergate scandal. Not surprisingly, his approval suffered. "My standing in the Gallup poll plummeted from a favorable rating of 71% all the way to 49" (Ford 1979: 176). Ford's experience also illustrates how watching approval wax and wane can take an emotional toll on presidents. Reflecting on the 1975 recession, Ford observed "86% of the respondents (in a Harris poll) expressed no confidence in my ability to turn the economy around. I felt pretty low about that" (Ford 1979: 221–222). Ford analyzed why his numbers varied so greatly. For example, he wondered why his Gallup poll rating leveled off at 47 percent despite his success on the economy and foreign policy (Ford 1979: 310). His tenuous grasp on the presidency led him to closely monitor the electoral horizon during the primaries, identifying what he called an "image versus substance" problem. In response he hired more political strategists and consultants and credited a public opinion–centered campaign strategy, which helped bring him to within one point of being reelected after trailing for most of the year to challenger Jimmy Carter (Ford 1979: 332–333, 338, 339, 396–399).

Even Jimmy Carter, one of the least "political" presidents, was well aware of how public opinion could affect his political standing.[3] He carried a copy of his pollster Pat Caddell's public opinion poll dealing with American attitudes toward a variety of issues relating to energy. The results of those polls directly influenced Carter's policy strategy (Carter 1982: 114ff).

Much of Ronald Reagan's, Bill Clinton's, and George H. W. Bush's administrations were poll driven. The Obama administration extended the innovative social media–based communication strategy that his campaign employed to good use in the 2008 election, but its effectiveness in the White House met with varied success (Heith 2012). Indeed, since modern public polling methodology was developed in the mid-1930s, presidents have engaged in elaborate use of private polls of public sentiment so as to gauge reaction to their policies, policy direction, and ultimately their own individual level of approval, albeit with great variation in what presidents do with that information and how successful they are (Eisinger 2003; Heith 2004).[4]

WHAT GOOD IS PRESIDENTIAL APPROVAL?
THE VIEW FROM POLITICAL SCIENCE

Presidents, their staffs, scholars, and pundits spend a lot of time studying presidential approval. Barrels of ink have been spilled trying to explain how and why approval changes, as well as what factors translate into approval. Not long ago, the Gallup Organization was nearly the only company that tracked public evaluation of presidents, and the Gallup approval rating remains the industry standard. Since then, many other companies and news outlets have begun to measure public opinion, with the result that presidential approval is increasingly ubiquitous. As media have become hypercompetitive in the age of the internet and social media, the frequency of polls has also exploded, affording anyone interested the opportunity to track presidential approval in a host of media and virtually in real time (Cohen 2008; 2009b). This has prompted organizations to poll the public more frequently than ever before. For example, Gallup moved from taking approximately ten to twelve observations per year to nearly one per day during the Obama administration.

It is worthwhile to recall that "average" approval is just that: an average. Much of the variance in approval is preset by partisanship.[5] Scholars have long observed that presidential approval is heavily conditioned by the partisan identification of the individual respondent making the evaluation. Respondents are increasingly polarized in their view of individual presidents, with partisanship being the primary culprit driving this divide. Democrats are more likely than ever to support a Democratic president, and the same is true of Republican identifiers' support of Republican presidents. Indeed, based on nearly every indicator available, the United States has become more polarized across the board.[6] The partisan gap in presidential approval between Democrats and Republicans, never lower than about 30 percent, widened substantially during the 1980s and 1990s and grew to more than 70 percent during much of George W. Bush's presidency. A month after Barack Obama was reelected, the difference between Democrat and Republican approval reached more than 80 percent (Gallup Poll 2017). But although party identification is a major factor in explaining aggregate approval ratings, presidential approval *does* vary, and much of that variation can be traced to changes in evaluations by political independents and the opposing party.[7]

Naturally, presidential approval plays an important role in determining how a president is perceived by the American public, but there is a limited window within which a president can act on any advantage he or she may glean from high approval. For example, presidents have difficulty influencing public opinion on their policy proposals, save for certain limited circumstances such as when policies are already popular and complex (Canes-Wrone 2006). The timing of policy proposals, speech making, and travel schedules is linked to presidential approval (Brace and Hinckley 1992). The conventional wisdom, played up in journalistic accounts and popular culture, is that popular presidents can virtually dictate the outcomes of policy disputes with Congress but that wisdom has been widely disputed in the literature.[8] Although presidents do try to use public approval, research shows that public approval has, *at best*, a mixed effect on areas of vital importance to presidents such as policy success in Congress.[9] In this vein and apropos of this book, Edwards argues that "public support gives a president, at best, *leverage*, but not control" (Edwards 1997).

Conceptually, it is not clear why popular presidents should necessarily derive policy advantage from their public standing. But there is reason to speculate that presidents will seek approval for a variety of reasons. For example, robust numbers may help with winning reelection in the first term or solidifying their legacy if lucky enough to get a second term. Still, given that Congress is comprised of 535 individuals with different parochial constituencies, it is not always clear why a national approval rating bears on individual decision makers. More to the point, why would a member of Congress (MC) who is affiliated with the Tea Party movement have cared whether President Obama had widespread national approval *if* the president was not popular in her constituency?[10] Regardless of the reason, presidential approval is sought by presidents, cited by pundits, and used for political advantage by opponents and critics alike.

CONTEXTUALIZING APPROVAL AS PRESIDENTIAL LEVERAGE

The presidency has been the clear beneficiary of a sort of extraconstitutional institutional inversion.[11] As the noted presidential scholar Elmer Cornwell wrote a half-century ago, "It has been the presidency, more than any other part of the system, that has enabled American democracy to succeed and flourish . . . And it has been the relationship between President and public that has given this office its power and importance" (Cornwell 1965).

But if the president is viewed in isolation, lacking a sense of embeddedness in a system of competing institutions, high or low presidential approval ratings measured in isolation convey only part of the story. If presidents are highly popular in a time when government itself is held in high esteem, trusted to do the "right thing," why should high approval lead to an increased likelihood of success? On the other hand, if they are popular at almost any level while at the same time government is discredited and trust in it is low, then they are the only, or best, game in town, and this can signal when presidents can legitimately use their standing to lay claim to political capital.

To clarify this relationship, consider the insights of David Easton. Easton's formulation of support into specific and diffuse can be used to simplify the concept of presidential leverage. In a series of articles and books that spanned decades, Easton developed a broad and influential basis for studying politics and developing empirical theory. Adapting a systems approach, Easton posited that among other inputs, specific and diffuse supports are vital to the long-term survival of a political regime (Easton 1965).[12]

Presidential Approval as Specific Support

Easton defined specific support as support for governmental leaders, presumably as a reaction to political outputs. Specific support focuses on individual leaders qua leaders and can best be conceptualized as an action-reaction chain. For example, a citizen evaluates a leader based on perceptions of outputs such as public policy or the state of the economy, or from behind a lens such as partisanship. This evaluation is followed by a reaction wherein support increases, decreases, or stays the same. Easton writes, "Specific support flows from the favorable attitudes and predisposition stimulated by outputs that are perceived by members [of the society] to meet their demands as they arise or in anticipation" (Easton 1965: 273). Clarifying the concept a decade later, Easton wrote that specific support is "closely related to what the political authorities do and how they do it" (Easton 1975: 437).

Holding partisanship constant, performance-based and contextual factors influence the degree of specific support, operationalized here as presidential approval. National tragedies and war generally increase the president's support from both parties, the so-called rally-around-the-flag phenomenon (Brody 1991). Other factors influence the level of support, such as economic conditions, policy orientations, peace and prosperity, and competence.[13] As long as presidents are perceived to deliver on their promises, approval can grow. This is a sentiment increasingly rare among opposition partisans in the time roughly coinciding with Clinton and growing through Bush 43 and Obama. A president's approval is derived from a sensitivity to the mass public (Quirk 2009). In turn, it may contribute to how presidents proceed. For example, various levels of approval may hint that the time is right to move on policy, maintain the status quo, or change governing strategies entirely, say from working through Congress or shifting to a more unilateral, administrative model of governance.

Generically, the public opinion component is one factor in political bargaining situations, and any advantage derived from "high" or "favorable" public opinion can be spun to his or her own advantage by any political actor, not just presidents. Congressional leaders acting on behalf of their party exploit moments of political leverage when the public context favors their position. For example, in January 2011, the Republican Congress and Democratic President Barack Obama were locked in a battle over raising the debt ceiling, which was set to expire later that year. Raising the debt ceiling is usually a routine matter, but during the Obama administration it became thoroughly politicized. House Majority Leader Eric Cantor (R-VA) invoked what he perceived as an advantage in the public mind (a newfound opposition to raising the debt ceiling) to go after dramatic spending cuts as a way to force the president to move toward their (the Republicans') position. In speaking to the House Republican caucus, he implored, "I'm asking you to look at a potential increase in the debt limit as a *leverage moment* when the White House and President will have to deal with us. . . . Either we stick together and demonstrate that we're a team that will fight for and stand by our principle, or we will lose that leverage" (Mann and Ornstein 2012: 11). Not only did Cantor take advantage of Congress's position as a coequal branch to apply pressure to the administration, but he explicitly referred to leverage born of public opinion.

On January 10, the day before Cantor made his plea to the Republican caucus, a poll showed 71 percent of Americans opposed raising the debt limit (Sullivan 2012). Cantor asked Republicans to exploit that leverage to go after spending cuts. If Obama did not acquiesce to deep cuts, the idea of leverage (in this case, congressional leverage) would put the president and his party on the defensive. Ultimately, everyone involved kicked the can down the road, and Republicans extracted a promise of greater spending cuts in the future; if those cuts did not materialize, "budget sequestration" would take place automatically on January 1, 2013. Thus, public leverage is not simply the province of any particular American institution. But presidents, as the most closely watched institutional actors, can use publicly generated leverage and the context of government in a sustained way. Thus, a president's approval rating can be thought of as tapping into and reflecting that degree of individual support.

Diffuse Support: Trust as Context

Whereas specific support is an input focused on individual political leaders, diffuse support is directed at the system itself. According to Easton, "This forms a reservoir of favorable attitudes for good will that helps members to accept or tolerate outputs to which they are opposed or the effect of which they see as damaging to their wants" (Easton 1965: 273). Expanding on the concept a decade later, he observed:

[Diffuse support] refers to evaluations of what an object is or represents . . . not what it does . . . Outputs and beneficial performance may rise and fall while this support, in the form of a generalized attachment, continues. The opposite is equally true. Where support is negative, it represents a reserve of ill-will that may not easily be reduced by outputs or performance. (Easton 1975: 444)

In this book, public trust is used as a measure of diffuse support. It is notable that, although Easton was writing generally, he was observing politics at a time of dramatic upheaval when trust in the American regime was at its lowest point. The country had just emerged defeated from the war in Vietnam and endured a constitutional crisis in the series of offenses collectively known as Watergate, which culminated in the only resignation of a sitting president. Consequently, trust in the system had just completed a decade-long freefall, and although it recovered some of that lost support, trust has never achieved the heights it occupied at the end of the 1950s and in the early 1960s.

Few scholars have done as much to explore the nexus between trust and government as Marc Hetherington. He cautions "political trust should not be confused with trust in a specific political figure. Political trust is a general evaluation of the entire federal government" (Hetherington 2005: 12). He also shows that trust is more than public attitudes toward government; it has real policy implications.[14] Although some argue that trust waxes and wanes with factors such as the economy and events (for example, Stimson 2004), others find trust remains persistently low, albeit subject to a fair amount of variation (Kamarck 2009; Keele 2007; Nye, Zelikow, and King 1997). Even if trust stays low, presidential leverage reflects the notion that presidents can find themselves at low or high points relative to that level of trust and therefore more accurately locate themselves in context of American politics and institutions. This conditions the types of policies and constituencies that can be targeted.[15] In addition, the separation of powers system presents challenges to the president more than to individual members of Congress. MCs respond to the moods of their constituencies, which is often more in line with their own policy preferences than the mass public is to the president's.[16]

Trust in institutions is the expression of public sentiment toward the state, particularly to the democratic state. Thus, trust is the nexus between state and society, akin to Easton's diffuse support. Even if low levels of trust persist, presidential leverage shows that presidents can find themselves at low or high points relative to that level of trust. Presidents are often caught up in this cycle as the decline in public support for presidents can be linked to an overarching lack of public trust in government (Hetherington and Globetti 2005).

As noted previously, presidents are, for many, the face of the American state. But they are not unmoored from other institutions that coexist and compete for power, including Congress, the courts, bureaucracy, and state governments. These institutions can be considered both as collections of progressively ambitious individual leaders and as unitary actors. The specific support they have in the form of presidential approval, generated by partisanship and policy output, is contextualized against diffuse support for the regime itself. Specific presidential support that rises above diffuse regime support affords presidents some autonomy and increased legitimacy because they come to personify the state. If specific support for individual presidents is up, the president takes on the mantle of the state; when diffuse support for the system is equal to or exceeds specific support for presidents, they have less autonomy with which to act.

Trust in government provides the larger systemic context within which to locate the individual president. As Elaine C. Kamarck put it, "The evolving American state is being powerfully shaped by negative attitudes towards government among Americans" (Kamarck 2009). In a separated system, trust affords the context for political action and signals whose values reign supreme. For example, trust is likely to be high when values of the political class coincide with those of the broader public. The role of trust in the context of presidential leverage is best thought of as a proxy for cultural affectation toward politics and authority in general. Presidential approval may be high or low in the short term, but trust is the "relationship between citizen and political authority" (Rockman 1984: 51).

Presidential Leverage: A Sketch

Consider the simple schematic diagram in Figure 2.1, which illustrates the dynamic of presidential leverage. Leverage is measured as the ratio of a president's approval to the public's level of trust in the federal government. The key advantage of conceptualizing presidential leverage in this way is that it maintains approval as a key component of presidential political capital but contextualized within a broader, more general public evaluation of trust in government.

Lower values of the coefficient mean less leverage. For example, if the index of presidential leverage falls below 1.0 (IPL < 1.0), then the president is in a range of "negative leverage," which occurs when trust (the denominator) exceeds the level of approval; in other words, when the public trusts government more than it approves of the president. In these situations, presidents are considerably weakened in the public mind. Approval is neither necessary nor sufficient for either high or low leverage because it is contextualized by measuring the relationship of the president to the

FIGURE 2.1. A schematic depiction of presidential leverage.

political system. When leverage falls below 1.0, presidents not only have no particular advantage, but they are held in lower regard as an individual than is the rest of government and have little or no public leverage on which to stand. As the value of the index approaches 1.0 (IPL ≈ 1), the position of the president is roughly equivalent to competing institutions; a president has no real leverage, but neither is he or she particularly disadvantaged. Finally, if leverage climbs above 1.0 (IPL > 1.0), the president enjoys positive leverage wherein the public places him or her above and perhaps distinct from the level of trust it places in the government writ large. The higher the value of the coefficient, the more leverage presidents have because their approval continually outpaces support of the system.

When presidential leverage decreases and the IPL falls in the "draw" or "negative" range, presidents are more likely to seize on constitutional leverage as well as the store of unilateral tools they have at their disposal. The framework predicts that lower levels of leverage will lead to increased reliance on constitutional or unilateral action, even controlling for institutional context, such as divided government and ideological divergence from competing actors.

Presidents do not derive leverage only when they are popular, but when government as a whole is beleaguered and they stand well above the fracas. In one of the most influential works on the presidency, Stephen Skowronek argues that "presidents stand preeminent in American politics when government has been most thoroughly discredited, and when political resistance to presidency is weakest, presidents tend to remake the government wholesale" (Skowronek 1993: 37). When government leaves the public disillusioned, leading to lower trust, presidents can leverage their position in the separation of powers and step into the trust/confidence breach to push an aggressive agenda or otherwise use the trappings of power to shape their political and policy paths.

The questions addressed in the empirical chapters derive directly from this idea. Does a president's "place" in the American political system have an impact on strategic decisions, and if so, how? Are presidents more autonomous, or at least do they act that way, if they enjoy public advantage over the rest of government? Alternatively, presidential leverage can influence presidents who find themselves challenged in one area, such as presiding over a stagnant economy, and able to compensate in other areas. Presidents who have low leverage can bolster their position by using other forms of constitutional or statutory leverage, such as the veto and executive orders. They may compensate for a lack of presidential leverage, which is dynamic, by employing other forms of leverage that are available to any president. An example is President Clinton's promise to use the veto when his public leverage had bottomed out. The decision to employ these other forms of institutionally based resources is largely influenced by presidential leverage.

CONCLUSION

This chapter has drilled down to further develop the concept of presidential leverage. Presidential leverage is distinct from constitutional and institutional sources of leverage, such as the veto or executive orders. The relationship is operationalized as the ratio of presidential approval to public trust in government. The higher the IPL, the more presidents can leverage political capital. Public standing can be used to shift blame or claim credit, forcing other institutions into retreat.

CHAPTER 3

The Quest for Presidential Leverage
The Presidency and the American State

ALTHOUGH THE CONSTITUTION ESTABLISHES Congress and national powers in Article I and the presidency in Article II, there has been an informal, but unmistakable, "institutional inversion" where the public expects much of everything from their presidents. However, this inversion has occurred while leaving presidents inadequately prepared to cope with heightened public expectations of the modern American state and the role of presidents within that state. The objective of the framers of the Constitution of 1787 that Congress be the primary lawmaking branch of government has yielded to a presidency-centered government after the mid-twentieth century.

The workings of presidential leverage, specific support, and diffuse regime support are integrated into the fabric of the American state by combining support for political leaders with trust in the system itself. The analysis presented here isolates on the concept of a fractured state and how it works against presidential success, particularly in domestic policy where presidents have fewer prerogatives than in foreign policy. Therefore, this chapter should be read with an eye to the weaknesses that inhere in the presidency and why presidents seek power sources outside the constitutional framework.[1] The presidency, existing as it does in a "fractured" state, armed with a small but potent arsenal of formal powers and institutional checks, needs leverage beyond "mere" approval to forge a power base, and developing an understanding of presidential leverage sharpens understanding of the extraconstitutional resources for gaining purchase in the American system.

MICRO- AND MACROFOUNDATIONS
OF PRESIDENTIAL LEVERAGE

The framers of the Constitution sculpted a presidency whose contours remain largely unblemished into the second decade of the twenty-first century. But despite the construction of the separation of powers, presidents are for many people the face of the federal government. More than a half-century ago, Fred I. Greenstein, a pioneer in the psychological facets of the presidency, observed, "The existence of this highly publicized national figure who combines the roles of political leader and head of state *simplifies perception* of government and politics" (Greenstein 1966: 35; emphasis in original). More recently, William Howell has written, "So great are the public's expectations of the president . . . that most Americans see their entire government as the presidency" (Howell 2013: 5). Although the public is clearly aware of the existence of the separation of powers and competition among institutions, these public expectations virtually assure that presidents will be held responsible not only for things they do or do not do but even for things they cannot do or are outside their control. One critical pathway for presidents to accomplish anything in the fractured American state is to acquire the resources with which to navigate the often turbulent waters of American politics. Although it may be advantageous in some respects for presidents to be the *embodiment* of the state, this perception brings with it many pitfalls as well. And that is where presidential leverage comes into play.

As an integral part of the state in America, presidents are hamstrung by the separation of powers, the set of institutional arrangements that poses formidable challenges for both real governance and academic analysis. The enduring contours of the state comprise the durable backdrop for political analysis. Political science in the mid-1980s found it necessary, or at least fashionable, to "bring the state back in" (Evans, Rueschemeyer, and Skocpol 1985). Some certainly questioned whether it had been gone in the first place. The idea of the "state" was not new to political science, as many scholars had long adapted sociologist Max Weber's famous definition of the state as the entity that enjoys a "monopoly on the legitimate use of force" in a given geographic region (Weber, Gerth, and Mills 1958). For Weber, the concept of the state was largely an administrative one, subordinate to and differentiated from the "ruler." But though the state was not new to political science, it had fallen out of favor first with the rise of the pluralist perspective on politics[2] and later the systems framework, which had much in common with the pluralists. These approaches, according to their critics, were "societally reductionist" in that they reduced the state to a mere arena in which conflicts by other, largely economic, interests played out. But this conscious effort to invite the concept of the state back to the table of political science accompanied another equally mindful effort to refocus attention on the organizational basis of politics, embedding political actors in a complex maze of political institutions.[3] Although the first enterprise faded with time, especially in comparative politics, the second, organizational focus and the role of key political actors has persevered; the effort to understand the "state," however conceived, has been the focus of a nontrivial amount of attention.[4]

POLITICAL SCIENCE, PRESIDENTS, THE STATE, AND LEVERAGE

Although political scientists have spilt much ink contemplating the state, many argue that the United States is not a "state" at all, at least not to the degree that states are analyzed in the comparative politics literature. Still, much work has been done on the American state, largely from a developmental perspective,[5] and this work incorporates not only bureaucracies and administration[6] but also legislatures[7] and shifting historical epochs, such as party and regulatory regimes.[8] Of course the presidency has been implicated as well, both in terms of the apparatus of the executive branch per se [9] and through the interplay of "human talents" (Skowronek 1982: 5) battling within and against institutional constraints.[10]

At one level, it does not matter whether the American state is an arena for channeling societal conflict, providing organized interests with an efficient means to maximize utility, or is an autonomous actor. What matters most distinctly for presidents and other American leaders is that the American state, fractured along the vaguely defined fault lines delineating the institutional badlands of the separation of powers, imposes significant transaction costs to efficient leadership. As such, the state is defined as that set of institutions that systematizes and channels political conflict; for current purposes the *state is most closely aligned with the president and the presidency.*

Perhaps the biggest difference in comparing the United States to other states, even many other "democratic states," is that the American state is more fragmented and fractured than most. Thus, the "problem" of the state in American politics is inherent in the separation of powers. To be sure, it is difficult to conceptualize the American system in the same way the "statist" theories of comparative political science did in the 1980s. Parliamentary democracies, for example, are more amenable to coherent leadership. In building on this observation, Charles O. Jones argues forcefully that the term *presidential system* is misleading, and the president is not the government in the same way that in a parliamentary system the government *is* the state. His argument is that Americans should think of the system as a "separated" one, emphasizing the fragmentation of the American polity (Jones 1994).

Still, the separation of powers organizes and channels political conflict on a number of fronts. Like almost all stable governments, the American separated system, though fractured, fulfills a fundamental obligation of the state, which is to establish the rules and context for routing competition and cooperation in economic transactions, as well as reining in political and social activity. Similarly, it navigates a paradox—where states and rules exist to minimize transaction costs of political and economic activity to maximize societal output,[11] however defined (for example, political, social, economic, and so forth), it is also true that America's fractured state erects significant obstacles to efficient policy making. The U.S. Constitution and the sum of American political history are rife with examples of mechanisms such as institutions to try to solve collective action problems and to provide an arena for the coordination and regulation of economic activity and to ensure some basic predictability within which to act, such as an economic system with single currency.

The theory underlying the system makes it difficult for leadership to take hold but also fragments power so that it is difficult for any single entity or collective to hijack the political process;[12] efficiency is not the goal of a separated system but rather a slow, considered compromise among institutions, parties, and groups where, theoretically at least, no one gets everything he or she wants from the political process, and few get nothing.[13] Numerous challenges confront presidents, but there are other constitutional and extraconstitutional structures that make navigating the American leadership project hazardous. The United States, organized as it is with fragmented institutions, a federal system, and set elections, makes for one characterized by multiple access points and, thus, a large and active interest group society. All of these can be used by the president but can also be employed by competing institutions to mobilize countervailing forces and block effective presidential action. Presidential leverage of any sort can help begin to mitigate these circumstances.

Historically, but with some notable exceptions, such as direct election of senators and a two-term limit for presidents, the contours of the separation of powers remain remarkably stable. A notable exception is the size of government, particularly the bureaucracy, which was not anticipated by the Constitution. But the most profound change has been the growth of the presidency as the central force in American politics. Though it still sits as it always has, nested within a "separated system of institutions sharing power,"[14] the American public focuses on the presidency in a way that both hinders and helps presidents in their quest to put their own stamp on American politics.

Making the Presidency and Presidential Leverage Explicit in the American State

Jimmy Carter's statement, cited earlier, that the president is the "personification of problems," is emblematic of the urgency found in the opening sentences of Charles O. Jones's master work on the presidency, "The president is not the presidency. The presidency is not the government. Ours is not a presidential system" (Jones 1994: 1). The presidency is, like all American and human institutions, limited in what it can achieve. Presidents, of course, are all too familiar with the limited nature of their influence, great though it can be from time to time. But Jones identifies numerous reasons that public attention is heaped on the president and explains why the occupant of the Oval Office becomes the de facto face of the state:

For presidents, new or experienced, to recognize the limitations of office is commendable. Convincing others to do so is a challenge . . . Media coverage naturally focuses more on the president: there is just one at a time, executive organization is oriented in pyramidal fashion toward the Oval Office, Congress is too diffuse an institution to report on as such, and the Supreme Court leads primarily by indirection. Public interest, too, is directed toward the White House as a symbol of the government. As a result, expectations of a president often far exceed the individuals' personal, political, institutional, or constitutional capacities. Performance never matches promise . . . The plain fact is that the United States does not have a presidential system. It has a separated system. (Jones 1994: 5)

Thus, the ease of access that many have to the president via media outlets, movies, books, television, and competing institutions works to the detriment of presidents because these tend to exalt presidents and therefore increase expectations. By focusing on the president, information costs for citizens decrease as well. It is far easier, as Jones notes, to focus on the one rather than the many. The offshoot is that it leads to serious distortions in citizen understandings of American politics. Presidents bear the brunt of this problem, with the public often demanding more of presidents than they can reasonably or legally deliver. Some would argue as well that presidents are largely responsible for their lot. Presidents weigh in on all manner of politics and policy, overpromise during the campaign phase, and then underdeliver when in office. Lowi argues that "social delivery" is the new basis of the relationship between the president and the public, replacing the representational aspect of the office. The public expects peace and prosperity, and presidents are trapped into playing games toward this end even though control over these objectives is largely outside of their control, even as their campaigns are spent promising great things in both arenas (Lowi 1985).

Presidents labor from a position of weakness in the American political system.[15] Presidents can exert political power in some instances but are generally frustrated by factors outside their direct control. This weakness is caused chiefly by the public's bloated expectations about what the president can accomplish and how those go unmet.[16] Richard Neustadt famously argued that presidents' use of the few powers of "command" they possess is tantamount to failure because the real power of the presidency lies in the president's ability to persuade others to do what he wants (Neutstadt 1960). Further, presidents' position in the American system all but guarantees that success will be limited and profoundly conditioned by the preferences and activities of their competitors in the American state. Others argue that presidents are often ill trained to do their jobs compared to prime ministers. Whereas presidents sometimes spend relatively little time in politics prior to their election, the British prime minister serves a long "apprenticeship" in government to prepare him or her for leadership (Rose 1991). This practical reality, that presidents are one among many rather than first among equals, increases the likelihood that the occupant of the White House will fail to satisfy expectations.

By way of example, consider the logic of coattails, often thought of as a source of leverage a president might have with members of Congress. This leverage is confounded by separate elections, which compounds the institutional fragmentation of the American system. Presidents and members of Congress are elected separately, and, although their electoral fortunes may be linked, it has more recently been to the detriment of the winning president. Coattails are rarely in play. The logic of presidential coattails as a source of presidential leverage holds that not only does a presidential nominee pull congressional candidates to victory as they ride his or her coattails to their own election, but that those newly minted members of Congress owe much to the winning candidate and are more likely to support what that president wants, possibly more than they would otherwise. But data do not support these claims and, in fact, point in the opposite direction. In the last six decades there have been only two elections (1956 and 1972) where the winning presidential candidate ran ahead of a majority of his party's successful House candidates (that is, received more votes in the House member's district). In every other instance, not only did the president run behind most of the winning House candidates of his party, but the difference between districts in which he ran ahead and those in which he ran behind was enormous. John F. Kennedy, for example, ran ahead of only twenty-two successful Democratic candidates for the House and behind 243. Similarly, the differential between Ronald Reagan running ahead/behind successful House Republican candidates was 38/150 in 1980 and 59/123 in 1984.[17] When successful presidential candidates run behind so many of their successful copartisans, the logic of "owing" the president anything disappears, as does any semblance of leverage he or she may derive from the election. Still, many members of Congress will support the president's position for other reasons, such as holding similar political preferences underscored by party label or because they seek intraparty harmony with a president, sometimes connecting their own political success with his, even though they do not "owe" him anything.[18] The fact that political parties are not always reliable bulwarks against presidential failure (witness the problems Carter and Clinton had with their own congressional copartisans, especially early in their administrations) is the basis for Richard Neustadt's observation that "what the Constitution separates our political parties do not combine" and is as true as ever (Neustadt 1960: 26).

Still, there are sophisticated studies that suggest presidents can create different types of leverage to gain a foothold in the American state and use the perquisites of office to act for both their own advance and that of other political actors. For example, David E. Lewis demonstrates that presidents create bureaucratic agencies in response to group-induced political pressures, but, if conditions are right, presidents can create agencies that are insulated from political attack and therefore persevere over time (Lewis 2008). Similarly, Terry Moe argues that bureaucratic structure is molded by presidents but that presidents act largely in response to political interests defined by political imperatives as presidents perceive them (Moe 1989). In other words, they can use their positions to influence political outcomes and maximize political advantage. After all, presidents make strategic political decisions to position themselves to increase their capacity to govern. The notion that presidents try to please various constituencies is no surprise. But that is far different from arguing that their actions, though perhaps constrained, are *determined* exogenously.[19]

Integral to the structure of the presidency and the incentives that flow to presidents is a set of checks and balances that theoretically reins in presidents and assures that presidents do not become the framers' worst nightmare—an American monarch or, worse, a tyrant. They created the system of separated powers and assured that presidents would face formidable challenges in gaining traction in the political system. As the separation of powers has developed over time and the wrinkles of the constitutional structure continue to be smoothed out in practice by Supreme Court decisions, congressional actions, and public expectations, the resulting system has been, as two leading presidency scholars put it, "brutal," to presidents (Lewis and Moe 2010). With competing institutions, access points, histories, interpretations of power, prerogatives, and separated elections, the American state can and does work at cross-purposes with itself.

For example, the case of executive branch bureaucracy demonstrates how even a simple categorization of differing institutions (legislative, executive, and judicial) is deceptively simplistic, wherein the president is only the titular head of his or her own branch and struggles to exert influence over a sprawling administrative state. The executive is interdependent with legislatures, courts, and the federal system, all of which work against establishing direction and achieving convergence of politics, policy, and purpose.[20] The presidency itself and its accompanying apparatuses, such as party structure and organization, allow incumbents to exploit political resources such as access and power as they create opportunities for leverage in the system. Some observers label the presidency as a "no-win" job in which the incumbent is doomed to fail (Light 1999; Lowi 1985) and analyze how presidents can or should adapt to the political system they inherit.[21]

Institutional Inversion: The Impact on the Presidency

One of the most profound changes in American politics has been an institutional inversion of the constitutional construction of the framers, who placed the legislative authority in Article I, the executive in Article II, and the judicial in Article III. This order reflects the framers' intentions as to how much power each institution would have at its disposal. It is no coincidence that the primary powers of the national government and the necessary and proper clause are to be found in Article I, which creates the legislative branch, making clear that Congress would wield most power (*Federalist 51*; see Hamilton, Madison, and Jay [1788] 1961). Notice that the president's most potent political check on the legislature, the veto, is not assigned in Article II but is placed in the legislative article instead. A major reason the framers partitioned Congress into two chambers was to install yet another check in a system of calibrated checks and balances that serve as a barrier against tyranny. Article II, which creates the presidency and a rudimentary bureaucracy, has only half as many words as Article I and, as it pertains to executive power, is ambiguous in the extreme. Most of the Article details presidential selection. Article III, shorter still, sets up the Supreme Court. But as Keith Whittington (2009) observes, the Constitution has not always "constrained" politics. He argues there are many paths by which the Constitution evolves to take on issues and meanings beyond its purview or control and therefore assume new meanings where existing meaning might be lacking. Although the constitutional requirements and prerogatives in Article II have changed, the development of the American state, bolstered by the courts and Congress, has developed to the point of *aggrandizing power to presidents*, and although that power is often seen as illegitimate or suspect, the populace continues to look toward the White House for leadership.

From the founding through the nineteenth century, Congress was "preeminent," owing to its station in the political system. But as the twentieth century unfolded, the presidency of Article II grew into the dominant American political institution without any real changes recorded in the Constitution; indeed, the only amendments that address the presidency directly (twelfth, twentieth, twenty-second, and twenty-fifth) deal with matters of presidential selection and succession and have only an indirect impact on presidential power. As the twentieth century progressed, the presidency replaced Congress as the most powerful branch (Cooper 2009).

The seeds of change were planted when Theodore Roosevelt and Woodrow Wilson pushed the boundaries of the presidency from leadership in times of crisis to a new mode of "politics as usual" and became, as Louis Koenig put it, the "asserters of bold undertakings in domestic and foreign affairs . . . gifted mobilizers of public opinion, and . . . inducers of congressional concurrence" (Koenig 1986, cited in Han and Heith 2013). New opportunities for leadership arose during Franklin Roosevelt's presidency as a dramatic expansion of national responsibilities and expectations of government solutions to seemingly intractable problems meant that the new responsibilities would have to be dominated by presidential action. This new era was characterized by deep changes in how presidents related to the public and media, the creation of enlarged capacities for doing so, and increased infiltration into the legislative process. These developments created a new relationship between the president and the Constitution but also between the public and the president. Presidents sought to push their public agendas in a way that would have seemed unreasonable just a few decades (or even years) earlier.[22]

The President as the Face of the State

The idea of a gap between political ideals (or expectations) and reality is certainly not new. In the preface to his seminal work on American politics, Samuel Huntington relates the story of his PhD oral exams and how Professor Samuel Beer posed a question about the relationship between political thought and political institutions. Huntington modestly confesses that he did not answer the question at the time but then went on to spend much his career grappling with it (Huntington 1981: vii). Exalted and often unrealistic expectations placed on the president are implicit in Beer's question to the young Huntington. In generic terms, the relationship between political ideals generated by the canon of political thought leads to expectations of the "good life" and how government will act, react, and in some cases refuse to act in the lives of its citizens. A gap between ideals and the actual performance of institutions widens because the political institutions and the individuals who inhabit them cannot or will not meet the subjective and often contradictory expectations of the public.[23]

The gap between what the public wants and what the president can deliver is rooted in the Constitution, statute, and even in historical precedent. The public demands action from presidents because the public views presidents as the face of the American state. This expectation of the president derives from the public's push toward governmental action, and the president's particular role in it. Perhaps no political scientist has summed up the relationships among the American polity, its government, and the presidency more cleanly than E. E. Schattschneider, who, during the earliest days of World War II, observed:

The President of the United States today receives a mandate to govern the nation and is responsible for the safety and welfare of the Republic . . . People are not interested in alibis for non-action, even when written by constitutional lawyers. They want results. The truth of the matter is that the American public has never understood the Constitution nor has it ever really believed in it, in spite of the verbal tradition of constitutionalism. With the rise of the plebiscitary presidency, making the president the one significant public officer elected by the country as a whole, the office has become the vehicle for the expression of a great simplification of the Constitution. By a popular political interpretation of the Constitution . . . the president is made responsible for the initiation, adoption, and execution of the policies by a mandate that merely ignores every known principle of the separation of powers and federalism. (Schattschneider 1942: 53)

The election of a president rarely signifies a clear policy-anchored mandate. In fact, research on mandates (for example, Azari 2014; Conley 2001; Grossback, Peterson, and Stimson 2006) agree that they are social constructions that depend on the "perceptions" of the media and political actors (Congress), and true mandates are rare or fleeting. For example, Julia Azari argues that presidents claim they have mandates when their actions are illegitimate; thus this claim is used when they are politically weak, not strong (Azari 2014). Schattschneider's observation is as relevant in the first quarter of the twenty-first century as it was in the middle of the last century, and his argument about public perception of presidential action devoid of the separation of powers is particularly trenchant and has since been borne out. In periods of divided government, the public holds the *president and his or her party in Congress* responsible for good or bad economic conditions, even though blame and credit could easily be distributed to both parties (Norpoth 2001). This adduces more evidence that, for the public, *presidents* are the face of the state.

In his presidential address to the American Political Science Association, Theodore Lowi provided an overview of the state in American politics, further developing his well-known partition of American political history into at least two epochs, or "republics." The "First Republic" set the constitutional relationship between the government and the polity as limited, and the "Second Republic," born of the New Deal and continuing today, saw government activity expand as a consequence of increasing political demands. Lowi argued that the "First Republic" was basically stateless and that government activity was as low in 1932 as it had been a century earlier. The combination of expanded national responsibilities in the midst of the Great Depression with heightened expectations that the national government would meet those responsibilities, and President Taft's desideratum of a "Whig" (that is, extremely limited) presidency was over. The development of new communication technologies transformed presidential elections and the relationship between the president and the public, particularly in the progressive era, and formed a closer bond between the president and the people. Consequently, the president further became the public picture of the state (Lowi 1992). Because presidents represent the state in the public mind, it is no wonder that this trend can be linked to the expansion of the so-called unitary executive theory, where presidents can take action largely unfettered by the separation of powers and the normal political processes and are thus in a better position to meet expectations.

Presidents have political and policy-related incentives to improve how the public perceives them. Public trust in government, for example, is related to the expectations gap; when trust is high, the expectations gap is low (Waterman, Silva, and Jenkins-Smith 2014). This is likely because when the public exhibits highly diffuse regime support, "labor" is divided among the branches and down to the states. But when trust is low, presidents bear the burden most directly, and trust in government has generally stayed low for more than four decades and has not come close to having fully recovered after Vietnam and Watergate.[24]

More problematic for presidents is that the fractured nature of the state itself obscures what presidential policy accomplishes. As Susanne Mettler points out, the fragmentation of the American state, designed to disperse power among competing institutions, obfuscates the policy-based relationship between government and citizen. She finds that many citizens are concerned that government does too much and they do not benefit personally from government policy. However, citizens take advantage of government services without realizing that they benefit directly from such popular programs as the home mortgage interest deduction, the earned-income tax credit, or guaranteed federal student loans (Mettler 2011).[25] If people do not see a personal connection to governance, then what politicians do in terms of policy becomes more tenuous. Because the media focus so much attention on the presidency and the political "horse race" generally, gauging who is "winning" or "losing," the public uses the president as a proxy for the government. The increasing fragmentation not only of the state but of the means by which the public gets and uses information means that presidents have to forge political battle armed only with what is immediately available to them, using whatever means are necessary to move politics forward in accord with their own ideas (Kernell and Baum 1999). Sometimes they will be successful, but often not.

On the other hand, expectations can also be a boon for presidents in the fractured state; presidents derive at least informal authority to act when a strict reading of constitutional or statutory texts would limit their range of action. For example, it has long been commonplace to expect presidents to actively propose legislation to Congress, and they pursue policy priorities as activist "chief legislators,"[26] whereas a strict reading of the Constitution resists such an interpretation.

In a real way, then, public expectations of the president are derivative of the fractured state. Public expectations of the Congress are low, and although the Supreme Court may have an advantage in terms of public approval, the nature of the Court's business is slower and more deliberate than what can be accomplished by the elected branches. Thus, presidents deal with expectations more so than others, not because the others are faceless but because it is more efficient to focus on the president as a single entity.

Capacity in the American State

A necessary if not sufficient condition for state autonomy is capacity. Capacity is defined as possessing the organizational or constitutional/statutory means with which to put preferences into action. Institutionalization is the process by which organizations adapt to their external environments, creating a space for themselves by delineating boundaries and putting themselves in position to absorb demands put on them. In short, it is the process of developing capacity. By institutionalizing support agencies and even the internal White House staff, presidents build political capacity for policy activity. There is variation in the degree to which presidents are successful in trying to do so, with success defined as the maximization of their ability to obtain what they want from the process.[27] Institutionalization of various support agencies within the presidential branch increase the capacity of presidents to get what they can in the political process (Hult 2000; Walcott and Hult 1995). Later chapters explore the effort to add to EOP staff, increasing responsiveness and politicizing the decision processes, and find that centralization and politicization are more actively pursued by presidents with low levels of presidential leverage.

With or without leverage, presidents must navigate and solve a series of "paradoxes." One of those paradoxes, already mentioned, is that although people want "powerful leadership that solves the nation's problems," the American ethos is inherently "suspicious of strong centralized leadership and the abuse of power" (Cronin and Genovese 2013).[28] To deal with this, presidents have taken advantage of the "executive power" vested in the president by the Constitution so as to tighten control over rule-making functions, implementation, and enforcement by expanding and exploiting some of the prerogatives at their disposal, such as an administrative presidency strategy branded by strategic use of political appointments, and the use of unilateral prerogatives such as executive orders.[29] Doing so can help presidents in their quest for institutional autonomy in the fractured state, especially presidents who do not enjoy strong public leverage. But even popular presidents can be blocked from asserting autonomy.

Consider an insider perspective. Lecturing to Henry Kissinger's International Relations seminar at Harvard in April 1962, Arthur M. Schlesinger Jr., a close confidant and aid to President Kennedy, discussed the development of presidential power and increased national responsibility:

Most people, I said, think that the president has grown more powerful because the national government has grown more powerful; but this is not necessarily the case. In certain respects, the President today is less free to act on his own (than) the President fifty or a hundred years ago. There were two reasons in particular for this: as the national government grew in size and function, so too grew (a) its dependence on appropriations and (b) its commitment to the federal bureaucracy. (Schlesinger 2007: 163)

Schlesinger, arguing from the perspective of both a historian and a White House insider, identified presidential "weakness" as lacking the leverage to overcome the advantages enjoyed by Congress. As the government grew larger and more dependent on appropriations, he argued, it relied on Congress to appropriate money, effectively transferring a veto over national politics from the president to the Congress. This was applicable to both domestic and foreign policy, with domestic policy particularly hamstrung by the "deadweight" of bureaucracy on presidential (as opposed to executive) action because the bureaucracy is composed of vested interests of its own. And as Kennedy, an activist president, sought to assert himself, the split personality of the permanent government (bureaucracy) and political government (elected officials) widened (Schlesinger 2007: 163–164).

Schlesinger was writing on the cusp of what would become a period of presidential reassertion and would soon resurrect itself in the form of increased politicization of the bureaucracy and internal White House development (Rudalevige 2005; Schlesinger 1973). Presidents with low presidential leverage are more likely to enhance responsive capacity. If presidents are going to be held responsible for what they do or do not do, they likely want to control the narrative of what emerges from their administration.[30]

Autonomy in the American State

In an early and more general treatment of state autonomy, Eric Nordlinger challenged the conventional wisdom that the American state was constrained by its institutional structure (Nordlinger 1981: 182–192). Although he concedes that the state, operationalized as those with governing authority (such as presidents), can be thwarted by dominant societal interests, he firmly asserts that the failure to enact policy in the U.S. context is more often due to the "sharing of dispersed powers [that] turns public officials into competitors for power, while their distinctive responsibilities help generate incompatible policy preferences" (Nordlinger 1981: 186). Nordlinger uses the example of Congress and its many access points as a foil for the idea that status quo public policy is state induced. Traditional state–society accounts could explain this by arguing that groups wishing to change the status quo are disadvantaged relative to those who wish to maintain the status quo given disparity in the number of procedural obstacles and veto points that the former have to overcome, whereas the latter need only prevent change at a single point (for example, one house of Congress does not pass a bill that the other favors). Nordlinger concedes this *might* reflect the relative ease with which affected interests can veto preferences of public officials, but he argues an easier explanation for the primacy of the policy status quo is that members of Congress (and presumably other public officials *including the president*) have a preference for maintaining the status quo, a preference that might be entirely consistent with those of veto players (Nordlinger 1981: 188).[31]

Whereas Nordlinger focuses on policy stasis, Jacobs and Shapiro (2000) argue that policy change takes place when politicians act autonomously to serve the greater good, even when their preferences differ from otherwise powerful veto groups and if they can persuade the public to support their vision of good public policy. Politicians, especially presidents, use public opinion polls not to pander to the public but to bring the median member of the mass public closer to the president's ideal point by formulating careful rhetorical strategies crafted from poll results. However, others have questioned how much power politicians have to move public opinion and implicitly connect the notion of an autonomous state where presidents are stymied in their inability to sway public opinion (Edwards 2003; but see Canes-Wrone 2006 and Rottinghaus 2010) or explicitly, where presidents pander to mass opinion and are consequently limited in the autonomy that they enjoy (Quirk 2009).

Others have argued that presidents have autonomy to act in the separated system. Recent work has sought not so much to supplant the earlier picture of presidential powerlessness but to round it out by calling attention to the considerable use of unilateral power. This viewpoint holds that presidential use of "command" power is not a sign of weakness but rather a set of alternate strategies that can be used to establish presidential authority and place in the separation of powers (for example, Mayer 2001; Howell 2003). To be sure, the George W. Bush administration's claim of wide expansive power gave scholars pause and allowed them the opportunity to reconsider the normative implications of a "unitary" executive.[32] These presidential command powers are not so much signs of failure as they are tools for presidents who strive to influence policy and politics in the constitutional separation of powers. With the fractured state embodying a difficult set of hurdles to overcome and achieve purposive action, a president has to take risks, and this sometimes entails the use of unilateral powers employed in pursuit of the administrative presidency.

The role played by institutions in the literature on the state cannot be overemphasized. It is difficult to think of a state apparatus if states are mere arenas of power within which to arbitrate societal conflicts. The state and the attendant presidential leadership projects attached to "moving" the state are more than simply a reflection of power politics. In the American context, this means that conflicts between Congress and the president, for example, are more than the sum of the aggregated interests and differential constituency perspectives asserted by each institution. One claim in favor of taking a presidential perspective is that the president is elected by a national constituency. In institutional terms, though, Congress represents all the people as well, albeit in a more fragmented way and with a necessarily different perspective. The conflicts inherent in the Congress over leadership, party, ideology, structure, and expression of policy direction produce outcomes that are more than the mere summation of the divergent preferences represented within the two chambers. So the efforts to match the Congress with the president to determine the degree to which institutions are autonomous in the realm of transforming preferences (public/society, government, and so on) into policy is helpful for understanding the role of the presidency in the American system writ large.

CONCLUSION

This chapter has surveyed the literature on the American state and has made an argument for how the presidency has come to be embedded in the state and how for many it has come to *be* the state. The Constitution creates a "fractured state" that renders leadership difficult and in which presidents must constantly fight to find a foothold. This fractured state is linked to heightened expectations on presidents. The separation of powers, supplemented by media attention that focuses on the Oval Office as the center of political attention, are the primary culprits driving these expectations. Citizens naturally gravitate to the presidency because of the singular nature of the president; they can reduce information costs by focusing their expectations on the president. This is particularly striking given the institutional inversion in the constitutional structure, wherein presidents, limited by the language in Article II, have seen their power grow both through their own efforts and the prodding of their otherwise competing institutions. It is in this context that presidents seek foothold, or "leverage," to justify their actions in the public realm. So while the separation of powers is part of the public mind, I am primarily interested in how presidents navigate a separated system with presidential leverage constantly shifting. Presidential leverage exposes important insights into when presidents are best positioned to take advantage of the tools of the political system for the movement of policy agendas and when they must pull on the reins or change course entirely.

CHAPTER 4

Measuring Presidential Leverage

THE INDEX OF PRESIDENTIAL LEVERAGE (IPL) combines a president's approval with public trust in government. To explore presidential leverage in American politics, this chapter describes the creation and trend of the index from John F. Kennedy to Barack Obama.

Recall that a president's leverage is conceptualized as the degree to which his or her public standing rises above the political scrum in American politics. Taken together as the ratio of approval to trust, the components of leverage signal when presidential status with the American public is greater or lesser compared to the political system in which presidents are embedded. Remember that Figure 2.2 showed that when presidents enjoy a level of approval that exceeds that of government as a whole, the value of the index increases and presidents have greater leverage from which to draw. Recall as well that a president need not be highly popular to have leverage *if* the public has little trust in government as a whole. The corollary holds as well—having high approval is neither a necessary nor a sufficient condition for presidential leverage if public trust in government is similarly high. In that case, presidents are not the only (or even the best) game in town and hold no special or elevated stature beyond that of the constitutional position they occupy. To be sure, this does not imply that presidents so situated are powerless; rather, they hold no publicly based leverage in dealing with issues of the agenda, policy making, policy output, or the use of unilateral tools available to the presidency.

CALCULATING THE INDEX OF PRESIDENTIAL LEVERAGE (IPL)

The IPL is straightforward and calculated in the following manner:

$$(4.1) \qquad IPL = \frac{\text{presidential approval}}{\text{trust in government}}$$

where IPL is the *index of presidential leverage*; *presidential approval* is either annual or quarterly presidential approval ratings, depending on the nature of the dependent variable used in the analysis; and *public trust in government* is, again, an annual or quarterly measure of aggregated opinion polls measuring various aspects of public trust.

It should be noted that this chapter traces approval, trust, and the IPL from John F. Kennedy's administration up through the end of Obama's first term given that several of the dependent and control variables used to estimate relationships in the empirical chapters are available only through 2012 as of this writing. However, to bring at least the IPL as current as possible, I measure the IPL into 2016, Obama's final year in office, and report these data in Chapter 7. Because the multivariate analyses in Chapters 5 and 6 extend only through 2012, this chapter calculates and reports descriptive statistics for Kennedy through Obama's first term.

Presidential Approval

The data to construct the IPL are extracted scores of presidential approval and trust, aggregated using James Stimson's WCALC algorithm, which he developed to calculate his widely used measure of public mood (Stimson 1991).[1] For Stimson's construction of *Mood*, scores above 50 indicate a desire for more liberal policy action, whereas those under 50 indicate a more conservative approach.[2] Here, I use the same algorithm to calculate trust scores and approval scores. To calculate the approval series, I used all measures of presidential approval between January 1961 and December 2012, as reported at the American Presidency Project[3] and again employed the WCALC algorithm to extract the scores.[4]

Political Trust

The trust data are slightly more complicated but in the end nearly as straightforward. On the trust scale, a value greater than 50 means the public trusts government more than it distrusts it, and below 50 means greater distrust. Accordingly, a score such as Nixon's late-term 39.5, just before his resignation, indicates a lesser level of trust than a reading of 45.

The trust data are extracted via the WCALC program from public opinion polls designed to tap the level of public trust in government.[5]

To minimize endogeneity, questions specifically referencing individuals such as individual presidents by name or members of Congress or the Supreme Court, or institutions such as "the presidency," or "the Congress" are *eliminated* from the data. To be sure, some polling organizations probe for opinions about the level of trust of a specific president, or of institutions such as Congress, the presidency, or the Supreme Court (Ragsdale 2014: Table 5-13, 332–333).[6] But eliminating questions with a specific reference to a president, an institution, or some other specific individual leaves the respondent free to interpret the "federal government" however she will, be it as an aggregated, undifferentiated collective or with reference to these institutions in her own mind. The point is that the respondent interprets the government on her own terms, without prompting from the pollster.[7]

Annual or Quarterly Data? A Caveat

The simple calculation in equation 4.1 yields president-specific IPL coefficients for the time period 1961 to 2012. For purposes of this book I have calculated both quarterly and annual indices, though most of the statistical analyses in Chapters 5 and 6 employ annual data.[8] The graphs provided at the beginning of each discussion of individual presidents highlight the term(s) of the president under consideration and plot quarterly data so as to produce as finely grained a picture of the ebbs and flows of presidential leverage as possible. When interpreting quarterly data, a word of caution is in order. Because the WCALC algorithm uses what it has available to it and can construct indices based on few observations, the annual reading is more valid, using public opinion polls throughout the year and thus basing its estimate from a larger pool of data than do the quarterly data. Still, almost all of the quarterly data meet standards of face validity, and so I will bring them into the discussion when necessary, though as noted their interpretation should be accompanied by an appropriate level of restraint.

Theoretically, the IPL has a domain of 0 to positive infinity. Observed values range from a low of 0.64 (Nixon in the first half of 1974) to 1.64 (Bush 41 in 1991 and Obama in 2010), with more variation in the quarterly data. In the quarterly data, we observe a low of 0.62 (Nixon's first quarter of 1974) all the way to 2.10 in the fourth quarter in 2010. This is another reason why the quarterly data are less valid. Although Obama definitely enjoyed high overall leverage in 2010, arguably allowing for the passage and signing of the controversial Affordable Care Act in March, he endured a low point at the point of the midterm elections in November 2010, when his Democratic copartisans lost control of Congress, a state of affairs Obama famously labeled a "shellacking" (see Lee and Thrush, 2010). Still, it is plausible that Obama had some leverage, perhaps more than people knew, because of the fact that his approval ratings were still in the mid-40s whereas trust in government was at an extremely low point.

The higher the value of the coefficient, the more leverage the president has as the dominant player in the political system. Relatedly, the higher the level of presidential leverage, the more political capital he or she enjoys. A low IPL indicates a president struggling for power, with little political capital outside the arsenal of constitutional leverage all presidents enjoy. What follows is a detailed exploration of the variation in and patterns of presidential approval and trust. The two components are then pooled as a ratio, generating the IPL, followed by a discussion of the patterns of presidential leverage from Kennedy to Obama.

DESCRIBING THE PATTERNS: A BROAD OVERVIEW

First, consider Table 4.1 and Figure 4.1. The average extracted presidential approval across the series, from Kennedy to Obama I, is 52.26. The

TABLE 4.1
Presidential leverage and its components.

	Descriptive statistics		
	N	Mean	Standard deviation
Annual approval	53	52.26	11.4
Annual trust	53	46.13	8.8
Index of presidential leverage (IPL)	53	1.15	2.4

Note: There are fifty-three observations because 1974 is represented twice in the data, once for Nixon and once for Ford.

Source: Approval data are from the American Presidency Project, available at www.presidency .ucsb.edu/data/popularity.php. Trust data are from public opinion polls and archived with the Roper Center for Public Opinion at http://ropercenter.cornell.edu/. All estimates were generated using WCALC. See text for details

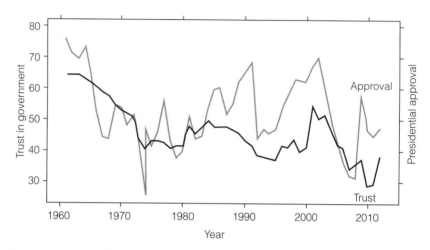

FIGURE 4.1. Presidential approval and government trust, 1961–2012.

Source: Approval data are from the American Presidency Project, available at www.presidency
.ucsb.edu/data/popularity.php. Trust data are from public opinion polls and archived with the
Roper Center for Public Opinion, available at http://ropercenter.cornell.edu/. All estimates were
generated using WCALC. See text for details.

standard deviation of 11.4 reflects a large amount of variation around
the mean. Average trust registered 46.1, with smaller dispersion (standard deviation of 8.8). Figure 4.1 shows that although approval and trust
move in similar fashion, they do not map perfectly on to one another,
with only about 30 percent of the variance in trust explained by approval.[9] Therefore, although the two series vary together in places, they
are ultimately distinct on both conceptual and statistical grounds.[10] As
already noted, for example, trust reflects questions about trust "in government" and cannot control for what a particular respondent has in
mind when asked about "government." The measurement of trust may
well include some respondents' evaluation of the incumbent president
at the time of the survey, but this is minimized by removing from the
calculation any question that asks specifically about institutions such as
the presidency or Congress. And as can be seen from the trend, trust is
different from approval.

Tracing the series, both presidential approval and trust in government were robust as the country moved out of the Eisenhower years
and into the 1960s. Soon, however, the Vietnam War and Watergate

overwhelmed the political system, and both measures declined dramatically. Trust, for example, fell more than three standard deviations in just thirteen years, from 64.5 in Kennedy's first year to just under 40 at the time of Nixon's resignation in the third quarter of 1974. Indeed, 1972, the same year the Watergate break-in occurred, was the last one in which trust registered at 50 or more until 2001 and the aftermath of the terrorist attacks on New York City and Washington, D.C. But even the observed score in 1972 itself was the culmination of an enormous decline in public trust from where it had been just a decade before.

Although the cumulative effects of Watergate and Vietnam battered political trust, the series eventually evens out and remains relatively flat throughout the Carter years, rebounding slightly during Reagan's two terms, especially during a brief period of divided government between 1983 and 1987. After this short-lived rally, trust fell throughout most of the second half of the 1980s and into the 1990s. The decline coincides with several developments in American politics, including the Iran-Contra scandal that plagued the latter part of the Reagan presidency and an extended period of congressional "gridlock" that laid bare the inability of Congress and the president to work together (and, incidentally, the inability of Congress to work with itself), mainly during the administration of George H. W. Bush, when it became clear in 1991 that he would have to break his "no new taxes" pledge. Bush's approval ratings remained high throughout this period as the Gulf War wound down but declined rapidly later in the year. As a recession began to take hold and public perception was that the economy was not going to get better in the near term, trust in government dipped from the lower 40s to the upper 30s by the first quarter of 1992, registering just over 37 percent in the first half of the year. This likely contributed to the rise of Bill Clinton, making his ascendency to the presidency possible. Trust continued to drop through the mid-1990s and again toward the end of George W. Bush's presidency, though the decline was more gradual. Still, trust in government dropped dramatically, from 51.8 in 2003 when the United States went to war with Iraq to just 28.6 in 2010, Obama's second year in office and the year in which he signed the Affordable Care Act.

Was 1974 Pivotal?

The preceding discussion gives rise to a methodological point derived from the proposition that the cumulative effect of Vietnam and Watergate were "different." In the data sets used for this book, 1974 is generally split into two parts, one coinciding with Nixon's presidency and the second with Gerald Ford. For Nixon, the approval data for January 1 through August 5 are parceled out and extracted in WCALC. The only poll taken in August was on August 5, just four days before he resigned, and that poll recorded Nixon's approval at 24 percent. The remainder of the year's approval ratings are assigned to Ford. Trust is calculated in the same way, using readings for the months January through July (Nixon), and August through December (Ford). Quarterly data are similarly partitioned, with both approval and trust in the first two quarters measuring Nixon and Ford reflected in the final two quarters.[11]

Simple *t*-tests for difference of means were performed on approval, trust, and leverage with one group measuring mean values during the Vietnam-Watergate era, which takes the value of 1 from the administrations of President Kennedy's through Richard Nixon's resignation in 1974, and the other coded 0 from Ford to Obama. These tests were used to determine whether there exists a statistically significant difference between these two time periods, which identifies any quantitatively distinguishable difference before and after trust plummets in response to Vietnam and Watergate. Table 4.2 shows the differences when the data are partitioned before and after the cut point in approximately August 1974. Inspection of the table shows that average approval and trust were both higher during the pre-Watergate phase. As will become clear later in the president-by-president comparisons, Kennedy, Johnson, and Nixon enjoyed high approval ratings at several points in their terms. But as the trends in Figure 4.1 show, they quickly declined, reflected in the higher standard deviations for both approval and trust in the pre-August 1974 era. There is an even more dramatic difference in the observed means in government trust. As argued earlier, trust in government dropped dramatically between 1961 and the first part of 1974 and never fully recovered. The highest reading in the post-1974 era is in 2001, the year of the ter-

TABLE 4.2
Averages in approval, trust, and leverage by time period
(Kennedy to Nixon, and Ford to Obama).

	Time period: Pre- and post-Vietnam/ Watergate	N	Mean	Standard deviation	*t*-Test for difference of means
Annual approval	Kennedy–Nixon	14	55.03	14.53	1.06
	Ford–Obama	39	51.26	10.13	
Annual trust	Kennedy–Nixon	14	56.42	8.03	7.12*
	Ford–Obama	39	42.44	5.58	
Annual IPL	Kennedy–Nixon	14	0.96	0.16	−3.86*
	Ford–Obama	39	1.21	0.22	

* *t*-test for the difference of means is significant at $p < 0.001$.

rorist attacks on New York and Washington, when trust registered 54.7, but this is still only 85 percent of the overall series high of 64.5, observed during Kennedy's first year in office.

Note as well that the mean differences before and after the Vietnam-Watergate era are statistically significant for *Trust* and the *IPL* but not for *Approval*. Mean approval differences fail to reach significance at the 0.05 level.[12] Thus, this difference is taken into account if and where differences in the statistical results (if any) emerge and are included in the analysis presented later in the book. To summarize, in the statistical analyses presented in the empirical chapters, I will first test to see if leverage measured as the IPL plays a part in presidential activity explored in this book. Second, if the IPL registers a statistical impact on presidential activity, I will then break it out from Kennedy to Nixon and from Ford to Obama by including and reporting (when appropriate and statistically significant) a dummy variable that separates pre- and post-Watergate (Nixon) time periods. If there is no difference, I will note that in the text and concentrate on the series as a whole.

So the answer to the question "Is 1974 pivotal?" is contingent; 1974 is pivotal in the sense that the dynamics of trust and the IPL differ significantly before and after the Vietnam-Watergate era. Approval does not. And as will become apparent in later chapters, these differences do not always manifest themselves in the larger statistical dynamic and in fact exhibit a very limited systematic effect with impact on only a precious few empirical analyses.

How does the concept of leverage map onto what we know about presidential activity? Table 4.3 displays the average extracted WCALC scores of both approval and trust in government. The fifth column is the core of the table and is the product of columns 3 and 4. Figure 4.2 presents the data in column 5 in graphic form. Again, the reader is referred to Chapter 7 for an update through 2016.

Z-scores, also known as "standard scores," are presented in column 6. Z-scores measure the distance that any one observation falls from the series average, expressed in standard deviation units. Standard deviations are expressions of variation in a distribution. The larger the standard deviation, the more spread out are the values in the distribution. Calculating Z-scores is an efficient way to identify outliers, as well as observations that fall closer to the mean of the series. The average annual IPL is 1.15, with a standard deviation of 0.24. In a standardized distribution,

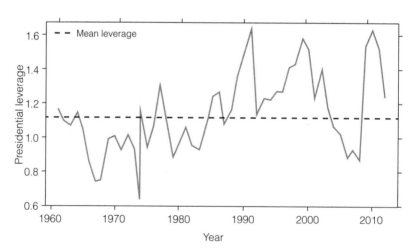

FIGURE 4.2. Tracking the index of presidential leverage (IPL), 1961–2012.

Source: Calculated by author. See text for details.

TABLE 4.3

Calculation of annual index of presidential leverage (IPL).

Year (1)	President (2)	Average approval (3)	Average trust in government (4)	Annual index of presidential leverage (IPL) (5)	Z-score IPL (6)
1961	Kennedy	75.72	64.50	1.17	0.10
1962	Kennedy	73.38	64.48	1.14	−0.20
1963	Kennedy	69.17	64.38	1.07	−0.31
1964	Johnson	73.81	63.76	1.16	0.04
1965	Johnson	65.83	62.44	1.05	−0.40
1966	Johnson	52.40	60.55	0.87	−1.20
1967	**Johnson**	**44.21**	**58.91**	**0.75**	**−1.69**
1968	**Johnson**	**43.67**	**57.56**	**0.76**	**−1.66**
1969	Nixon	54.98	55.34	0.99	−0.66
1970	Nixon	53.81	53.01	1.02	−0.57
1971	Nixon	48.13	51.84	0.93	−0.93
1972	Nixon	51.61	50.30	1.03	−0.52
1973	Nixon	40.86	43.18	0.95	−0.86
1974	**Nixon**	**25.19**	**39.58**	**0.64**	**−2.16**
1974	Ford	49.23	40.82	1.21	0.04
1975	Ford	40.85	43.18	0.95	−0.86
1976	Ford	46.66	43.23	1.08	−0.29
1977	Carter	56.13	42.78	1.31	0.70
1978	Carter	44.07	40.80	1.08	−0.29
1979	Carter	36.91	41.67	0.89	−1.12
1980	Carter	39.98	41.54	0.96	−0.79
1981	Reagan	51.41	48.32	1.06	−0.36
1982	Reagan	43.59	45.38	0.96	−0.80
1983	Reagan	44.17	47.40	0.93	−0.92
1984	Reagan	53.07	49.71	1.07	−0.34
1985	Reagan	59.49	47.78	1.24	0.41
1986	Reagan	60.45	47.42	1.27	0.54
1987	Reagan	51.76	47.66	1.09	−0.26
1988	Reagan	54.82	46.78	1.17	0.10
1989	GHW Bush	62.24	45.79	1.36	0.90
1990	GHW Bush	65.58	43.51	1.51	1.53
1991	**GHW Bush**	**68.56**	**41.78**	**1.64**	**2.10**
1992	GHW Bush	43.92	38.72	1.13	−0.06
1993	Clinton	47.11	38.17	1.23	0.37
1994	Clinton	45.74	37.42	1.22	0.32
1995	Clinton	47.15	36.96	1.28	0.54
1996	Clinton	53.33	41.92	1.27	0.53
1997	Clinton	57.86	40.95	1.41	1.13
1998	Clinton	62.94	43.84	1.44	1.23
1999	**Clinton**	**62.71**	**39.64**	**1.58**	**1.85**
2000	Clinton	62.47	41.21	1.52	1.57
2001	GW Bush	67.21	54.65	1.23	0.35
2002	GW Bush	70.44	50.22	1.40	1.08
2003	GW Bush	60.73	51.82	1.17	0.10
2004	GW Bush	50.57	47.13	1.07	−0.32
2005	GW Bush	43.71	42.56	1.03	−0.51
2006	GW Bush	36.18	40.85	0.89	−1.12
2007	GW Bush	31.95	34.13	0.94	−0.90
2008	GW Bush	31.41	35.86	0.88	−1.16
2009	**Obama**	**57.63**	**37.43**	**1.54**	**1.67**
2010	**Obama**	**46.86**	**28.60**	**1.64**	**2.09**
2011	Obama	44.68	29.25	1.53	1.56
2012	Obama	47.57	38.25	1.24	0.41

Source: Calculated by author. Outliers are presented in **bold**. See text for details.

the series average (that is, the "mean"), no matter its actual value, is set to zero with a standard deviation of one. Column 6 displays the Z-scores, or a precise estimate of how far away from the average score of 1.15 each president falls in a given year. As an illustration, Lyndon Johnson's IPL in 1964 is 1.16, which is very nearly equal to the average of the series, as indicated by his Z-score of 0.04, meaning his IPL registered 0.04 standard deviations above the mean.

But even more useful, Z-scores are expedient for quickly identifying outliers. Take for example Nixon's 1974 score. Given that he was in the middle of Watergate and on the cusp of becoming the first president in history to resign the office, his IPL registered a series low of 0.64, 2.16 standard deviations below the mean. Finally, Z-scores are useful for identifying "surprises," those that fall well below or above the average, or to make comparisons reasonably straightforward. For example, it may not be surprising that George H. W. Bush's 1991 IPL was among the highest of any president, registering a staggering 2.10 on the heels of the quick U.S. victory in Desert Storm. But when the economy was plagued by persistent recession and Bush was (perhaps wrongly) held accountable, his 1992 IPL fell to 1.13, just below average for all presidents. In Table 4.3, outliers are presented in **bold**, highlighting years in which a president's Z-score reaches at least positive or negative 1.64, the cutoff for the .05 level of confidence in one-tailed tests, the tests that are employed in the empirical analyses.[13]

Annual trust scores exhibit a range from a high of 62.73 in the first year of Kennedy's term to its nadir of 28.6 in the second year of Obama's first term.[14] Because extracted approval ratings correlate highly with the raw data ($r = 0.98$), the extracted scores are treated as percentages. Between the table and the graph, we have both an overview of the series and a more detailed look at the actual scores.

Figure 4.2 tracks the annual coefficients of presidential leverage for President Kennedy's first term through President Obama's, recalling from Table 4.1 that the average IPL over the entire series is equal to 1.15 (the horizontal dotted line). Presidents who register above 1.0 are relatively stronger, and those who fall below the line are weaker given that an IPL of 1.0 means that specific support and diffuse support are equivalent;

that is, when approval equals trust. The IPL hovers around the average at the beginning of the series, which is somewhat surprising given that Kennedy's and Johnson's approval ratings were well above average; approval ratings in each year from 1961 to 1964 yielded Z-scores more than two standard deviations above the mean, and 1965 registered nearly as high with $Z = 1.85$.

This apparent anomaly is a simple reflection of the fact that, although approval of the president may have been high, so too were public evaluations of trust. The IPL is a contextual, relative measure such that high approval ratings do not necessarily translate to high leverage. Presidents with low approval measures can still have high leverage if public trust in government is even lower.[15] Like the raw approval measure, the lowest IPL value registers 0.64 in the last year of Nixon's presidency.

After the IPL declines during the 1960s, the first major peak occurs in 1977, President Carter's first year in office. Watergate was over and all of Nixon's men, including Gerald Ford, were gone from the political scene.

The IPL finds its second, and highest, peak in 1991, the year of George H. W. Bush's triumph in the Gulf War. Government trust was lower even than it was in Carter's first year, registering 41.78, but Bush's average extracted approval was 68.56, yielding an IPL of 1.641, the highest in the series, and besting Obama's 2010 IPL of 1.639. But a persistent recession doomed Bush's reelection prospects as the IPL dipped from the highest annual observation (1.64) in 1991 to well below average (1.13) in 1992, clearing the way for Bill Clinton's ascent to the presidency.

Clinton's IPL follows no consistent pattern, but it is clear that he enjoyed high presidential leverage even as the impeachment process in 1998 and 1999 were at full throttle. His extracted approval in 1999, for example, was 63 percent, the second highest reading of his administration. However, public confidence in Congress was abnormally low,[16] which drove aggregate trust down more than 4 points and boosted his IPL to 1.58. Thus, even during impeachment, Clinton registered IPLs in 1998 and 1999 that well exceeded Jimmy Carter's 1977 score and three of four Obama scores (save for 2010) but fell short of Bush's 1991 leverage rating.

George W. Bush's IPL began high and increased throughout 2002 but dropped precipitously during the rest of his administration. Indeed, no president's leverage was as widely dispersed as was Bush's, and by 2008 the country was ready for Barack Obama's rise to the Oval Office. Obama's IPL during his first term was strong, even though he suffered near-record defeats in the midterms of 2010. Appendix A displays his quarterly IPLs as particularly robust, coinciding with the president's signing of the Affordable Care Act in March 2010, at the beginning of the second quarter. The annual IPLs drop in 2011 and 2012, though 2012's index remained well above the series average, paving the way for his reelection.

INDIVIDUAL PRESIDENTS AND PUBLIC LEVERAGE

This section takes a microscopic look at each president considered in this book. To both facilitate the individual experiences of each president as well as place each president in context of the others considered here, graphs are provided displaying quarterly readings for approval, trust, and the IPL for the entire series, highlighting the individual president under consideration. In each "a" graph, the black solid line indicates the degree of trust, whereas the line-fill shows presidential approval. For comparative purposes, the "b" graph highlights each president's IPL.

John F. Kennedy, 1961–1963

After the economic recession of the 1950s ended and the Korean War was won, but before the United States became increasingly involved in Southeast Asia, Presidents Eisenhower (not shown here) and Kennedy enjoyed the political perks of peace and prosperity. But because trust in government was also high they did not record high IPLs and had no special advantage in the political system. Kennedy's aggregate average approval during his term was just over 70 percent, whereas public trust averaged 62.7. Thus, contrary to what might be expected, Kennedy's IPL was a relatively moderate, even slightly below average, 1.12. In fact, the patterns observed during his administration are illustrative of how the IPL is measured in *relative* terms. Recall that among all presidents considered here, Kennedy recorded the highest average approval ratings; indeed, 1961 was more than two standard deviations above the mean. Like all presidents, his approval declined as his term progressed, moving

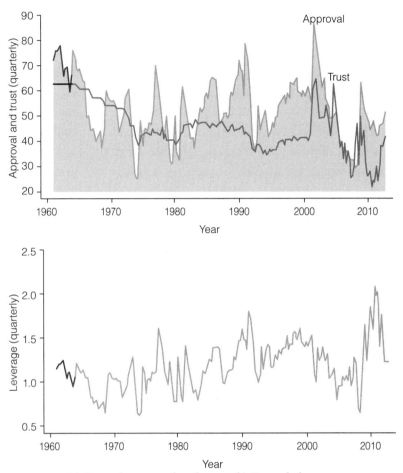

FIGURE 4.3 (a) Kennedy approval and trust. (b) Kennedy leverage.

Sources: (a) Approval data are from the American Presidency Project, available at www
.presidency.ucsb.edu/data/popularity.php. Trust data are from public opinion polls and archived
with the Roper Center for Public Opinion, available at http://ropercenter.cornell.edu/. All estimates
were generated using WCALC. See text for details. (b) Calculated by author.

from a high of about 78 percent in the first quarter of 1962 to just below
60 percent shortly before his death, though still well above the average
approval ratings of other presidents at the same points in their presidencies.[17] Even the debacle at the Bay of Pigs in April 1961 failed to damage
Kennedy's stature. His approval was all but unaffected, declining almost
imperceptibly from 76 percent in the first quarter to 75.7 percent in the
second. (See Figures 4.3a and 4.3b.)

Despite Kennedy's consistently vigorous approval throughout his term, his IPL is mediocre because trust in government was similarly hearty. As the recession of the late 1950s abated and unemployment hovered just under 6 percent, gross domestic product (GDP) came storming back to previously strong levels. As many have noted, both the objective state of the economy and its evaluation by the public are major components in influencing levels of trust (Hetherington 2005; Weatherford 1984). During the three short years of Kennedy's presidency, GDP increased by an annual average of 4.3 percent. In addition, Kennedy had an optimistic leadership style; from the very beginning in his inaugural address, he consistently argued that government could and would do great things (Hetherington 2005: 19).

Unlike later presidents, particularly those under whom trust declined, Kennedy's "average" IPL may be a difference of kind and not just degree. Measures of variation for both approval and leverage show a high level of consistency (his IPL standard deviations were third lowest in the series, and for approval he was fifth lowest). It is difficult to sustain an argument that Kennedy was hamstrung by both approval and high trust. He was able to put through major legislation, particularly in his first year,[18] enjoying high levels of congressional concurrence, though he was never able to pass federal aid to education, his signature domestic initiative, nor other domestic initiatives, even as he served with Democratic majorities in both houses of Congress.

Lyndon B. Johnson, 1963–1969

Lyndon Johnson assumed the presidency in shocking fashion on November 22, 1963, and rode the waves of extremely high approval ratings due to the public impact of Kennedy's assassination. Overall, his one-plus term as president registered an aggregate 54.5 percent approval rating, whereas trust averaged 59.5, plunging his average IPL of 0.91 into negative territory and well below-average.[19] Indeed, his final two years in office are negative outliers in the IPL, registering −1.69 in 1967 and −1.66 in 1968. (See Figures 4.4a and 4.4b.)

Although trust in government was generally high in Johnson's term, it began to decline almost from the day he took office. Like Kennedy, Johnson

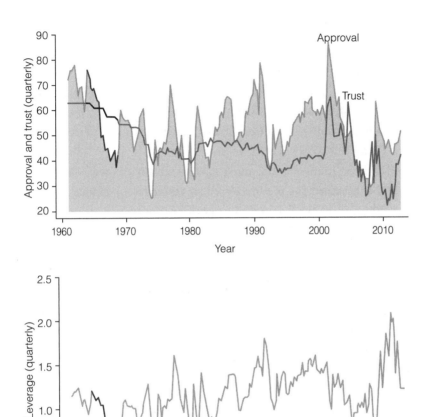

FIGURE 4.4   (a) Johnson approval and trust. (b) Johnson leverage.

Sources: (a) Approval data are from the American Presidency Project, available at www
.presidency.ucsb.edu/data/popularity.php. Trust data are from public opinion polls and archived
with the Roper Center for Public Opinion, available at http://ropercenter.cornell.edu/. All estimates
were generated using WCALC. See text for details. (b) Calculated by author.

generally articulated a positive role for government and sought to forge a
"Great Society." Trust in government was rather high in the mid-1960s,
principally because the Vietnam War was still popular. Americans by and
large framed the war in heroic terms, interpreting the war as one in which
United States sought to stave off communist aggression in Southeast Asia.
The economic recovery that began during Eisenhower's administration

and accelerated under Kennedy continued unabated throughout LBJ's administration, with unemployment declining from 5.2 percent in 1964 to 3.6 percent in 1968. Because the measure of political trust minimizes the direct effect of the presidency, these issues interacted in a way that kept trust high, even as it gradually declined. Specifically, trust declined slowly but constantly, from 62.7 on November 22, 1963, to 55.9 on the eve of Richard Nixon's election in 1968.

What hurt Johnson's IPL most was the dramatic decay in his approval. He assumed the presidency under tragic circumstances, and average approval for the first full quarter of his presidency reached nearly 76 percent. By the time of his landslide reelection in November, 1964, he was still extremely popular and enjoyed an approval rating of nearly 70 percent. This number reflected his management of the war after the August Gulf of Tonkin episode, and the signing of the Civil Rights Act of 1964. But as the nation became entrenched in Vietnam and antiwar protests increased in number and intensity, his approval dropped to below 50 percent at the 1966 midterm elections. When antiwar candidate Eugene McCarthy pulled 42 percent in the New Hampshire primary in March 1968, a wounded LBJ announced he would not seek another term, and his approval fell below 43 percent. His approval ratings over his one "long" term exhibit the eleventh highest variation of the thirteen administration terms covered in this book. Consequently, his average IPL fell to 0.91 overall, well below the average for all presidents in the series and slightly below the 0.97 average of the three pre-1974 presidents (Kennedy, Johnson, and Nixon).

But Johnson's annual IPL was far below these averages in the period after the midterm elections in 1967 and 1968, registering 0.75 and 0.76, respectively. The variation of his IPL is the ninth highest in the series. With low approval ratings and high trust in government, a measure that likely exempted him from its calculation, he announced his decision to step aside.

Even so, Johnson enjoyed considerable domestic policy success, particularly in the areas of civil rights and antipoverty legislation. The number of legislative requests in 1965 alone registered more than 3 standard deviations above average. But his grasp on the presidency was clearly slipping, and his approval ratings increased in only six quarters of his entire presidency.[20] His IPL did increase in nine quarters, albeit in very small increments, and in only four quarters did he match or exceed the average IPL and not at all after the first quarter of 1965.

Still, much of Johnson's presidency was ambitious and productive in both absolute and relative terms. But LBJ struggled with low levels of presidential leverage and most of the big issues that he is known for in the areas of civil rights and other social programs were accomplished *before the decline* in his IPL. Hetherington (2005) shows that periods of high trust are more likely to generate policy accomplishments in areas targeting race and the economy. Johnson's inability to rebound and capitalize politically is due partly to his strategic sense that the administration had to move rapidly on his agenda, as much as it could by the 1966 midterms, but his declining approval relative to declining levels of trust is also to blame, driving his outlier years of 1967 and 1968.

Richard M. Nixon, 1969–1974

Though his presidency would end in resignation amid dismally low approval ratings, Richard M. Nixon was generally a popular president during his first term. His approval averaged 54.4 percent, while trust registered 53.23. This gives Nixon a "draw" in the leverage space (IPL = 1.02), with very little variation. His IPL ranges from a high of 1.03 in 1972 to 0.93 in 1971, with a standard deviation of 4.9. But Nixon remained popular despite a sluggish economy; GDP had slowed to just 0.2 percent annual change in constant dollars, and he cruised to a historic reelection in 1972. He won one of the most lopsided contests in history, defeating Senator George McGovern (D-ND) with almost 61 percent of the popular vote and a stunning 520 electoral votes. (See Figures 4.5a and 4.5b.)

Those numbers changed dramatically in Nixon's second term, when his average approval fell to 36.4 percent and was subject to the widest variation of all the presidents included in this study (standard deviation = 13.76). He began his second term with relatively high approval ratings, reaching nearly 60 percent, but soon after they declined swiftly. Although only half of the country (52 percent) had heard of Watergate before the 1972 election, some 85 percent had heard of it just four months later in

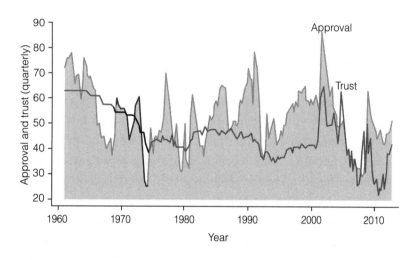

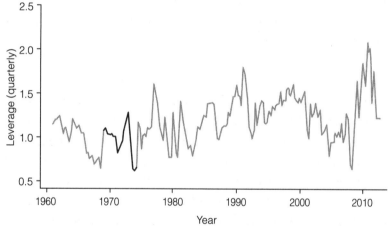

FIGURE 4.5. (a) Nixon approval and trust. (b) Nixon leverage.

Sources: (a) Approval data are from the American Presidency Project, available at www .presidency.ucsb.edu/data/popularity.php. Trust data are from public opinion polls and archived with the Roper Center for Public Opinion, available at http://ropercenter.cornell.edu/. All estimates were generated using WCALC. See text for details. (b) Calculated by author.

April 1973, and by August fully 98 percent knew of Watergate. Nixon's approval ratings fell as quickly, from 60 percent in the fourth quarter of 1972 to 45 percent by the second quarter of 1973, and, by the time the year ended, he labored under a crushingly low 27.8 percent. They tumbled even further in 1974.[21]

If government trust had started to fall during Johnson's term, it was driven off the proverbial cliff during Nixon's six years in the White House, particularly during the second term. Trust fell from approximately 54.3 percent at the beginning of Nixon's term to just below 50 percent by the 1972 election. But Watergate and the continuing national tragedy that was Vietnam badly damaged the public's trust in government. It took just two years between 1972 and Nixon's resignation in August 1974 for trust to decline from 50.3 to 38.2. The quarterly data are even more striking. In the final quarter of 1972, trust registered 60.4, and by mid-1974 it had fallen to 38.2. The decline in trust during this period is by far the steepest and quickest of any period in the series.[22]

Nixon's IPL decreased intensely throughout his shortened second term. His IPL slips from a hefty 1.30 in early 1973 to under 1.0 by the end of the second quarter, the steepest one-quarter decline up to that point. Even with trust in government falling, Nixon quickly lost footing, and by the time of his resignation his IPL registered a dismal 0.66, the largest outlier in the series with a Z-score of −2.16. The only reason leverage "increases" at all from the first to the second quarter in 1974 is that Nixon actually "enjoyed" a very slight uptick in approval (from 25.2 to 25.4) while the reading for trust in government fell from 40.9 to 38.2.

Gerald R. Ford, 1974–1977

Ford moved into the Oval Office under unique circumstances, becoming the first person to serve as both president and vice president of the United States having been elected to neither office. As such, his constitutional leverage was mixed. He served in a period of divided government, never an easy task for presidents. Things only got worse for the president in the 1974 midterm elections, just three months after moving into the White House, when congressional Republicans lost forty-eight seats in the House and five in the Senate. Consequently, the veto became his most successful tool with which to try to induce direction to his policy agenda. Additionally, he had a lackluster economy to deal with, with inflation a particular concern. Ford tried to transform inflation into a winning opportunity with lapel pins proclaiming support for WIN (Whip Inflation

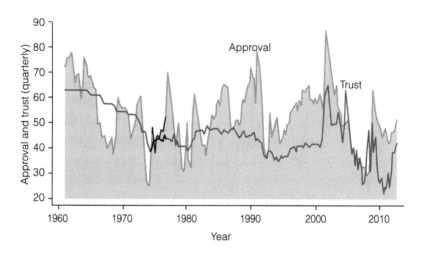

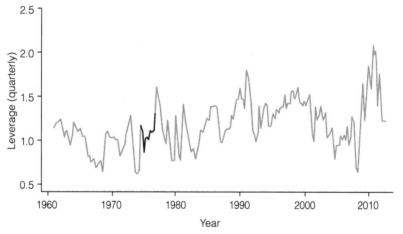

FIGURE 4.6. (a) Ford approval and trust. (b) Ford leverage.

Sources: (a) Approval data are from the American Presidency Project, available at www.presidency.ucsb.edu/data/popularity.php. Trust data are from public opinion polls and archived with the Roper Center for Public Opinion, available at http://ropercenter.cornell.edu/. All estimates were generated using WCALC. See text for details. (b) Calculated by author.

Now), but his presidency faced formidable challenges no matter what he did. (See Figures 4.6a and 4.6b.)

Throughout most of his short term, Ford's quarterly approval hovered below 50 percent (roughly 46 percent), with very little variance. The standard deviation for his approval rating (4.1) was the second lowest of any president in the series, just behind Clinton's second term. By way of comparison, Kennedy, who served only slightly longer than Ford, registered the fifth-lowest variation. Ford began his term with significantly higher approval ratings than his predecessor (Ford's first-quarter approval rating was more than 20 percent higher than Nixon's last), and, like most presidents, his individual approval ratings were initially high, reaching 71 percent in a Gallup survey just a week after taking office. Still, Ford found it difficult to distance himself from Watergate, and he did himself no favor when in September 1974 he granted Nixon a full and clear pardon, leading many to wonder whether there had been a deal between Nixon and Ford. Though Ford vehemently denied there had been such a deal, his approval ratings dipped 16 points almost overnight, into the mid-30s by early 1975. Still, his approval crawled steadily upward throughout the remainder of his term and settled at nearly 50 percent in the quarter just prior to his loss to Jimmy Carter in 1976. Interestingly, his approval rating peaked at 53 percent barely over a month after losing the election.

Trust in government stayed roughly constant throughout Ford's abbreviated term. Average trust in the series was stable at about 46, and during the Ford years it stayed around 43. Though the standard deviation on trust was only fifth lowest during his term, it needs to be pointed out that, for the fourteen terms and ten presidents covered in this book, eight of them had standard deviations under 2 and nine under 3.

Ford's IPL for his term was 1.08, slightly below average, but his quarterly IPLs move into high leverage territory during 1974. Whereas Nixon had left office with an IPL of 0.64, Ford's nearly doubled to 1.21 between August and December. However, the sluggish economy and his pardon of Nixon dramatically reduced his leverage, which plunged into negative territory throughout 1975 and into 1976. Ford's IPL increased briefly to 1.08 in the election year, but the same basic pattern reveals itself in the quarterly data as well, remaining around a "draw" for most of his presidency, which helps explain his dependence on constitutional leverage.

Jimmy Carter, 1977–1981

Jimmy Carter had a rough presidency when approval and trust are considered in isolation. Although there has been a substantial amount of Carter revisionism (for example, Hargrove 1988), the Carter presidency was certainly a beleaguered one, enduring seemingly everything from stagflation (simultaneously high levels of unemployment and inflation) to a perception of weakness when confronting the Iranian hostage crisis. His average approval over the entire term, 44.9 percent, was the third lowest of any term studied here, trailing only the second terms of both George W. Bush and Richard Nixon. Average trust was fourth lowest in the series, registering just ahead of the readings in Bill Clinton's first term, George W. Bush's second term, and Barack Obama's first term. This low trust in government helped produce a relatively high IPL in 1977, but events soon overwhelmed Carter, and his overall 1.08 IPL was slightly below average. Perhaps more telling, although we often think of Ford as among the most beleaguered of presidents given the peculiar circumstances of his presidency, Carter's IPL over his four years was exactly equivalent to Ford's. (See Figures 4.7a and 4.7b.)

Initially, Carter's quarterly approval was even more impressive, as it hit nearly 70 percent in the first quarter of 1977, declined slowly at first, and then continued to decline at an accelerated rate. By the 1978 midterms his approval dropped into the 40s. At the same time, congressional Democrats lost fifteen seats in the House of Representatives and three in the Senate. Soon afterward, his approval plummeted further, into the 30s, and it never recovered except for the quarter just after the onset of the Iranian hostage crisis. But that rally-around-the-flag effect decayed quickly, and Carter's approval dipped back into the 30s and remained there for the duration of his term.

The IPL's first peak appears in 1977, the first year of his term, which is explained by the fact that Carter was the first truly post-Watergate president. His pledge that "I will never lie to you" brought with it a new timbre of hope for a weary polity. Of course, by the time Carter assumed the presidency, presidential power had presumably been scaled back by Congress with the passage of the 1974 Budget and Impoundment Control Act and the War Powers Resolution, which passed over Nixon's veto. Still, government trust was relatively low in 1977, registering 42.8, well below the series average. Carter's annual approval that year was a robust 56 percent, producing an annual IPL of 1.31, which was up to that time the highest index recorded. Indeed, if we examine quarterly data,

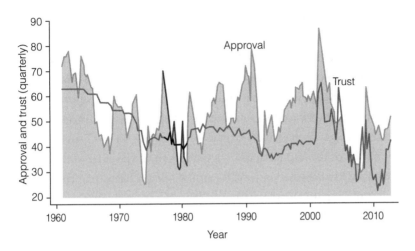

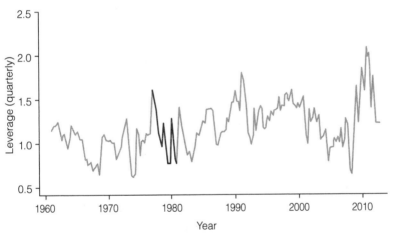

FIGURE 4.7. (a) Carter approval and trust. (b) Carter leverage.

Sources: (a) Approval data are from the American Presidency Project, available at www
.presidency.ucsb.edu/data/popularity.php. Trust data are from public opinion polls and archived
with the Roper Center for Public Opinion, available at http://ropercenter.cornell.edu/. All estimates
were generated using WCALC. See text for details. (b) Calculated by author.

Carter's initial IPLs are even more impressive, reaching 1.6 in the first
quarter of his presidency. Thus, when placed in context, the observation
that Carter registered such an immediate spike is not terribly surprising,
especially because the coefficient declines throughout the rest of his term.

Trust had not yet begun to recover after the dramatic declines of the
1960s and early 1970s. Carter's IPL fluctuated throughout in spite of that

fact, but he never again came close to reaching the same levels as in his first year. After the midterms, though, Carter's IPL was nearly always in negative territory. To be sure, his quarterly IPL reached 1.28 in the period just after the American embassy in Tehran was seized. But the IPL dropped as quickly as it had risen, and by the very next quarter it dropped to 0.93 and kept falling during the remainder of his presidency. His inability to free the hostages coupled with crippling stagflation led to Carter's defeat at the hands of Ronald Reagan by 7 percent in the popular vote, and he was thoroughly flattened in the Electoral College. The salt in the wound was that the Senate Democrats found themselves in the minority for the first time since Dwight Eisenhower's first term.

Ronald Reagan, 1981–1989

Ronald Reagan's first term, like Carter's, began with optimism. Where Carter had played the role of "president as teacher," warning Americans of a crisis of the American soul in his so-called malaise speech of July 1979, Reagan campaigned on a more positive note, telling Americans that government, rather than conspicuous consumption, was the root cause of the problems, and he turned that optimistic message into an easy 489 to 49 win in the Electoral College. However, much of Regan's first term was plagued by persistent economic problems, including a recession, and his average first-term approval fell below 50 percent. Ironically, given Reagan's antigovernment rhetoric, trust in government actually *increased* to the mid-40s, and his first term IPL was 1.08, about the same as Ford's and Carter's and only slightly higher than George W. Bush's beleaguered second term. Reagan's second term was much more vital, though. Even while he endured a late-term scandal over arms-for-hostages (the so-called Iran-Contra episode), his second-term approval averaged about 56 percent, trust stayed constant, and his IPL was a healthy 1.21, the fifth highest of the presidential terms in this book. (See Figures 4.8a and 4.8b.)

Quarterly approval reveals the patterns in a bit more depth. Reagan's approval was high to begin with (57.26 in the first quarter) and rose even higher, due in part to the failed assassination attempt at the end of March 1981. But as the recession took hold, his approval ratings declined dramatically, and he was unpopular at the midterm (41 percent), reaching a

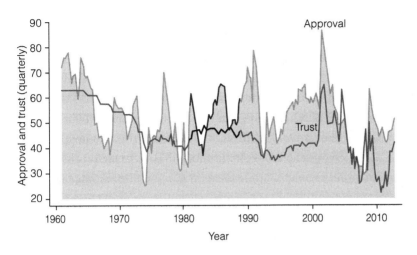

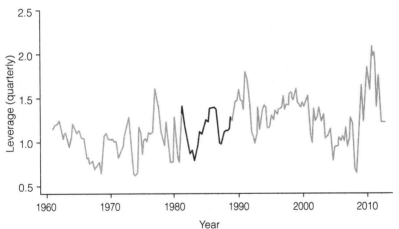

FIGURE 4.8. (a) Reagan approval and trust. (b) Reagan leverage.

Sources: (a) Approval data are from the American Presidency Project, available at www
.presidency.ucsb.edu/data/popularity.php. Trust data are from public opinion polls and archived
with the Roper Center for Public Opinion, available at http://ropercenter.cornell.edu/. All estimates
were generated using WCALC. See text for details. (b) Calculated by author.

low point of 36.8 in early 1983. Over time, though, he rallied and was
in the mid- to upper 50s around the time of his easy reelection in 1984.

Reagan's second-term leverage was a marked increase over the first
term. At the 1986 midterm, his IPL was 1.37 but plunged as word of the
Iran-Contra arms-for-hostages scandal began to break. The electorate
returned the Senate to the Democrats. His IPL remained slightly below

average in the quarters after the election and turned into negative territory in the second quarter of 1987. Still, by the time he left office in 1988, his annual IPL was a slightly above-average 1.17.

George H. W. Bush, 1989–1993

George H.W. Bush, the first man to be elected directly to the presidency after serving as vice president since Martin Van Buren in 1836, came to office with relatively little left to do on the domestic agenda. Many programs that could be cut had in fact been cut under Ronald Reagan, and Bush was relegated to overseeing a caretaker presidency. He was perhaps best known for his "no new taxes" pledge, which he promptly had to break. His greatest triumph was in the Gulf War, in which the United States engaged in a twenty-eight-day confrontation that liberated Kuwait from Saddam Hussein's Iraq after the dictator invaded that country in August 1990. Although a recession raged through much of the early part of Bush's presidency, he was largely correct when he argued that the economy was recovering, even while most of the public did not yet agree. Therefore, depending on one's perspective, it may or may not be surprising that: (a) Bush had annual approval ratings above 60 percent in the first three of his four years as president, and (b) he lost his bid for reelection in 1992. (See Figures 4.9a and 4.9b.)

Trust in government dropped during Bush's four years in the White House, which coincided with the rise of the code word *gridlock*, a term that began to spread throughout Washington, the media, and into the public. Gridlock described public perception of the federal government, which was that politics was dysfunctional and, worse, very little if anything could be done to correct the situation. Bush had a relatively small domestic agenda (although he was able to pass the Americans for Disabilities Act and the Clean Water Act), but foreign policy and the Gulf War victory kept his approval high, and thus he maintained considerable public leverage, particularly in 1990 and especially in 1991. In fact, Bush's IPL of 1.64 in 1991, an outlier at nearly 2.4 standard deviations above the mean, is tied with Obama's 2010 for the highest IPL in any year of this study. But in the course of one year, though the recession appeared to be easing, Bush fell from a high of 68.5 percent approval to 43.9 per-

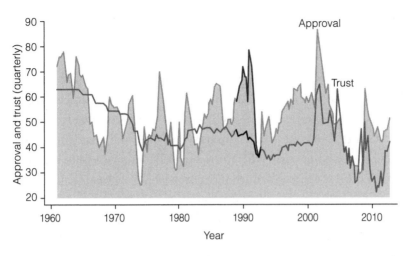

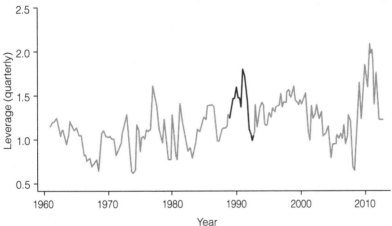

FIGURE 4.9. (a) George H. W. Bush approval and trust. (b) George H. W. Bush leverage.

Sources: (a) Approval data are from the American Presidency Project, available at www .presidency.ucsb.edu/data/popularity.php. Trust data are from public opinion polls and archived with the Roper Center for Public Opinion, available at http://ropercenter.cornell.edu/. All estimates were generated using WCALC. See text for details. (b) Calculated by author.

cent. Consequently, his IPL dropped from 1.64 to 1.13, even though trust in government was falling at the same time. Bush's public standing was falling faster and further even than trust. His decline in approval, IPL, and trust, as well as the on-again/off-again candidacy of billionaire Ross Perot as a high-profile, well-financed third-party candidate in the 1992 presidential race, combined late in Bush's presidency to pave the way for Bill Clinton's election.

Bill Clinton, 1993–2001

Almost immediately after Bill Clinton defeated the incumbent president, his administration stumbled. It seemed that everything from social policy (for example, gays in the military), to the more mundane (a $400 haircut that held up air traffic at the Los Angeles airport), to the firing of the White House travel office staff, broke against the administration, leaving the wonkish president struggling to find his voice. An initially popular health care reform proposal soon lost major support once the details of the plan became public, and Clinton saw his political fortunes plummet. Average approval for his first term was just below 50 percent and would have been even lower had it not been for his political resurrection in 1996, described in Chapter 1. Average trust hovered in the 30s during his first term, the third lowest in the series, trailing just behind George W. Bush's second term. To be sure, this is understandable enough. The perception of gridlock was firmly ensconced as a descriptor of American politics as the Republicans reaped the rewards of the 1994 "wave election," taking control of the House of Representatives for the first time in four decades and reclaiming the Senate it had lost eight years prior. Perhaps no other single episode illustrates that perception better than the two government shutdowns that the public pinned squarely on the Republicans. Thus, although Clinton infamously had to plead that the "president is still relevant," his actual leverage was not very low. In fact, his first-term IPL registered a strong 1.31. Clinton's IPLs for the first two quarters of 1994 were actually quite robust, but, as the midterms grew near and perceptions increased of Clinton's inability to work with the Democratic majority in Congress, the IPL plunged from a high of 1.40 to 1.17 on the eve of the midterms elections. Although Clinton's IPL was still slightly above average by November, the contrast was striking. (See Figures 4.10a and 4.10b.)

As described early in this book, Clinton saw his political fortunes increase radically throughout 1995 and especially 1996. His average approval in the second term was 60 percent, the second highest rating of

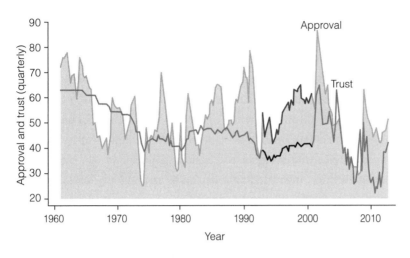

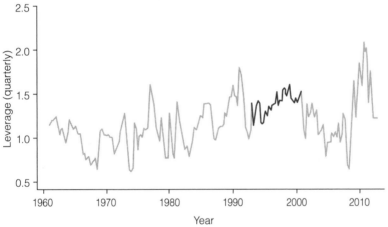

FIGURE 4.10. (a) Clinton approval and trust. (b) Clinton leverage.

Sources: (a) Approval data are from the American Presidency Project, available at www
.presidency.ucsb.edu/data/popularity.php. Trust data are from public opinion polls and archived
with the Roper Center for Public Opinion, available at http://ropercenter.cornell.edu/. All estimates
were generated using WCALC. See text for details. (b) Calculated by author.

the presidents considered here, just behind George W. Bush's first term,
which had benefited tremendously from rally support after 9/11 and its
aftermath. The government trust reading also improved to 40 percent,
but the huge increase in the IPL's value to 1.48 was due mainly to Clinton's 12-point turnaround in average approval. This turn of events seems
counterintuitive given that Clinton was impeached in his second term

and spent much of it embroiled in the Monica Lewinsky scandal. A likely reason for the high IPL is it grew as the mixture of low government trust and high approval, which was likely due to public dissatisfaction with Kenneth Starr's investigation of the Lewinsky affair and public distaste for Starr himself, coupled with skepticism about Republican efforts to impeach Clinton. Clinton's average approval throughout scandal-plagued 1998 was in the 60s. Consider that during the last quarter of 1998, when the midterm elections were closing in and Clinton was on the cusp of impeachment, and into the first quarter of 1999 when he was acquitted in the Senate, his approval ratings were 64 percent and 65 percent, respectively.[23] Indeed, Clinton's average IPL in 1999 was 1.58, another outlier at nearly two standard deviations above the series mean, and declined only slightly in 2000, his last year as president. Trust remained flat at just above 40 in both quarterly and annual observations. Thus, Clinton enjoyed high public leverage, although he was stymied by congressional use of its constitutional prerogatives, especially in the latter part of his presidency.

George W. Bush, 2001–2009

George W. Bush came to the White House having won a Supreme Court decision after losing the popular vote to Vice President Al Gore. *Bush v. Gore* stopped vote counting in Florida, thereby sealing the presidency for Bush who squeaked by with 271 electoral votes, one more than necessary. Many in the public protested the outcome of the election for the first several months of his presidency, and he struggled for legitimacy. That all changed in tragic fashion on September 11, 2001, when the United States was attacked on its own soil by terrorists. The public rallied around the commander in chief in the days after the attacks, and Bush's job approval soared above 90 percent in some polls. Even so, his IPL, although large, was not as extraordinary as might be expected with such a huge approval rating because trust in government was similarly high. (See Figures 4.11a and 4.11b.)

Bush's average approval throughout his first term was a healthy 61 percent, which is actually somewhat low given how high his approval ratings were in 2001 and 2002. Additionally, given the extremely high early

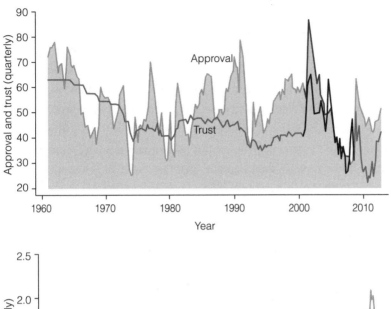

FIGURE 4.11 (a) George W. Bush approval and trust. (b) George W. Bush leverage.

Sources: (a) Approval data are from the American Presidency Project, available at www. presidency.ucsb.edu/data/popularity.php. Trust data are from public opinion polls and archived with the Roper Center for Public Opinion, available at http://ropercenter.cornell.edu/. All estimates were generated using WCALC. See text for details. (b) Calculated by author.

ratings early on and how low they fell after a small uptick in response to the American invasion of Iraq in March 2003, there was enormous variation over the course of his first term. Gary Jacobson (2008) shows that, although Bush enjoyed astronomical approval ratings after the September 11 terrorist attacks, almost all of the variance in the 40 percent decrease in his first-term approval ratings (from a high of about 90 percent to about 50 percent) is accounted for by declining approval among Democrats and Independents. In the months just after the attacks, Bush's approval ratings soared among all three partisan groups. Independents approved of his performance by nearly the same percentage as Republicans (close to 90 percent), and even Democrats registered nearly 80 percent approval. By the end of 2005, Bush's approval among Republicans fell slightly to 83 percent, whereas his advantages among Democrats had practically disappeared (13 percent approval), and less than one in three (32 percent) Independents approved (Jacobson 2008).

Bush's approval did not dip below the 60 percent mark until the third quarter of 2003, when questions about the wars in Iraq and Afghanistan dominated the political landscape, and from 2003 to 2004 his average approval fell ten points. Trust in government also fell, from 49 to 43, though it rebounded by the time of the 2004 election in which Bush faced off against Democratic challenger Senator John Kerry (MA). Though battered and bruised, he was narrowly reelected in spite of the fact that his quarterly IPL registered 0.79, easily the lowest in the series for a president winning reelection.[24]

Bush's second-term approval, trust in government, and his IPL were among the worst of any president examined here. Much of the negativity directed at the president and the political system was driven by public anxiety over the legitimacy of the war in Iraq as questions surfaced regarding the circumstances under which the president took the nation to war in 2003, specifically whether Iraq really harbored weapons of mass destruction. Bush's approval also suffered in the wake of his handling of the aftermath of Hurricane Katrina, as well as revelations of a scandal that culminated in the trial and conviction of Vice President Cheney's Chief of Staff Scooter Libby.[25] Consequently, Bush's approval stagnated below 40 percent at the time of the 2006 congressional midterms. Because trust in government was low during this period of unified government, Democrats enjoyed the fruits of a wave election that allowed them to retake both the House and Senate. Bush's IPL was volatile; variation in the index during his second term was the second largest of any president examined here, just behind Obama's first term.

Barack Obama I: 2009–2012

If Kennedy's experience constitutes a concrete example of the relative nature of the IPL measure, Barack Obama's first term is a veritable poster child. No president examined in this book came to the office with greater expectations for "hope" and "change." Obama's ascension to the presidency was as incredible as it was unlikely. Barely a decade had passed since he first won a special election for the Illinois state Senate. In that time, he won reelection twice (1998 and 2002), ran unsuccessfully for the U.S. House of Representatives (2000), and ran for and won a seat in the U.S. Senate (2006). Scarcely a year later, he launched a long-shot bid for the presidency. But his campaign gelled quickly as he inspired a young, energetic team that exploited opportunities in the new and developing world of social media. Obama raised record amounts of money and, in one of the great intraparty upsets in American political history, defeated Hillary Clinton, the heavily favored former first lady and sitting U.S. senator from New York, for the Democratic nomination. Riding a wave of discontent engendered by the collapsing economy and excitement generated around the prospect of electing the first black president and facing a weakened Republican challenger in Arizona Senator John McCain, whose candidacy was marred by numerous mistakes, real or perceived,[26] Obama cruised to victory, winning by more than 7 percent in the popular vote on his way to a 365 to 173 victory in the Electoral College. Obama's inauguration on January 20, 2009, attended by some 1.8 million people,[27] brought with it feverish expectations for a new type of presidency. In some ways, there was no place for the new president to go but down. (See Figures 4.12a and 4.12b.)

Obama's approval in his first year averaged nearly 58 percent, which, though high, was still lower than that of Kennedy, Johnson, and both Bushes, and barely higher than Carter's. Still, 58 percent approval is well above average, but it proved to be the high point of his presidency as he saw his approval ratings tumble through the remainder of his first term, rebounding slightly in the reelection year.[28] His first term averaged 49.3 percent, locating him almost exactly in the middle of the presidents examined here, recording higher than Nixon II, Ford, Carter, Clinton,

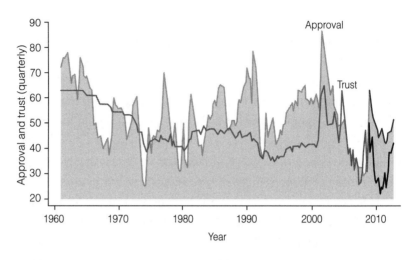

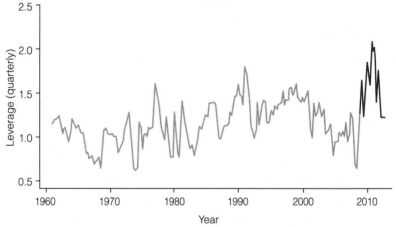

FIGURE 4.12. (a) Obama approval and trust. (b) Obama leverage.

Sources: (a) Approval data are from the American Presidency Project, available at www. presidency.ucsb.edu/data/popularity.php. Trust data are from public opinion polls and archived with the Roper Center for Public Opinion, available at http://ropercenter.cornell.edu/. All estimates were generated using WCALC. See text for details. (b) Calculated by author.

and Bush 43 II, and almost exactly equal to Reagan I. Although his approval ratings were middling, Obama still recorded extremely high IPLs as a product of the fact that the public consistently displayed a stark lack of government trust, and two of the four years considered here are positive outliers. Furthermore, trust over the course of his first term was 32.19, by far the lowest reading observed during any of the presidential terms studied here. For purposes of comparison, the next lowest trust score was in the second term of Bush 43, part of a general erosion of public trust over time. Indeed, the only two years in which trust dips below 30 are in 2010 and 2011, the midpoint of Obama's first term.

Trust in government proved to be extremely unstable during Obama's first term. Out of all the presidential terms in this book, average trust was at its lowest during the Obama administration, averaging just over 30. With a standard deviation of 8.5, it also exhibited the second-highest variation, just behind that of George W. Bush's first term. Obama inherited low trust, which continued to decline as "politics" in its most pejorative sense prevailed. Fallout from the passage of the Affordable Care Act, also known as Obamacare; the rise of the Tea Party as a national force during and after the 2010 midterm elections; brinksmanship between the White House and Congress on otherwise routine matters such as raising the debt limit; the so-called fiscal cliff negotiations, where deep cuts to the federal budget would be automatically triggered and meted out across the board if preset fiscal goals were not met; and the nearly constant threat of government shutdowns drove trust in government to their lowest levels in history. Public perception of government solidified around the general idea that government was broken and that politics, rather than good policy, seemed to be the endgame of Washington politicians (Mann and Ornstein 2012).

Accordingly, Obama's leverage scores are as fascinating as they are instructive and reinforce why specific support via presidential approval must be contextualized relative to diffuse public evaluation of government as a whole. In three of the four years of his first term, both approval and trust fell well below average. Only in Obama's first year did his mean approval climb above the series average. But while the mean approval over four years averaged a Z-score of −0.27, trust was well below the overall mean ($Z = -1.45$), yielding Obama's first-term IPL of 1.6, the highest of any president examined here. In only a few other instances (Ford in 1974 and Clinton from 1993 to 1995) did a president's IPL move into *above*-average territory when both approval and trust were *below* average.

Clinton's 1995 rating reached the highest (IPL = 1.28; Z = 0.54). Obama's average approval rating fell below the series average in the last three years of his first term after hitting near-record highs for a president in the first year of his first term. But public trust was extraordinarily low for all four years, and in 2010 and 2011 stagnated nearly two standard deviations below the mean. Though Obama's approval ratings were close to or exceeded $Z \cong -0.40$, trust was always nearly one standard deviation below the mean, reaching its nadir in 2010 (Z = −1.99), closely followed by 2011 (Z = −1.92). Because of this, though, Obama's IPLs were among the highest of any president, including 2010, the year he signed the Affordable Care Act and in which the Republicans picked up a startling sixty-three seats in the House of Representatives and six in the Senate, giving them back the majorities they lost in 2006. But Obama proved successful in passing major legislation and in fighting to stalemate in the face of a rejuvenated, though internally divided, Republican Congress. On May 1, 2011, for example, mere months after the Tea Party wing of the Republican party set up shop in the U.S. Congress after winning back control of both chambers, Obama scored a major foreign policy coup when he announced that, after nearly a decade on the run, Osama Bin Laden had been killed by American forces. Obama's approval increased by nearly 2 percent in the second quarter of 2011; though trust in government also rose, he registered his single highest IPL (2.02), clearly an outlier in the series.

Later, Obama and Congressional Democrats fought the Republicans to a draw in negotiations on raising the debt limit, though Obama was a "weakened" president if one examines his low raw approval scores. To be sure, he did not get all he sought in the negotiation, but with the combination of his leverage and the fact that the House Republicans were internally divided, he was able to fend off defeat and settled for what was destined to be an ineffectual congressional "super committee" charged with trying to hit deficit-reduction targets. The committee tried to impose structure and discipline by creating the so-called fiscal cliff by imposing structure and discipline to the process. It did so by setting a target deadline of January 1, 2013, notably after the 2012 elections, to reach predetermined budgetary goals or face "sequestration," a series of across-the-board budget cuts. The result of the negotiations displeased an already disillusioned public. As a result, Obama's approval rose slightly in the fourth quarter of 2011, but trust in government fell from 30 to 24, yielding Obama a well-above average IPL of 1.76.

Though during the 2012 election season Obama's leverage was the lowest of his term, it was well above average of all presidents considered in this book. Trust rebounded slightly but still yielded Obama an annual IPL of 1.24, the second highest for any of the presidents who ran for and won a second term.[29] The IPL for the remainder of Obama's administration will be considered in Chapter 7.

CONCLUSION

President Obama's experience illustrates the general thrust of this book. Although raw approval is certainly an indicator of how presidents are viewed by the public, a more nuanced portrait emerges if we take a deeper look at that approval in context of the public's level of government trust. Although approval is an important indicator of public estimations of the president, presidential leverage, measured as the IPL, is a deeper, far more contextualized view of how presidents are situated in the public mind, a measure of presidential "place" in the political system. Presidents who exhibit low leverage as measured by the IPL find themselves in a different place altogether than presidents who enjoy high support relative to diffuse regime support in the American political system, and this different vantage point produces different incentives. Presidents will almost always seek to increase or maintain strong approval ratings, but the manner in which that approval, or lack thereof, is interpreted is different depending on the changing public dynamic of trust in government. Presidents may seek different strategies for building autonomy and capacity in a system seemingly stacked against them, and the way in which they do so may vary depending on where they find themselves situated in the public mind. How they try to build capacity and assert autonomy manifested in the politics of policy formation, agenda setting, and use of unilateral prerogatives ebbs and flows with presidential public leverage. This can be illuminated in ways that are not always found by examining approval in isolation. In the following two chapters, the IPL is used to explore the relationship between leverage and several features of presidential action in both the macro- and micropolitical spheres.

CHAPTER 5

Presidential Leverage and the Creation of Public Policy

PRESIDENTS CAN FIND SUCCESS OR FAILURE in many different ways. In the constitutional context, presidents are "one among many" in the American state. To cope, they can exploit presidential leverage and whatever advantages they have to push their agenda, where many of the prospects for successes and failures lie. Certainly, presidential success is ultimately evaluated by how presidents place their stamp on the American political landscape and what their legacies looks like. President-specific policy monikers such as the New Frontier (JFK), Great Society (LBJ), or simply giving pride of place in the American system to presidents themselves (for example, the "Reagan years" or "the Obama years"), highlights presidents and their programs at center stage. Policy output defines presidents and their terms of office as much and in some cases more than other presidential gauges such as public opinion. This chapter argues that presidential leverage is related to the success presidents enjoy in stamping the landscape with *significant policies* that are of their own making and therefore are parts of their legacy that they can truly call their own.[1] It also argues that presidential decisions on unilateral action and agenda size are conditioned through presidential leverage as well.

When it comes to creating significant, large-scale, and lasting public policies, the stakes are high. Features such as the political context (for example, divided or unified government) influence individual bargaining conditions and condition the likelihood of success on key issues. As noted in previous chapters, presidents are hampered by public expectations, which almost invariably hold them and their party responsible for "bad" systemic conditions such as the economy (Norpoth 2001), but these expectations also work to a president's benefit. If presidents are held responsible for the bad, they are often given excess credit for the good. They bring their own bargaining skills and situational strategies to bear, but whether they can unite or divide the country may be contingent on the political circumstance in which they find themselves, such as the degree of presidential leverage they have at any given time.

Scholars have employed variables such as public approval, political and policy ideology, and partisan control of government as key indicators of policy output. This chapter contributes to that line of inquiry by trying to determine if and how presidential leverage bears on presidents' public policy activities in three major areas: the proportion of major legislation (as defined by Mayhew 1991) whose origin can be traced to the White House rather than Congress, the size of the president's public agenda, and executive orders as broadly representative of the "unilateral presidency" that has become prominent in presidential agenda activity. Much of the variation in securing a legacy through significant public policies is driven by presidents with high or increasing IPLs, whereas weakly leveraged presidents drive the use of unilateral executive action and agenda size.

MACROPOLITICS, POLICY, AND PRESIDENTIAL LEVERAGE

The linkage between American politics qua politics and public policy focuses on the output of the American political system and has come to be known as "macropolitics." The study of macropolitics deals with the production of government output over time and includes contextual information on the political environment.[2] It is concerned with tracking aggregate policy output produced by institutional players on the national stage, and scholarship has focused most prevalently on Congress (Adler and Lapinski 2006; Cooper and Brady 1981). Still, the enterprise of macropolitics makes no claim that one institution is "more important" than another. Even the Supreme Court, Hamilton's "least dangerous branch," is implicated given that many scholars maintain that courts do indeed "make policy" (compare Dahl 2003, 153–155; Canes-Wrone 2006). And, of course, the presidency takes its prominent place as well, advocating, pushing, prodding, defending, passing, and defining public policy (Erikson, MacKuen, and Stimson 2002).

Examining the macropolitical environment by focusing on the president sorts out both circumstances that were peculiar to a particular president and those that are shared more or less by all presidents. Indeed, presidents are often judged by the nature and scope of policies pursued and passed under their watch. Presidents' degree of public leverage matters greatly for creating the large-scale public policies that they need to secure their legacies.

A second part of presidential action pertains to agenda setting (Cohen 1997, 2012; Light 1999). Presidents are constrained in their decisions to pursue policy magnitude and tenor of their agendas only to the degree of their commitment to deliver legislation and policy direction, including symbolic politics, within the time available. Presidents with high leverage are more or less free to offer policy proposals given that public pressure as measured by trust works against Congress (or the government in general) rather than the president, leaving a strategic president able to adjust and readjust as the nature of time and political circumstances demand. Of course, there is an outer bound to what presidents will want to propose.[3] Thus, although the leverage framework suggests that presidents will do more in times of high leverage, growth is bounded at some point such that they will try to avoid losing comparative advantage. Indeed, Ostrom and Simon (1985) show that more popular presidents are ones who focus more and attempt less. This state of affairs occurs in concert with other factors such as a president's ideological compatibility with Congress, a White House/EOP staff with limited attention and resources, and other exogenous factors such as the state of the economy, all of which place limits on what the president can realistically do.

PRESIDENTIAL LEVERAGE AND THE CREATION
OF SIGNIFICANT PUBLIC POLICY

Presidents are unlikely to be oblivious to structures or conditions that bode well, ill, or neutral for the strategies of agenda success. Accordingly, I explore a measure of the proportion of significant legislation that originates with the president, as opposed to arising in Congress. Presidents with high leverage are more likely to see important policies pass that address significant issues as part of the overall governmental agenda. Because so much of the literature on the relationship between presidential approval and success in Congress shows contradictory evidence as to whether presidential approval has any systematic impact on presidential success (see, among others, Bond and Fleisher 1990; Edwards 1989; Fett 1994; Peterson 1990), I examine the degree to which presidential leverage has an impact on not presidential success in Congress, but specifically on the proportion of big, important legislation as defined by David Mayhew (1991, update through 2012) that a president can rightly and truly take credit for—a true "legacy" issue.

Thus, the dependent variable in the following analysis is the proportion of significant issues identified by Mayhew that were actually developed in and proposed by the White House. This is a measure of how much of the political landscape is shaped by the president's policy legacy. The theory implies that, as leverage increases, the president's preeminent position leads to the conditions for pushing significant legislation. When presidents propose major policy initiatives, members of Congress might be more likely to concur with them, and thus the set of significant legislation in a given year should be more heavily populated by presidential initiatives in high-leverage years and less so in times of lower leverage.

It is possible that large-scale, enduring macropolitical output plays a role that, left unmeasured, may obscure important information about the relationship between presidential leverage and policy agendas. Because much of the literature on presidential approval and success in Congress leads to contradictory findings (Edwards 1989; Bond and Fleisher 1990; Peterson 1990), the following analysis explores whether presidential leverage has any impact on policy, specifically those policies identified by David Mayhew as important issues (Mayhew 1991, updated).[4] In his seminal work, Mayhew employs a two-stage process, which he calls "sweeps," to uncover policies that have weathered the test of time and were both important at the time of their passage and continue to be considered highly or unusually important into the present day. I examine the proportion of significant issues identified by Mayhew that were not only presidential priorities but were *developed in and proposed by the White House* as opposed to those that were congressional initiatives. This yields a measure of the president's direct fingerprint on the American political landscape. Although most presidents are successful in obtaining a high percentage of legislative success from Congress, the final product is not always exactly what they want. Thinking about presidential leverage leads to the expectation that high-leveraged presidents are more likely to get large-scale policy enacted into law, rather than simply "pile on" and pad their records with smaller issues or issues that originated elsewhere, such as Congress, and already likely to pass (see Peterson 1990). The analysis addresses the question: Do presidents with high leverage have that ability to use their standing with the public to attest to what Skowronek has called "warrants for action" and what Jones calls "leeway"? Does success in Congress on high-ticket items reflect that leeway, or is there no extra benefit to be derived from this high public place?

Thus, the following hypothesis:

H5.1 *As presidential leverage increases, so will the proportion of important issues that pass through the congressional process and are signed into law that were presidential (as opposed to congressional) initiatives.*

The method for identifying the dependent variable is a two-step process. The variable measures both the proportion of legislation that counted as major legislation by Mayhew *and* that were presidential proposals (rather than originating in Congress). To determine whether the significant policies were proposed by the president, each important policy identified by Mayhew was cross-referenced with the comprehensive list of presidential proposals compiled by Andrew Rudalevige (2002 and updated), and often, when ambiguities arose, an exhaustive search of presidential speeches, news reports, and other secondary sources. The decision rule was straightforward: if the legislation deemed important in Mayhew was also on Rudalevige's list of presidential proposals, it was counted as a presidential victory and included in the data set. In most cases, where coding was difficult to ascertain, these were cross-checked with secondary sources. Where Rudalevige's data ends in 2002, I rely exclusively on secondary sources, memoirs, and statements made by the president at bill-signing ceremonies to determine origin. If the origin of a policy could not be verified one way or the other, it was *not* included in the data set. Thus, the measure is a conservative estimate of policy origin.

To illustrate the method, consider the Equal Pay Act. This policy was identified by Mayhew as significant and also appears on Rudalevige's list of presidential proposals. To confirm, secondary sources were consulted. In this case, Kennedy appointed labor activist Esther Williams to head the Women's Bureau in the Department of Labor. He urged her to establish the Presidential Commission on the Status of Women to move in the direction of achieving equality. In February 1963 she presented a draft bill on behalf of the Kennedy administration (National Park Service, 2015). Because this bill began life in the Kennedy administration, even though he delegated responsibility to an agent in the bureaucracy, it was included as a presidential policy.

Consider as well a counterexample, namely when a president actively supports a bill already in the works by Congress. In cases such as this, the policy is not included in the data set. For example, Nixon endorsed and actively supported amendments to the Federal Election Campaign Act in 1974, but neither he nor any department or agency in the executive branch promulgated or submitted it to Congress. It was already being considered. Similarly, the minimum wage increase during Carter's administration is not counted as a presidential proposal, even though he vocally supported its passage, because it was a pet project of congressional Democrats and Carter fell in line behind it. To be sure, he loaned important presidential support to the cause, but it was not a proposal that was developed in his White House. Therefore, because Carter did not actually propose it as part of his legislative program, it is not counted in the measure of significant legislation.

Similarly, if a bill substantially incorporates part of a president's proposal in legislation considered and passed by Congress, it is *not* included in the analysis. For example, the Defense Reorganization (Goldwater-Nichols Act) incorporated a significant amount of Reagan's proposals, but the structure of the bill was already largely in place. Likewise, if a president calls for legislative *action* in the State of the Union but simply urges Congress to work on an issue as opposed to the president submitting draft legislation, it is not included in the data set. For example, Reagan called for passage of the Family Support Act in his State of the Union address in 1988, but the bill was not his nor did he significantly shape it, so it was not included.

In sum, if there is any ambiguity to where a proposal originated, the policy is not included as presidential.[5] This conservative approach establishes a high bar militating against rejection of the null hypothesis. Therefore, if a statistical relationship is found amid circumstances that make it more difficult, there is heightened confidence that the relationship exists.

Figure 5.1 displays the trend for policies that originated in the White House, EOP, or the bureaucracy. A full list of these policies is provided in Appendix C. Examining the data closely reveals interesting patterns. For example, in the half-century within which these data are measured, the number of *presidential* initiatives deemed important or significant ranged between zero and twelve whereas the total number of laws so considered (presidential plus congressional) ranged between two and sixteen. The average number of pieces of significant legislation per year was 6.19, with the average of those originating in the presidency registered at just over three per year. In terms of percentages, the average president broke even, with just over 50 percent of significant legislation originating in the White House, and presidential success traversed the gamut from 0 to 100 percent. Percentages are the appropriate measure to examine because they take into account the entirety of significant policies. Whether we consider years in which there were few significant pieces of legislation overall (for example, two in 1981) or many (for example, sixteen in 1970), the measure encompasses major, enduring policies identified by Mayhew. However, as will be explained later, the statistical results are basically identical if one models the *number* of significant policies as opposed to the percentage. The focus here is on percentages because they demonstrate how much of the imprint on the macropolitics of the American system emanates from the president, which can be missed when focusing only on the number of proposals.

Control Variables: Political/Contextual

Several theories of presidential action maintain that presidents need to be cognizant of the historical circumstances in which they serve and accurately recognize the connections inherent in the times in which they govern (for example, Skowronek 1993; Hargrove 1974; Hargrove and Nelson 1984). In addressing these concerns, a set of controls is constructed that tap some of the dimensions of the political and contextual landscapes within which presidents move. The controls are broadly representative of the countless contexts presidents face at any time in their presidency.[6] The controls used to model the context change slightly across analyses, but in general the most prominent arenas in which presidents act and through which leverage is filtered are taken into account.

Institutional Contagion

First, I control for the congressional context by estimating ideological compatibility between the president and Congress. In doing so, I adapt the findings of a number of studies that show a large number of presidential copartisans in Congress is neither a necessary nor sufficient condition for presidential success on a number of dimensions (for example, Jones 1994; Bond and Fleisher 1990; Mayhew 1991; Krehbiel 1998). Because presidents cannot always count on partisan support even when their party enjoys majority control (Jimmy Carter comes to mind), an alternative measure of presidential "strength" is employed. Presidents who are ideologically compatible with Congress may find that a higher proportion of the important legislation proposed in their administration passes than when presidents with low leverage occupies the White House. *Congressional Compatibility* is measured as the absolute value of the president's DW-NOMINATE score from that of the median member of Congress. DW-NOMINATE scores measure the ideologies of MCs and recently have been applied to presidents. They array political actors along a continuum from -1 to $+1$, with scores closer to -1 indicating liberalism, scores closer to $+1$ reflecting more conservative views, and those close to 0 representing moderation.[7] I am agnostic about the direction of the relationship; indeed, if results are consistent with previous findings, we may well observe a null result.

Nonetheless, given the degree of political contagion that may emerge from a situation in which a president is ideologically distant from the median member of Congress, a negative sign is expected.[8]

Party Control of the White House

To control for the fact that party control of the White House was fairly evenly split during the time period covered in this study (Democrats controlled the White House for twenty-four years; Republicans for twenty-eight), I control for the party in the White House. For reasons specific to agenda size and explained later on, I use a simple dummy variable to account for the party of the president (1 = Democrat; 0 = Republican).

Budgetary Constraint

To control for the effect of economic conditions, I measure the size of the cumulative budget debt relative to gross national product (GDP). The reasoning is straightforward: as deficits grow and accumulate in debt, presidents are constrained as to what they can legitimately propose, whether substantively or symbolically. In times of budget retrenchment, politicians (not just presidents) may adjust their policy strategies accordingly, especially in light of the findings that the public often sees the economy as its most important problem, and the budget is one important way of at least symbolically dealing with economic conditions. Thus, I include a control for *Debt/GDP*, which is simply the size of the cumulative budget debt relative to gross national product[9] and expect a negative sign.

Time of Term

Empirical research has shown that presidents often decrease activity later in their terms so as to concentrate on what has been done and to focus their efforts as they prepare for reelection in the case of first-term presidents and, for second termers, shape their legacy (for example, Light 1999). Therefore, I include a simple term counter that takes the value of the year of the president's term in which the observations were made (that is, take a value that ranges from 1 through 8, depending on the president).

In keeping with previous research that finds presidents do tend to do less as their terms grow older, I expect a negative sign.

Mood

Public *Mood* measures the idea that the context of representational capacity waxes and wanes over time and taps into the public's desire for either activist or conservative policy change (Stimson 1991). First, it measures whether major policy innovations and the liberal–conservative dynamic explain presidential proposals and their ensuing success in passing important policy legislation, the volume of the president's public agenda, and the use of unilateral power, all of which are analyzed in this chapter. Second, *Mood* is practical because some scholars use it as a proxy for the public's revealed preferences. For example, Krehbiel (1998: 62, 68) argues that the measure reflects Mayhew's (1991) notion of a "public purpose." *Mood* can be considered one measure of time, as the public's tolerance for policy innovation waxes and wanes over the series (see Erikson, MacKuen, and Stimson 2002). Stimson and his colleagues employ it as a global measure of policy-related opinion and argue: "Mood is the major dimension underlying expressed preferences over policy alternatives in the survey research record . . . [the] measure represents the public's sense of whether the political temperature is too hot or too cold, whether government is too active or not active enough" (Stimson, MacKuen, and Erikson 1995: 548).

War

Whether the nation is at war has been shown to be a significant predictor of presidential resources, such as public opinion (Erikson, MacKuen, and Stimson 2002; Mueller 1973; Ostrom and Simon 1985). The variable *War* is simply a dummy variable that captures whether the United States is engaged in war during the year for which the dependent variables were measured. The variable is coded as a dummy because my interest is in determining whether the existence of foreign conflict systematically affects presidential decisions on agenda setting, not on how war per se affects a president's popularity level. Thus, it is coded as 0 to 1, taking a value of zero if the United States was not engaged in war and a value of one for years in which it was.[10]

Watergate Effects

Reflecting the findings in Chapter 4, a dummy variable was constructed to account for the differences in the pre- and post-Watergate eras. The measure is a simple dummy variable (1 = Kennedy to Nixon; 0 = Ford to Obama) and was included as a predictor for all models in this chapter. However, it was subsequently dropped so as to preserve degrees of freedom because it was found to be statistically insignificant in all analyses.

Methodology: Error Correction Modeling

Before proceeding to the analysis, two statistical issues need to be addressed, both of which apply to this chapter as well as to some of the analyses in Chapter 6: the appropriate estimation technique and issues with multicollinearity. Most of the rest of the analyses in this book deal with time series issues. Error correction models (ECMs) are increasingly employed in political science to deal with these data (for example, De Boef and Keele 2008; De Boef 2001; Box-Steffensmeier et al. 2014, chapter 6). There are a variety of reasons to employ ECMs, which can be estimated with ordinary least squares (OLS) regression analysis, but the central reason is succinctly put by Kelly and Witko: "The primary motivation for using an ECM . . . is that it is a general time series model that imposes the fewest possible restrictions" (2012: 421n6, drawing from De Boef and Keele, 2008). A single-equation ECM is estimated as:

$$\Delta Y_t = \alpha_1 Y_{t-1} + \beta_1 \Delta X_t + \beta_2 X_{t-1} + \varepsilon_t.$$

Following Kelly and Witko (2012: 421), two values of each independent variable (a differenced and a lagged value) are estimated, and each can be dropped from a final equation if it is found to be statistically insignificant. The coefficient on the differenced variable (β_1) represents the "short-term" effect, meaning that the coefficient occurs at a given point in time. The coefficients on α_1 and β_2 estimate the longer-term "error correction." An indication that error correction is occurring is when $\alpha_1 < |1.0|$ and is significant at the 0.05 level. In most of the rest of the analyses in this book,[11] inspection of the α_1 coefficients yield evidence of error correction taking place, and thus the models are estimated with an ECM.

One other issue that arises with ECMs is that they quickly consume degrees of freedom. Given that all (or almost all) of the independent variables are differenced *and* lagged, it is even more incumbent on the analyst to model the relationships parsimoniously. In the case of most of the analyses presented in this book, the number of observations is near fifty, one for most years between 1961 and 2012. This presents a statistical and theoretical trade-off. On one hand, an analyst should employ controls to measure various contexts that may theoretically have an impact on the dependent variable and the independent variable of interest. But in a case where the number of observations is relatively small and the number of potential controls is large, as is the case within this book, multicollinearity is often present. Multicollinearity is a statistical issue rather than a theoretical one and can arise from at least two conditions, both of which are dealt with in this book. First, and most pertinent for an ECM, if the number of predictors relative to the number of observations is large, the variance of some right-hand side variables can become artificially inflated, increasing the likelihood of committing a Type II error (failing to reject a false null hypothesis).

The second way in which multicollinearity can arise is when two or more of the independent variables are highly correlated with one another, again increasing the likelihood of a Type II error. One method for dealing with multicollinearity is not to deal with it at all. An argument can be made that if two variables that happen to be highly correlated with one another are included in the analysis but the inclusion of each is theoretically justified and "should" be in the model, then the researcher can or should leave them in and ignore the multicollinearity. After all, a Type II error is a conservative one, and therefore if a researcher finds statistically meaningful relationships when the deck is stacked against such findings, given the artificial variance inflation, then the more confidence can be had that the findings are robust. On the other hand, it can be argued that the researcher should choose carefully or create other variables that capture the essence of the relationship or remove one of the offending variables, run the analysis, then remove the remaining one and reinsert the previously omitted variable and compare the results.

A larger problem occurs when there are too many control variables relative to the number of observations. This problem is more difficult to resolve because it requires the researcher to pick and choose from among a variety of contextual control variables. As noted earlier, this is a problem for the ECM because each independent variable is measured twice (differenced and lagged), and thus they multiply very quickly. Both methods are used in this book when ECMs are employed, and the choices made in the research strategy will be made clear.

Results

Diagnostics confirmed error correction, though barely. Indeed, technically, the full form model's error correction term is −1.0, which is barely outside the acceptable range. However, as already noted, an ECM is amenable to removing statistically insignificant predictors. Once that is done, the reduced form model, which is the model that will be interpreted in all the analyses in this chapter, meets the ECM criteria. However, given the marginal circumstances under which an ECM is considered appropriate, I ran a number of alternative model specifications to determine whether the results were driven by the type of analysis or are robust across model techniques and model specifications. In each instance, the results were substantially the same.[12] Thus, error correction is occurring in each of the following models, ECMs are used to generate the statistical estimates. The error correction rate (−0.99) indicates that the series takes very little time to return to equilibrium after a shock, with 99 percent of the series returning to equilibrium after one year. (See Figure 5.1.)

Table 5.1 displays the results of the analysis on legacy issues. As the public mood increases, meaning it is in the "mood" for more "liberal" or active legislation, presidents benefit. They are less successful, of course, when institutional contagion is controlled. As *President–Congress Polarization* decreases, significant legislation that bears the imprint of the president also declines. Therefore, and not surprisingly, the structure of Congress is a factor, both in terms of what is proposed to address the problems at hand and in asserting itself into those periods. The coefficients on

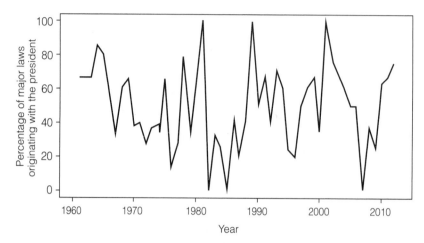

FIGURE 5.1. Proportion of major laws drafted by the president or executive establishment that became law per year.

Source: Calculated by the author using data derived from Mayhew (2001 and updated), Rudalevige (2002), and and various sources. See text for details.

Democratic President shows that they are less successful in the short run and have a smaller significant impact over time. The budget constraint has no statistically discernable effect. *Time* has a negative impact on presidential legacy, which makes sense given that, as the presidential term ages, presidents are less likely to experience large, impactful policies. The political system has begun to move on, much of what presidents do at that time is based on preserving rather than manufacturing legacy (except in times of crisis), and the presidential election season has taken hold. Finally, the variable that captures the pre- and post-Watergate/Vietnam era was not significant in any of the analyses in this chapter, so it was excluded.

So what of the impact of leverage on the passage of significant policy? Turning to the results for the impact of the IPL on presidential leverage, the short-term, immediate impact of a change in presidential leverage is statistically insignificant. However, the long-term impact of presidential leverage (IPL_{t-1}) unambiguously advantages presidents. Presidents are more successful in placing their imprint on the American political landscape, creating large significant legislation over and above that of Congress. Because it is rare for a president to move an entire point in the IPL (for example, from 1 to 2), the substantive results are

TABLE 5.1
Presidential leverage and proportion of major legislation proposed by the president.

Variable	Full model	Reduced form
Constant	−43.64	−59.62**
	(45.38)	(35.44)
Percent of major legislation originating with the president$_{t-1}$	−0.1.00***	−0.99***
	(0.13)	(0.13)
Presidential leverage		
Δ Index of presidential leverage	−11.86	
	(17.85)	
Index of presidential leverage$_{t-1}$	36.56**	44.49***
	(16.67)	(12.62)
Political context		
Δ Mood	1.68***	1.75**
	(0.74)	(0.67)
Mood$_{t-1}$	1.41***	1.29***
	(0.70)	(0.54)
Δ President–Congress polarization	−54.91*	−42.55*
	(37.73)	(31.38)
President–Congress polarization$_{t-1}$	−27.15	
	(35.27)	
Δ Democratic president	−33.80**	−36.21***
	(17.03)	(13.59)
Democratic president$_{t-1}$	5.21	
	(13.70)	
Budget constraint		
Δ Debt to GDP	0.56	
	(0.79)	
Debt to GDP$_{t-1}$	−0.14	
	(0.52)	
War		
Δ War	10.33	
	(8.72)	
War$_{t-1}$	−5.07	
	(9.19)	
Time		
Δ Year of term	−5.20***	−5.89***
	(1.79)	(1.61)
Year of term$_{t-1}$	−2.78*	−4.46**
	(1.74)	(1.64)
JFK–Nixon dummy	N.S.	
Adjusted R^2	0.71	0.68
Standard error of estimate	17.30	18.14
N	53	53

Dependent variable is Δ Proportion of Mayhew's Major Laws Originated with the Presidency. See text for details. Standard errors in parentheses.

*** $p < 0.01$

** $p < 0.05$

* $p < 0.10$ (one-tailed tests)

interpreted with reference to a shift of one standard deviation. A one standard deviation change of the IPL (0.24) is associated with a cumulative predicted increase of 10.68 percent. Multiplying this by the error correction rate (0.99) means that about 10.57 percent of this increase occurs in the first year. This is not surprising given that inspection of Figure 5.1 shows little trend in the series and that individual presidents may see their fortunes vary wildly within a given term. So we would expect that most of the impact of a standard deviation shift in the IPL would occur in the first year, with the remaining predicted values distributed slightly over time. Thus, as presidential leverage increases, presidents have the political leverage to execute large, significant policy issues in a short period of time.

In addition to estimating an ECM with only a lagged value of significant policies and the differenced and lagged values of the IPL as predictors as described earlier in note 12, I also ran a variety of model techniques and model specifications to be sure that the impact of presidential leverage was consistent across these various iterations. The direction and significance of the IPL was confirmed. The lagged value of the IPL was positive and statistically significant regardless of estimation technique. Some examples include the following. I ran a full ECM after removing the insignificant war variables. The ECM is appropriate, and the IPL coefficient registered 41.84, $p = 0.000$. Employing a more traditional time series configuration and including a lagged dependent variable as a right-hand side predictor, the coefficient on lagged IPL is 50.8, $p = 0.002$. Finally, I ran a negative binomial count model based on the quasi-likelihood Markov estimator, using the number of significant policies that originated in the executive per year (rather than as a proportion), with a lagged value of the log of the dependent variable as a control to account for serial interdependence (see Wood and Webb 2011). The IPL coefficient is 0.85, $p < 0.01$.

President Obama is an instructive example. As his leverage reached stratospheric levels, he was able to propose and pass significant legislation. For example, even with unified government, his relationship with the Senate minority was contentious. Although Democrats controlled nearly sixty seats, which would have fended off a filibuster if all Democrats plus Bernie Sanders (I-VT) and Joseph Lieberman (R-CT), both of whom caucused with the Democrats, banded together and were able to persuade Republican moderates such as Olympia Snowe (R-ME) or Ben Nelson (R-NE) to come along. From the beginning, it was clear that Republicans were in no mood to cooperate. And even keeping Democrats unified proved difficult, as Lieberman, who had briefly been considered as a running mate for Republican nominee John McCain, often broke with his party. To complicate matters, it was always far from certain that the few moderate Republicans would fall in line with their Democrat counterparts. Nonetheless, Obama was able to accomplish much in a relatively small period of time, when his IPL was highest. This included the stimulus act (some of which had been negotiated under Bush), as well as a series of proposals incorporated in legislation that regulated the financial services industry, repealed "Don't Ask, Don't Tell" military policy restricting the rights of gay servicemen and servicewomen, and others.

The hill that the Affordable Care Act (ACA) had to climb became even steeper after the death of Senator Edward Kennedy in late 2009. Republican Scott Brown shocked the political world when he won Kennedy's seat, and the switch of that seat from Democrat to Republican made it harder for Senate Democrats to fend off a filibuster. However, in the end, the ACA passed through a series of parliamentary maneuvers and congressional cajoling. Consequently, Obama signed the ACA in March 2010, when his IPL was extremely high. This was early in an election year in which the Tea Party rose to become a prominent political force, ousting the Democratic majority and asserting powerful influence over the Republican establishment. The proportion of significant legislation that passed in 2011 and 2012 was even more striking, when Obama no longer had majorities in either house of Congress. Still, he was able to push forward bipartisan compromise using Vice President Joe Biden, and although the total number of significant issues was down in 2012, virtually all of them came from the White House, a significant victory given that it was Obama's reelection year and Republican incentives clearly matched those of Senate Majority Leader Mitch McConnell's stated goal of making Obama a one-term president. Obama's IPL, though declining from its earlier highs, was still significantly above average.

THE UNILATERAL PRESIDENCY: EXECUTIVE ORDERS

President Obama was about to preside over his first cabinet meeting of 2014. Throughout his presidency, he felt that his efforts, aimed at helping the lower and middle classes caught in the economic downturn of the late 2000s and early 2010s, had been consistently blocked by congressional Republicans. Just before heading into the White House meeting, he quipped that he had a "pen and a phone," the tools he would use to sign executive orders and to mobilize interest groups to advance his agenda when Congress refused to act (Eilperin 2014). Obama was referring to the power of unilateral prerogatives as weapons presidents can use to mitigate weakness in the face of an intransigent Congress and to exert some measure of strength.

Presidential leverage helps set the conditions for unilateral action. The experience of President Obama is an illustration. Although much of the political punditry and public praised or excoriated the president (depending on their point of view) for using so many executive orders, he actually used fewer than many of his predecessors, though his IPL registered far greater. For example, Obama issued thirty-nine (2009), thirty-five (2010), thirty-four (2011), and thirty-six (2012) orders, respectively, in his first term. His IPL scores all were well above the mean IPL for presidents analyzed in this book. Compare this with Ronald Reagan, for instance. Reagan issued sixty-three total orders in 1982 when his IPL was 0.96, well below the mean and bleeding slightly into the realm of "negative" leverage. When his IPL was substantially higher (1.27) in 1986, he issued only thirty-seven orders. Obama issued thirty-six in 2012 when his IPL registered 1.24. Although we should be cautious in comparing these presidents one-to-one (for example, Obama was in his reelection year, where Mayer [2001] shows that presidents tend to issue fewer orders anyway), the comparison is telling.

Richard Neustadt argued that a president's power lay in his ability to persuade others to do what is in their best interests anyway and that resorting to "command" authority indicated a presidential failure (Neustadt 1960). But in the past decade or so, scholars have challenged that claim, at least as it pertains to the present day. In particular, William Howell has led the charge arguing in effect that unilateral actions, a kind of "command authority," are now another weapon in the president's arsenal (Howell 2003). Executive orders have taken pride of place in the search for presidential power (Mayer 2001; Warber 2006). Indeed, so much literature parses presidential action that it is difficult to cover it all. Space and time constraints preclude a full consideration, so I briefly focus only on executive orders, though the following analysis could be applied in future across a range of unilateral actions.

Presidents often deal with the institutional context they inhabit by embracing an "administrative presidency" strategy that includes a large component of unilateral action, action that can be taken by administrative measures as opposed to going through the political/congressional process (Nathan 1983; Waterman 1989). In a separated system where presidents govern from a position of weakness, presidents have to do what they can to place their mark on the political landscape. When presidents find themselves stymied by competing institutions such as Congress, the temptation to use unilateral action as a way around the political obstacle course is strong. To examine one aspect of this strategy, variation in the number of executive orders issued in a given year is examined in the following paragraphs. Studies of executive orders have become more numerous recently than was the case in the past. Additionally, work on the unilateral presidency covers more than simply executive orders. For example, signing statements have been the subject of increasing attention (for example, Conley 2011; Kelley and Marshall 2010).[13] The analysis here does not delve into executive orders as comprehensively as these other works do, but, consistent with the other analyses in this book, is meant to explore whether presidential leverage links the context of the presidency at a particular time to unilateral action.

President Obama directed his use of execution actions to a variety of topics, none as contentious as immigration reform, particularly in his second term. This in turn prompted a debate on how much (or little) these unilateral actions are used, for what purposes, and with greater than ever public awareness of executive orders than perhaps at any other time in American history. In November 2014, no less a social and political barometer than *Saturday Night Live* (SNL) weighed in with a satirical skit based on the popular "School House Rock" cartoon, probably the first and only time executive orders appeared on that show, though they were routinely highlighted in shows such as *The West Wing* and *House of Cards*. Although SNL got it wrong (Obama's immigration orders were not "executive orders" at all but rather two presidential memoranda and an administrative directive),[14] the public outcry both in opposition to and defense of the orders led to a vigorous debate about unilateral action. Therefore, for analytical purposes here, executive orders are used as a proxy for other high-profile executive strategies and used to explore the relationship between leverage and unilateral action.[15] Consequently, the next hypothesis is stated as:

H5.2: *The use of unilateral action in the form of executive orders will be inversely related to presidential leverage*

Method

Executive orders as reported in the *Public Agendas Project* and Ragsdale (2014) are employed as the dependent variable. Some scholars argue that attention should be paid to the type and tenor of orders in addition to or instead of counting the raw numbers of orders (Cooper 2002; Warber 2006). I do not disagree. However, for this analysis I take my cue from the outcry over the Obama administration's executive actions given the renewed public and scholarly interest in unilateral power.[16]

Figure 5.2 displays the trend in all executive orders, regardless of type or policy significance. The mean number of orders in the series is 51.34 with a standard deviation of 16.49 and range from 26 in 2005, the first year of George W. Bush's second term, to a high of 99 in 1980, Carter's last year in office.

Turning to the statistical analysis, consider Table 5.2. The same model used in the previous analysis was employed to estimate an ECM. The coefficient on the lagged dependent variable confirmed that error correction is occurring. Additionally, because the mean of the series is reasonably high, OLS is an appropriate estimator because we can interpret the coefficients more directly.[17] Again, all models were originally estimated with

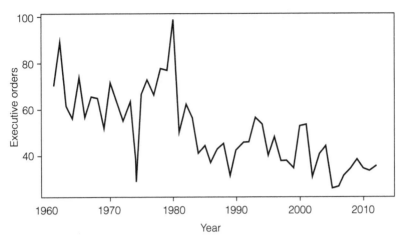

FIGURE 5.2. Executive orders.

Source: Policy Agendas Project.

the JFK–Nixon dummy variable, but it was never statistically significant and was therefore dropped from all subsequent models.

Impacts of Controls

The long-term impact of public *Mood* is positively related to the number of executive orders. Presidents respond to either symbolic or substantive context by issuing orders. *Congressional Compatibility* performs as might be expected, with more orders issued as presidential polarization increases.[18] One reason may be that presidents are less likely to be able to move their agendas in the face of a hostile Congress. As for presidential party, the findings are consistent with others (Mayer 2001; Fine and Warber 2012), who find that *Democrats* are more likely to issue executive orders than are Republicans. *Debt* decreases the use of executive orders, as might be expected given that presidents are less likely to expand their use of agenda activity in the face of economic downturn. Finally, the long-term effect of *War* is negatively related to the use of executive orders.

Now consider the impact of leverage on unilateral action. Like policy legacy, the error correction of 0.88 is quite high, meaning that about 88 percent of the series returns to equilibrium within a year. The coefficients on

TABLE 5.2
Presidential leverage and the issuance of executive orders.

Variable	Full model	Reduced form
Constant	34.22	32.73
	(29.34)	(22.57)
Executive orders$_{t-1}$	–.94***	–0.88***
	(0.15)	(0.125)
Presidential leverage		
Δ IPL	–26.49***	–21.93***
	(10.71)	(8.46)
IPL$_{t-1}$	–19.71**	–16.93**
	(11.11)	(9.65)
Political context		
Δ Mood	0.25	
	(0.44)	
Mood$_{t-1}$	0.94**	0.77***
	(0.42)	(0.29)
Δ President–Congress polarization	13.37	
	(21.99)	
President–Congress polarization$_{t-1}$	49.90***	48.12***
	(20.61)	(14.43)
Δ Democratic president	18.43**	13.33***
	(9.88)	(4.67)
Democratic president$_{t-1}$	33.19***	31.98***
	(8.39)	(6.41)
Budget constraint		
Δ Debt to GDP	0.71*	0.61*
	(0.47)	(0.38)
Debt to GDP$_{t-1}$	–1.15***	–1.08***
	(0.31)	(0.27)
War		
Δ War	–2.64	
	(5.28)	
War$_{t-1}$	–2.502	
	(5.75)	
Time		
Δ Year of term	–1.082	
	(1.09)	
Year of term$_{t-1}$	–3.980***	–3.34***
	(1.11)	(0.86)
Adjusted R^2	0.52	0.56
Standard error of estimate	10.12	9.65
N	51	51

Dependent variable is Δ Executive Orders. Standard errors in parentheses.

*** $p < 0.01$

** $p < 0.05$

* $p < 0.10$ (one-tailed tests)

Source for dependent variable: Policy Agendas Project.

the IPL are negatively related to the use of executive orders. This is generally consistent with research demonstrating that popular presidents issue fewer executive orders (Mayer 2001: 97–102). Thus, it is not surprising that, as presidential leverage decreases, the issuance of executive orders increases. Weaker presidents are more likely to issue executive orders so as to gain some purchase and mobilize their agendas by bypassing competing institutions, particularly Congress. In the truncated model in Table 5.3, a one-standard-deviation increase in the IPL leads to 5.26 fewer orders. The long-term lagged coefficient indicates that a full unit shift in the IPL predicts a decline of nearly 17 orders cumulatively, or 14.9 in the first year with the rest distributed over time. When we account for the fact that few presidents shift one full unit, this can be normalized to predict a drop of just over 4 orders cumulatively, with about 3.6 fewer in the first time period with the rest distributed accordingly. Orders are an efficient means to move an agenda given that courts are not likely to overturn executive orders and Congress even less so (Mayer 2009). Stronger presidents, as measured by the IPL, are less likely to have to turn to executive orders.[19] As presidents grow stronger in the American political system, they use executive orders less frequently. Thus, presidents use "power without persuasion" (Howell 2003), though as far as executive orders are concerned, they are more likely to do so when their power, or leverage, is low.

HIGH-PROFILE AGENDA SIZE

The magnitude of the president's high-profile agenda is the final area explored in this chapter. For this analysis, *high-profile agenda* is defined as a president's public agenda, formulated in the White House, publicized in the State of the Union address. There is a substantial literature concerning presidents and agendas.[20] Indeed, it is not a stretch to say that most research on the presidency touches on what presidents do and how they do it. This strand takes many forms, but can be termed, however loosely, as agenda setting and/or advertising of that agenda. Presidents can influence public agendas as well as those of competing institutions. Cohen's (1995, 1997) analysis of State of the Union addresses reports that presidents influence public opinion on what the public deems its "most

TABLE 5.3
Presidential leverage and State of the Union requests (agenda size).

Variable	Full model	Reduced form
Constant	−15.18 (14.88)	14.37** (7.20)
State of the Union requests$_{t-1}$	−0.76*** (0.14)	−0.79*** (0.13)
Presidential leverage		
Δ IPL	−9.69* (5.91)	−10.21** (5.07)
IPL$_{t-1}$	0.99 (5.32)	
Political context		
ΔMood	0.24 (0.23)	
Mood$_{t-1}$	0.01 (0.24)	
Δ President–Congress polarization	6.05 (12.24)	
President–Congress polarization$_{t-1}$	23.39** (11.55)	22.98*** (9.52)
Δ Democratic president	11.60** (5.46)	8.98*** (2.7)
Democratic president$_{t-1}$	9.78** (4.56)	9.41*** (3.16)
Budget constraint		
Δ Debt to GDP	−1.13*** (0.28)	−1.16*** (0.25)
Debt to GDP$_{t-1}$	0.30** (0.17)	0.34*** (0.12)
War		
Δ War	3.75* (2.83)	4.6** (2.49)
War$_{t-1}$	8.01*** (3.11)	8.03*** (2.7)
Time		
Δ Year of term	−1.69*** (0.60)	−1.41*** (0.49)
Year of term$_{t-1}$	−1.06 (0.56)**	−1.00*** (0.52)
Adjusted R^2	0.43	0.46
Standard error of estimate	5.58	5.42
N	52	52

Dependent variable is Δ Total State of the Union requests. Standard errors in parentheses.

*** $p < 0.01$

** $p < 0.05$

* $p < 0.10$ (one-tailed tests)

important problem" but that this influence is mostly gone by the end of a year after the State of the Union.[21] But presidents are influenced as well. The notion of a presidency constrained by place in the broader context of the American system, especially if this is determined by public perceptions of the president relative to trust in government, suggests that presidents will engage in strategic behavior. Do presidents tailor their actions to how they fare in the American polity at a given time? Does their leverage in the system influence the outcome?

In formulating their agendas, presidents make decisions as to how much or little to pursue and to how much they publicly commit themselves. The justification for studying the State of the Union as an indicator of presidential activity is well documented (Cohen 1995, 1997; Light 1999; Hoffman and Howard 2006). With the exception of crisis messages, the State of the Union address epitomizes the president on the public stage. Presidents decide to "go public" (Kernell 2007) with policy proposals.[22] Presidents use the State of the Union as a public platform from which they publicize their agenda. Unlike others, though, I examine the volume of policy activity embodied in the message, rather than its content, using the address as a proxy for presidential policy priorities. It might be costly for presidents to put forth a large number of requests, only to fall short of achieving their goals as publicly stated in the address. Thus, high-leverage presidents would wish to focus attention on achievement. Low-leverage presidents may seek to put forth more in the way of high-profile requests so as to mollify their constituencies and gain public leverage. After all, there may be something of a cycle at work here: Low-leverage presidents who put forth little are likely to feed the perception that they are politically ineffectual, which in turn may send their leverage even lower.

This is not to argue that stronger presidents do not have to mollify constituencies; every president has to. But presidents with lower leverage have greater incentive to push more out in the form of proposals. Low-leveraged presidents have incentive to try to propose more because of the necessity of reclaiming a place in the American system. High-leveraged presidents already have that luxury and therefore can focus on perhaps a relatively smaller set of proposals. To be sure, they have every incentive to please constituencies and further their agenda, both symbolically and substantively. But like other analyses presented in this book, the argument is that most of the variation in the number of requests is likely to be driven by weaker presidents. Putting forth proposals in the State of the Union establishes a public record that later can be subjected to careful (and not so careful) scrutiny by journalists, political adversaries and allies, and the general public.[23]

Thus:

H5.3 *The size of the president's agenda as measured by the number of legislative requests in the State of the Union is inversely related to presidential leverage.*

Figure 5.3 traces the number of legislative requests made by the president that were cleared in accordance with the president's program and mentioned in the State of the Union address. The issues included here are not merely suggestions for future action but rather the issues that the president and staff or others in the executive branch have created, passed through legislative clearance, and then proposed to Congress in the SOTU address, which is the public rollout of the president's agenda. The series ranges from a low of 4 (Reagan 1988) to a high of 38 (LBJ

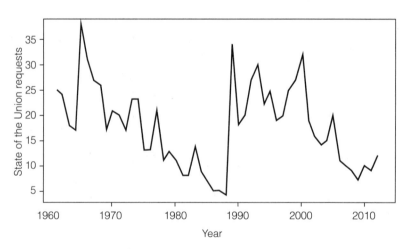

FIGURE 5.3. Presidential requests in the State of the Union address, 1961–2012.

Source: Ragsdale 2014: Table 9.3, 522–524.

1965), with an average of 17.7 requests per year and a standard deviation of 8.17. Although like executive orders, this is technically a count model (that is, a count of the number of agenda items proposed); the mean of the dependent variable is greater than three and high enough that one can profitably interpret the coefficients via OLS (see also Eshbaugh-Soha 2005; Cohen 2012). The model estimated is identical to those in the two previous analyses save for the dependent variable.

Impact of Controls

Table 5.3 displays the statistical results. As might be expected, *Mood* affects agenda setting in a positive way, though statistically insignificant.[24] As expected, *Democrats* request more. Historically, Democratic presidents are more active in terms of the sheer volume of legislative requests and the attendant strategies, such as messages to Congress (Light 1999). Nathan (1983) argues that some presidents, such as Nixon, felt that the bureaucracy leans left and is thus stacked against Republicans. Thus, if being a Democratic president has a systematic effect on the size of the presidential agenda, modeling should take it into account. A difference of means was performed on both the number of presidential proposals sent to Congress and the number of messages to Congress.[25] In both cases, Democrats exhibited systematically higher rates of activity than their Republican counterparts. This holds even when Lyndon Johnson, whose volume of legislative requests in 1965 was nearly 3 standard deviations above the mean, is removed from the analysis. Interestingly, the measure of presidential–congressional ideological polarization indicates a long-term increase in the volume of State of the Union requests. This suggests that when presidents and Congress are less polarized, presidents will put forth less because they can also rely on congressional copartisans to carry some of the burden; thus presidents can call for Congress to take action on some policy area without themselves putting forth as many proposals. In periods of greater ideological distance between the president and Congress, presidents will propose more so that they can shape the agenda and perhaps put Congress on the defensive.

The result for *Debt* is a mixed bag. The lag value indicates the existence of a short-term impact, when the shock of the change in the variable is absorbed all at once. As would be expected, the sign on the coefficient is negative, signifying that presidents will propose less in times of greater budget constraint. However, the long-term value indicates that they will ask for more over time, though the impact is much smaller than the long-term component. *War*, again as might be expected, is positively associated with proposals, meaning presidents increase their requests in both the short and immediate terms as well as in the longer term during wartime.

Turning now to the results on presidential leverage, we see that the short-term impact of leverage is positive but not statistically significant. But the long-term results are striking. As the IPL *decreases*, the model predicts an *increase* in the number of requests, suggesting that the variation in proposals tends to be driven by low-leveraged presidents.[26] Again, because a president who experiences a shift of one on the IPL scale is rare, I calculate the change in terms of a one-standard-deviation shift. An increase of one standard deviation is associated with a decrease of 2.44 proposals in the reduced form model. So, once again, a decrease in leverage is associated with increased agenda size, with presidents hoping to regain some traction in the American state.[27] It is worth noting that this robust negative relationship persists even if we remove the outliers of Johnson 1965 and Bush 1992. In an analysis not shown here, I removed the outlying observations of 1965 and 1992, in essence making it more difficult for the theory to be supported. The substance of the negative relationship remained roughly the same, and therefore we can have even more confidence that the pattern is robust. The regression coefficient on the variable Δ IPL when both LBJ 1965 and George H. W. Bush 1992 are excluded from the data set is -8.6, $p < 0.10$. This is notable because both presidents had dropped from very high IPLs to average or below-average IPLs at the same time they recorded the highest frequency of requests.

Consider Figure 5.3 in light of the findings in Table 5.3, especially the enormous amount of requests by Lyndon Johnson. This is not necessarily surprising. Johnson was well known for his ambition to be a great president, and he knew that he had only a limited amount of time after his election in 1964 to move policy. It is also at this time that leverage was waning, though by the time of the State of the Union, the country had not yet escalated its presence in Vietnam as a consequence of the Gulf of Tonkin resolution. Still, as the trends presented in Chapter 4 showed, Johnson had begun his free fall. Although he was still quite popular, trust in government was high, and his leverage had dropped more than a standard deviation, from 1.21 after Kennedy's death to 1.14 in the first quarter of 1965. Moving through the series, presidents tempered their legislative requests, through Watergate and into the Carter administration. But in 1992, with the persistently sluggish economy weighing on the public's mind and as the political system moved again into election season, George H. W. Bush asked for twenty-seven different items. His leverage had fallen dramatically in the nine months since he had won the Gulf War, from 1.81 in the first quarter of 1991 to a below-average 1.12 in the first quarter of 1992.

What happens when we include the raw measure of presidential approval rather than leverage? Appendix B shows interesting results. Like the IPL, $\Delta Approval$ exhibits a negative, statistically significant relationship. In an innovative and important study, Eshbaugh-Soha finds minimal support for the effects of lagged approval. In one subset of the agenda (what he calls "minor" policies), approval is negative, though not statistically significant. He finds approval to be positive though statistically insignificant in "metoric" and "incremental" policies and weakly positive in "total" and "major" categories. This is not inconsistent with my findings, as Eshbaugh-Soha finds varying patterns for approval when he divides up the agenda into categories. Here I am interested in the effects of the State of the Union, and I find consistently negative relationships for the immediate (that is, differenced approval) ratings and positive, statistically significant for the long-term effect.

It can be argued that this is to be expected, as much of the hype around the State of the Union address focuses on evaluations such as the president's approval rating. For example, in 2002, President Bush's abnormally high approval rating was well-publicized just before his State of the Union, the first in the post-September 11 era. However, so was Congress's. "With Bush's approval rating at 80%, and 54% approving of the job performance of the Democratic congressional leadership, both branches of government have the goodwill of majorities of the public" (Pew Research Center, 2002). A half-decade later, the story was far different.

"Mr. Bush's overall approval rating has fallen to just 28 percent, a new low, while more than twice as many (64 percent) disapprove of the way he's handling his job" (Roberts 2007). President Obama's fortunes were similarly subjected to close scrutiny. In 2014, Obama's approval ratings on the eve of his State of the Union were 46 percent, with 50 percent disapproval. The following year, his approval ratings were on the rise as the address approached. The *Washington Post*/ABC News poll reported a 50 percent approval rating of Obama among respondents, a nine-point increase from December (*RT*, 2015). The following year, the story was largely the same, with a thorough appraisal of the president's public standing. For example, "Americans are largely split on whether President Barack Obama is doing a good job . . . While 46 percent approve of Obama's job performance, 47 percent disapprove, roughly in line with where the president has stood in January 2014 and January 2015" (Gass 2016). In short, it is not surprising that approval is also significant.[28]

CONCLUSION

This chapter examined presidential action as macropolitical policy output. The analyses are not meant to be comprehensive but suggestive of situations wherein presidential leverage might be useful and assert explanatory power. Three general areas of presidential action were surveyed: presidential legacy, operationalized as the proportion of large, important laws that originated in the White House; unilateral action in the guise of executive orders; and volume of presidential requests in the State of the Union on policies that were promulgated by the White House. In the first two analyses, the IPL is unambiguously a better and stronger predictor of presidential action; in the third, it was nearly as strong a predictor as approval. This finding is important and suggests an interesting distinction, namely that when the public presidency is most on display (such as the State of the Union) and much of the hype around it centers specifically on presidential approval, then approval may have slightly more predictive capacity than the IPL—but, again, only slightly more. This finding further suggests that scholars will do as well or better in explaining presidential action if they contextualize presidential leverage as opposed to simply using approval lacking context.

One way to evaluate presidential history is to examine the public policies produced by an administration, particularly those that maintain a lasting impact. Although important, enduring policies are often controversial, they can be thought of as bold answers to large and enduring questions. Actions of strongly leveraged presidents might be interpreted as asserting leadership to unite the country. However, such a conclusion must be tempered by the fact that regardless of how one measures institutional contagion, there is a strong and significant party factor at work. As presidents are more polarized from Congress, they encounter partisan obstacles in loading the agenda with large and significant policy. Still, the impact of presidential leverage indicates that strong presidents can mitigate these obstacles and make lasting and significant contributions to the policy epochs characterizing presidential history. Although presidents can and often try to work to unite the country, they may divide it as well or at least play partisanship (see also Wood 2009). This conclusion is further buttressed by the impacts that new regimes and new presidents make, as with some caveat, these presidents so situated in time also make a lasting impact on the macropolitical regime.

The evidence presented in this chapter supports the theoretical argument that to understand a president's place in the system, one needs to understand how that "place" situates the president in relation to public perception and trust in the government as a whole. When presidents make their mark on American politics, the leverage they have affects how much more successful they are at making their impression on American politics with substantively important, lasting policy legacies. It also affects their proclivity to use the unilateral presidency, and they are emboldened on the front end of the agenda-setting process. In each of the latter cases, the relationship of leverage to action is an inverse one, suggesting that, as presidential leverage decreases, presidents are more likely to use executive orders and propose more in the State of the Union, perhaps to distract from their weak status and appear stronger by proposing more policy action.

CHAPTER 6

A Refuge of Low-Leveraged Presidents
Politicized Capacity and Policy Centralization

"THE PRESIDENT NEEDS HELP" is one of the most iconic sentences ever written about the presidency (President's Committee on Administrative Management, 1937: 1).[1] Because it was penned during Franklin Roosevelt's first term, presidents have tried to balance building political capacity with which to negotiate the myriad obstacles that can waylay presidential policy against symbolic commitments to save money and trim the size of the executive branch. Political capacity is defined here as the organizational resources and personnel close to the president in the executive office of the president (EOP) and the White House staff (WHS) that keep his or her political interests at the vanguard of any policy effort and act to protect political interests. To be sure, policies may be pursued for their own instrumental purposes, but the political staff is tasked with trying to align policy with the politics of the situation, satisfying, or at least failing to unduly antagonize, politically important constituencies such as Congress or the president's electoral bases.

Building the political staff to do this has not always been easy, and the Constitution as written is of little or no help for it does not explicitly provide presidents with staff support. The only overt reference to the president's executive branch is in Article II, Section 2, which authorizes presidents to "require the Opinion, in writing, of the principal Officer in each of the executive Departments, upon any subject relating to the Duties of their respective Offices." Like Article I, where the framers created a Congress that consisted of empty houses, later furnished with committees, party structures, leadership structures, and routinized modes of doing business, the Constitution is largely silent on the administrative configuration of the presidency in part because the framers were loath to create anything that smacked of tyranny, and an overly staffed presidency, with the capacity to bulldoze competing institutions, would do just that. Or so they feared.

To shape policy, politics, and legacies, presidents have used various strategies to win support and approval so as to mold a positive legacy for themselves in the annals of history (Heith 2004). Whether they do so internally within the White House (such as communications strategies) or look outside for support, factors such as electoral politics, policy accomplishment, and representation pose constant challenges for the occupant of the Oval Office. Presidents have systematically and predictably cultivated the intersection of these values in part by employing various models of policy-making location (primarily within the White House, designated primarily for bureaucratic agents, or some mixture of the two), depending on the nature of the policy at hand, the degree to which departments and agencies are to be affected, the locus of presidential commitment to a policy, and other factors (Ponder 2000; see also Rudalevige 2002). Politics and policy often flow in parallel streams, and it is the task of presidents and their administrations to manufacture "canals" that connect these streams (Kingdon 1984). Presidents are proactive (and not simply reactive) actors in a system that is comprised of institutions that can be ambivalent or impermeable to presidential leadership. Successful presidents react in systematic ways to strategize and implement optimal processes that help to shape the macropolitics of their time, which is crucial because they often govern in political times that constrict rather than liberate their actions (Skowronek 1993).

LINKING LEVERAGE TO RESPONSIVENESS AND AUTONOMY: THEORETICAL CONSIDERATIONS

For more than a century after the founding, Congress was stingy when allocating money to the presidential office, declining to appropriate money for even the most nominal staff support. Recognizing that they could not go it alone, presidents often used their own personal resources to hire at least one assistant or relied on relatives to help with office duties and other administrative chores. This hindered presidents for decades, and it was not until the administration of the hapless James Buchanan on the eve of the Civil War that Congress finally allocated funds, albeit only for a single secretary. Not until Herbert Hoover committed the heresy of trying to expand the size of his staff did presidents aim to increase their administrative and political capacity through legislation. Even though Hoover's efforts were mild (he requested a grand total of four new hires), his actions triggered a backlash from those worried that presidents had begun to overflow their constitutional and statutory boundaries by drawing power in toward themselves, preparing for a full frontal assault on the political system (Walcott and Hult 1995: 1–2).[2]

By the end of his second term, Franklin Roosevelt had weathered many of the same storms first visited on Hoover, and he was successful in creating the executive office of the president (EOP), composed of support staff agencies designed to provide the "help" that the president so desperately needed. Presidents now had the basis for building capacity to manage and sustain relationships with myriad institutional and noninstitutional actors (such as interest groups, the public, and so forth), but that capacity did not mature overnight. Instead, there were fits and starts in how the EOP was structured, how the emergence of a more formidable White House staff would be integrated into the executive establishment, and with what consequences.[3] Presidents sought out "neutral competence" by promoting the creation of agencies such as the Bureau of the Budget (later renamed as the Office of Management and Budget), whose first responsibility was to the *presidency*, not the president. The concept of neutral competence traces its roots to the Weberian politics–administration dichotomy wherein bureaucrats develop and manage policy in a quasi-scientific manner, relying on expert opinion and objective criteria unburdened by political or partisan ties.[4] Over time, this focus on neutral competence was scaled back when presidents sought to increase responsiveness to their own initiatives and political preferences. Questions of internal political capacity and, to a lesser extent, autonomy became paramount as expectations increased and emerged coterminous with technological advances that made it more difficult for presidents to coexist in, much less dominate, the political landscape (Moe 1985).

Leverage and Political Responsiveness

Public expectations of the presidency can play a major role in presidential decisions to centralize policy making and maximize responsiveness. Low-leveraged presidents are more likely to increase the responsiveness of the EOP and to pull policy making into the White House. Why? The capacity for purposive action is primary for presidents trying to lead in a hyperpolitical system with fragmented power bases and political stakes tied to the outcome of numerous policies, whether that outcome is policy defeat, transformation, or passage (in whatever form) of policy mixed in with politics.[5] Characterized by Samuel Kernell as "individualized pluralism," this system is a complicated web of political actors who compete with the president for policy and political relevance. Thus, the politics of bargaining and compromise among a few concentrated elites such as the president and party leaders in Congress, or what Kernell called "institutionalized pluralism," has become a thing of the past, and the ideal forms of bargaining and compromise have become more difficult to implement as the number of key players has increased dramatically (Kernell 2007: 11–45). This suggests that presidents will attempt to decrease transaction costs more efficiently by trying to persuade constituencies to sign on to their position by going over and above the heads of political competitors (for example, Congress) directly to the public as a means to apply pressure to reach agreement, even as the process of achieving consensus or tentative bargain has become increasingly unpredictable in the face of fracturing coalitions.

Whereas political capacity is necessary for presidents to navigate institutional, extrainstitutional, and electoral waters, their power positions ebb and flow in the face of numerous factors, including the power stakes of their institutional competitors. For example, presidential policy goals may be thwarted when they conflict with the competing policy, constituency, and electoral interests of members of Congress (MCs). Presidents have the means not only to assert their political and policy goals but to act on them. Presidents with low leverage are likely to try to enhance their prospects for success by centralizing policy making in the White House, a defensive strategy that seeks to protect their political interests from hostile competitors (Rudalevige 2002; Ponder 2000).[6]

Linking the Public and Institutional Presidencies: Centralization and Decentralization of Public Policy Formulation

Terry Moe argued that the gap between public expectations heaped on the office of the presidency and the inability of individual presidents to meet those expectations is linked to important developments in the institutional presidency, including the tendency for presidents to tightly control content by centralizing policy making in the White House (Moe 1985). Moe focused attention on institutional dynamics in the presidency, arguing that presidents react to the gap between public expectations and their capacity to meet those expectations by controlling policy making and implementation. Many scholars soon evaluated various components of Moe's framework (for example, Lewis 2008; Ponder 2000; Rudalevige 2002; Rudalevige and Lewis 2005; Weko 1995). At the same time, many scholars looked deeply into the public presidency (Edwards 1983; Kernell 2007), though few have linked these two areas of research.[7] Moe comes close as his argument explicitly involves both the public component (expectations gap) as well as the institutional (centralization and politicization).[8]

The remainder of this chapter explores the degree to which the public presidency (via presidential leverage) informs our understanding of some aspects of the institutional presidency. Presidential leverage plays a significant role in influencing location of public policy making, and this determination is a strategic short-term advantage for presidents. Building on the theoretical linkages established earlier, the leverage framework suggests that, as leverage *decreases*, presidents will centralize more because their standing with the public means that they are often beleaguered as weak presidents, or simply as one of several individuals or institutions with a stake in the political action. Conversely, strongly leveraged presidents can construct complex, new, large-scale policies that cut across departmental or agency jurisdictions. Because of this complexity, high-leverage presidents are less likely to centralize. Like politicization, centralization is a rational response to presidential incentives structured by both dynamic and static contexts in the larger political system, not least the decline of political parties (for example, Moe 1985; Weko 1995).

Not all policies are centralized, of course. Presidential resources such as time and the use of the White House staff and EOP are at a premium. The staff in particular are hardly immune from pathologies of "bounded rationality," the concept that humans are limited by both time and cognitive capacity and therefore must often forego the opportunity to systematically determine the "best" possible alternative. Instead, they "satisfice," finding the first alternative that is acceptable for immediate purposes (Simon 1947).

Elsewhere, I developed a framework for analyzing and categorizing the use of the White House staff according to the incentives, interest, and use of the presidents (Ponder 2000).[9] That analysis posits that presidential preferences are conditioned by the incentives existing in the American political system. It is useful to think of presidential preferences as having at least two related but distinct components. First, presidents have "pure preferences," which are those they would implement if they were a "dictator" and confronted no political or policy opposition. The second component is dubbed "realistic preferences," which are plausible outcomes based on modified pure preferences and are more or less possible given the political context, the timing with which presidents choose to push policy ideas, and the location of policy construction. Taken together, these form the incentive structure within which presidents operate. These incentives, like "realistic" preferences, are variable, change over time, and are at least partly influenced by circumstances outside the White House. The incentives (or disincentives, as the case may be) include the congressional context, party politics, interest group pressures, public opinion, and other considerations.

Linking leverage to the institutional presidency is related to the logic of presidential incentives to centralize or decentralize policy processes. Presidents are faced with a decision to centralize, mix, or decentralize policy, and, although presidential staff play an important part in any and all of these processes, the nature of staff involvement shifts depending on factors individual to each president (agenda priority, for example) or contextual considerations such as political environment and issue complexity (see also Rudalevige 2002).

Stronger, high-leveraged presidents are given more leeway when acting on their "warrants" to make and implement policy (Skowronek 1993). The mechanism driving the decision to locate policy construction in the White House or elsewhere stems from the overlap of public opinion and leeway. Consider the case of the "weak," or lower-leveraged presidents as measured by their IPL. They have less political capital and therefore are likely to centralize to protect their policy proposals. "Political concerns become so intractable that the technical substance of policy is used as a bargaining tool between the political and policy dimensions" (Ponder 2000: 8).

Of course, not all presidents who centralize are politically weak; indeed, there is wide variation in the propensity to centralize policy making within and across presidencies as a function of the size of the IPL. Presidents who centralize often have to sacrifice policy expertise to control the political definition of policy, but, as Rudalevige demonstrates, control often dissipates as centralized policies are less likely to be passed in Congress (Rudalevige 2002). Of course, congressional success cannot always be equated with political success.[10] Nonetheless, presidents who lack public leverage are more likely to pull policy making into the White House so as to protect their agenda from being diluted outside the White House or EOP.

Stronger presidents have the luxury of relying on the bureaucracy to frame policy proposals, taking advantage of information gains from trade.[11] Expertise is the primary good that presidents can offer to presidents. Thus, presidents have access to a sort of responsive expertise, which reinforces policy fealty buttressed by an increased likelihood of prevailing in the legislative process (Rudalevige 2002). Bureaucratic expertise can work to the president's advantage in a number of ways, but only if the president can assert political control over policy content against competing institutions and to score political points with the public (Ponder 2000). Here the public dimension overlaps with policy construction. Examples gleaned from the literature on presidential policy and public activities illustrate the point. For instance, presidents who enjoy greater credibility with voters are more successful at raising the salience of an issue (Larocca 2006). Eshbaugh-Soha (2006) argues that presidential speeches are efficient signals to bureaucrats and others about the president's true objectives. The concept of presidential leverage adds to this literature by proposing that high-leverage presidents have more credibility with the public, and this enables them to control the definition of issues. Consequently, they are thus able to use "excess" leverage and burn some capital by using staff as a powerful *monitor*, leaving much of the policy content to bureaucratic agents but under the watchful eye of the president's policy staff (Ponder 2000).[12]

Presidential priorities are likely to be more centralized (Rudalevige 2002). For high-leverage presidents, this reflects an incentive to centralize those priorities mixed with a tendency to look to complex items that may have larger impact. Thus, whereas members of Congress are likely to use public cues such as approval for decreasing uncertainty, presidents can use leverage as a way to gauge the likelihood of seeing clearly their opportunities for action.

Strategies of Presidential Policy Making

Extending Kernell's (2007) insight that Washington politics is now best described as "individualized pluralism" and applying it to presidential policy making, an atomistic system implies that presidents will delegate policy making to the executive branch well outside the cozy confines of the EOP but that White House staff activity will always be prevalent, though not always as the coordinator or primary manufacturer of that policy. Thus, "staff shift" suggests that policy making will run the gamut from fully centralized in the White House to fully decentralized to the bureaucracy (though in the latter case, it is likely to be only to agencies that are sufficiently politicized). Staff involvement shifts in accordance with presidential preferences located within a strategic context. Detailed in the following subsections are those categories, which mirror the coding of the dependent variable, estimated later (Ponder 2000).

Staff as Director   Politically charged issues are likely to be centralized, and staff acts as the "director" of policy making so as to ensure a high degree of responsiveness. Bureaucrats in the executive branch are thus largely responsible for implementation rather than a source of independent authority.

Staff as Facilitator   If a policy cuts across numerous department or agency jurisdictions, presidents centralize less often, preferring to obtain gains from expertise and thus act as "facilitators," coordinating the work of departments and agencies, playing a developmental role themselves, but by necessity neither controlling nor fully delegating the formulation of a particular policy.

Staff as Monitor   Finally, policy formulation can be fully delegated to external agencies. Under this strategy, the White House staff often maintains a role in supervising policy content in a process of what might be called "decentralized centralization." In other words, departments and/or agencies can make policy, but the White House staff monitors the content and maintains "creative control" over the final outcome. As an example, think of this as similar to the process of legislative clearance wherein policies are cleared with the White House to ensure they are consistent with the president's program. When presidents enjoy high leverage, staff are likely to monitor bureaucrats on policy items and therefore benefit from information advantages held by bureaucrats, combined with political imperatives in the White House. Bureaucrats do not have reelection incentives, of course, but a president's leverage and the leeway that comes with that leverage ground and guide executive decision makers. The public component plays an important role but not in the same way Congress uses public opinion as a means to decrease uncertainty as to the consequences of their votes on policy. Rather, leverage is a signal of presidential *capital*, and this can provide the necessary information for MCs, the media, and other interested parties.[13]

If presidential leverage influences the decision to centralize policy making, the arrow of causality flows from leverage to centralization. However, it should not be interpreted that leverage itself represents a public preference for or against centralization; rather leverage provides the president with capital such that he is less threatened by the political context, making it more likely that policy will be decentralized. With the exception of high-profile policy initiatives (such as the Clinton and Obama health care reform efforts), the public is unlikely to know (or even care) whether the policy proposal is centralized or decentralized.[14] Clinton's effort at health care reform was scuttled in part because political opposition successfully branded the process as closed off and elitist; in short, political opponents were successful at redefining what the president was trying to do, much to the detriment of the administration and its reform effort.[15]

Presidents often claim credit for policy making, and when the stakes are high it is to the president's advantage to decentralize policy making for political reasons such as cultivating inclusiveness or for policy expediency, such as when the issue is complex or cuts across department and agency jurisdictions (see Ponder 2000; Rudalevige 2002).[16] Presidents who have thoroughly politicized the relevant bureaucracies are less likely to centralize because they simply do not need to do so. Conversely, if they do not have presidential loyalists in place in the executive branch, they are more likely to pull policy making inward to the White House, controlling policy from the center. Adding a public component to the politicization argument, Villalobos and Vaughn (2009) show that presidents with higher policy-specific approval are more likely to politicize the executive branch.[17]

Combining these two perspectives, the expectation is that presidents who enjoy higher levels of presidential leverage will centralize less because they are more likely to have a responsive executive branch. On the other hand, presidents with low leverage are incentivized to reinforce their political staff, in part to help bolster their efforts in an often unfriendly political environment. Though results are weaker and inconsistent than other analyses presented in this book, I provide evidence below that higher-leveraged presidents do not generally reduce the numbers in the EOP, but they do not significantly add politicized agents, either. One reason is that they may already have adequate political responsiveness in the executive branch, in the EOP, or in the White House staff. Most of the variation in EOP size is to be generated by lower-leveraged presidents. Here a paradox emerges, though, because whereas centralization is often used by publicly weak presidents to play defense, a centralized policy is less likely to find success in Congress than a decentralized one (Rudalevige 2002). Still, as Ponder (2000) argues, presidents closely guard the nature and definition of their program, particularly when they are weak and can make this argument publicly. If they are going to lose on a policy issue, then they have incentive to publicly control the definition of that loss and control the content so they can plausibly argue that though they "lost," they were faithful to their core beliefs.

The expectation that emerges from this discussion as it relates to centralization is that strongly leveraged presidents will be more likely to rely on a politicized bureaucracy to manufacture policy content. Thus, the hypothesis:

H.6.1: *Presidential leverage is inversely related to centralization; low-leveraged presidents will be more likely to centralize than presidents with high leverage.*

Variables and Measurement

The analysis adapts Rudalevige's (2002) framework to that of presidential leverage to explore the linkage between leverage and the processes of presidential policy making in the White House. Accordingly, the dependent variable is Rudalevige's measure of centralization, which is analogous to Ponder's (2000) concept of staff shift, discussed earlier in this chapter. Rudalevige's measures correspond nicely to the staff shift framework, as he codes unique policy proposals for whether they were staffed out to the bureaucracy (equivalent to staff as monitor), a mixed strategy in which the White House staff or EOP coordinates the process among several participants (Ponder's "facilitator" category), or fully centralized in the White House staff (corresponding to staff as "director"). In particular, the dependent variable is an ordinal measure that takes a value of 0 for fully decentralized and 3 for fully centralized in the White House or EOP, with the values of 1 and 2 reflecting mixed strategies.

The independent variable of primary interest is the IPL, measured in the quarter previous to the announcement of a policy. This provides lead time in which a president makes a determination of the situation and deploys staff resources as he or she sees fit.

As is the case with other analyzes in this book, other contexts are controlled as well, such as *Divided Government* (1 = Divided; 0 = Unified) and *Congressional–Presidential Polarization*, which is the absolute value of the distance between the President's DW-NOMINATE score and that of the median member of Congress.

Other controls come largely from Rudaleivige (2002: chapters 4 and 5), and the reader is referred to that source for a full accounting of their inclusion, as well as to Appendix D of this book. However, one final caveat needs to be noted. Because of data limitations on both the primary independent variable (leverage) and the dependent variable (centralization), the analysis incorporates an update of the centralization measure as coded by Jose Villalobos (Villalobos 2008, 2013), which brings the analysis into the Obama administration.[18] Thus, what follows should not be interpreted as a direct replication and extension of Rudalevige's results but simply as an exploration of the linkage of the IPL to policy centralization.

FINDINGS AND IMPLICATIONS

Although Rudalevige's covariates were used as controls in modeling centralization, the discussion of the findings is generally limited to the hypothesis linking presidential leverage to policy centralization. Although the data are more truncated than in Rudalevige, the results are strikingly similar. Table 6.1 displays the results of an ordered probit estimation whereas Table 6.2 displays the marginal impacts associated with the probit coefficients.

Impact of Control Variables

The main purpose of this analysis is to evaluate the impact of leverage on centralization. But it is worth noting that divided government has no systematic impact on centralization, though Democratic presidents and increased presidential–congressional polarization are more likely to increase the likelihood of centralization. Size of the EOP, crosscutting jurisdictions, reorganization proposals, new items, priority items (not significant), salient items (not significant), and budget impact (not significant) are more likely to increase centralization, whereas the percentage of federal employees under merit protection, complexity (not significant), foreign policy, crisis (not significant), and month of the term are less likely to lead to centralization.

Presidential Leverage and Policy Location

Moving to an analysis of leverage, Table 6.1 shows that the IPL, lagged one quarter, is strong and statistically significant. Indeed, when an ordered probit was run using only the IPL as a predictor, it was nearly as strong. The probit coefficient was -0.60, $p = 0.60$, with a log likelihood of -325.14. The other covariates explain centralization in much the same way that they did in Rudalevige (2002), but it is clear that the IPL adds to the explanatory power of policy making location.

Table 6.2 shows the probabilities of a fully decentralized (0) and fully centralized (3) policy proposal. A unit increase in the IPL leverage increases the probability of decentralizing policy making to a department by nearly 0.17 of one percent. Recall that presidential leverage is measured in continuous discrete units, so if leverage were to increase from 1.0 to 1.10, the probability of full decentralization increases by 1.68 percent. Similarly, the same shift in leverage *decreases* the likelihood of full White House Office/EOP centralization by approximately 1.8 percent. Thus, the centralization hypothesis is strongly supported; presidential leverage is a significant predictor of the probability of centralization. The higher the degrees of presidential leverage, the less likely presidents are to centralize. Conversely, more weakly leveraged presidents are more likely to bring policy making into the White House. One implication is that presidential leverage provides a context within which presidents do not have to centralize policy to maintain authority over the policy-making process. Although it is possible that there is a reciprocal relationship at work here (high leverage leads to more decentralization, which in turn implies openness to government policy making and thus further reinforces presidential approval, which often leads to higher leverage), the findings offer strong confirmation of the impact of the strategic presidency. The findings also persist in the presence of partisan and contextual covariates.

The Obama Presidency as an Illustration

Perhaps no other administration highlights the trends just described as well as President Obama's first term. Policy-making efforts, particularly early in his presidency when his leverage was extremely high, bear this out most directly. Obama initially sought out information from a variety

TABLE 6.1
Probit estimates of leverage and associated contexts on policy centralization.

Independent variable	Coefficient
Public context	
Presidential leverage (lagged one quarter)	−0.62**
	(0.34)
Partisan/congressional context	
Divided government	−0.14
	(0.27)
Democratic president	0.32*
	(0.24)
President–congress polarization	1.44*
	(0.96)
Executive capacity	
EOP size	0.001***
	(0.0002)
Merit percent	−0.08***
	(0.02)
Programmatic	
Crosscutting jurisdictions	0.16***
	(0.03)
Reorganization impact	0.36***
	(0.10)
Complexity	−0.07
	(0.08)
Policy type (foreign/domestic)	−0.07**
	(0.04)
New item	0.37***
	(0.14)
Priority item (State of the Union)	0.03
	(0.16)
Policy salience	0.08
	(0.16)
External context	
Budget situation (deficit as percent of GDP)	0.006
	(0.04)
Crisis	−0.04
	(0.19)
Temporal context	
Month of term	−0.006*
	(0.004)
N	392
Log-likelihood	−499.82
Likelihood ratio chi-square	84.54
Prob > χ^2	0.000

*** $p \leq 0.01$

** $p \leq 0.05$

** $p \leq 0.10$ (one-tailed tests; coefficients are ordinal probit estimates; standard errors in parentheses)

TABLE 6.2

Impacts of explanatory variables on likelihood of policy location, 1961–2010.

Independent variable	Level of centralization			
	0 Department	1 Mixed (Department)	2 Mixed (EOP)	3 (WHO/EOP)
Public context				
Presidential leverage (lag 1 quarter)	**0.169**	**0.077**	**−0.067**	**−0.179**
Partisan/congressional context				
Divided government	0.038	0.018	−0.015	−0.041
Democratic president	−0.085	−0.040	0.032	0.093
President–Congress polarization	−0.394	−0.181	0.157	0.418
Executive capacity				
EOP size	−0.0002	−0.0001	0.0001	0.0002
Merit percent	**0.021**	**0.010**	**−0.009**	**−0.022**
Programmatic				
Crosscutting jurisdictions	−0.043	−0.020	0.017	0.046
Reorganization impact	−0.097	−0.045	0.039	0.103
Complexity	0.018	0.008	−0.007	−0.019
Policy type (foreign/domestic)	**0.020**	**0.009**	**−0.008**	**−0.021**
New item	−0.103	−0.043	0.042	**0.104**
Priority item (State of the Union)	−0.007	−0.003	0.003	0.008
Policy salience	−0.021	−0.010	0.008	0.024
External/fiscal context				
Budget situation (deficit as percent of GDP)	−0.002	−0.0007	0.001	0.002
Crisis	0.011	0.005	−0.004	−0.011
Temporal context				
Month of term	**0.002**	**0.0007**	**−0.001**	**−0.002**

Note: Figures indicate percentage change in the probability of obtaining a result in the indicated category, from least to most centralized, given a unit shift in the particular independent variable, or a shift from 0 to 1 in the case of dummy variables. Statistically significant coefficients (at least $p < 0.10$) are in **bold**.

of sources, pledging to run a less politicized White House and pursue a "multiple advocacy" approach to governing, wherein presidents seek, cultivate, and use advice proffered by multiple sources of information from both inside and outside the White House. But by the end of the second year of his presidency, with his IPL in gradual decline (though still relatively high compared to many of his predecessors), his closest advisers in the White House fell victim to internal dysfunction when his political and policy teams clashed. An outwardly directed form of policy making was employed in the first two years of his administration, wherein advisory systems from across the government were part of the policy-making process, and in a variety of contexts, including the Affordable Care Act (ACA). However, the pathologies of such a strategy began to manifest themselves in the advisory configuration of Obama's White House. As a consequence of the clash between the ideological team on the inside and the pragmatists on the outside, the speed with which policy making progressed decreased. A strategy of increased centralization, directed by a small, tight-knit group whose membership shrank over the course of his first term, emerged. As his IPL fell, the inclination toward centralization by Obama's more ideological advisers located in the White House increased, just as the leverage framework suggests. In Obama's case, it was more a matter of his IPL decreasing relative to his early, extremely high ratings, rather than falling to "low" or "average" territory, but the pattern in his first term illustrates the incentives and general patterns uncovered over all presidents considered here.[19]

BUILDING CAPACITY: A CAUTIONARY TALE

Systemic theories of policy making, including the leverage framework, generally contend that increased fracturing and growing polarization of the political system have decreased how predictable the structure and consequences of American politics can be. Long gone are the days of close, personal president–MC relations, and mounting antagonisms both between MCs and presidents as well as among MCs within Congress itself dissolve into greater uncertainty for understanding and predicting how a policy proposal might work in practice. To decrease uncertainty, presidents may well find it in their interest to increase the size of the political staff to gain capacity as a buffer of sorts against the strong headwinds in the American political system.

Thus, this section examines one simple means of exploring capacity building, via the size of the EOP. One method of doing so is to examine the number of *units* in the EOP. But adding units for presidents takes time, and the distance between proposal and creation of the unit might not reflect the political situation at a particular moment. A short-term proxy is to look at building presidential capacity by adding political personnel.

Thinking of the EOP is not as straightforward as one might hope. As Andrew Rudalevige argues in his work on centralization, not all EOP units should be considered part of a "centralized" policy system, serving the president and his political/policy agenda. For example, the Office of Economic Opportunity (OE), which existed from 1963 to 1975, and the U.S. Trade Representative (USTR) are operating agencies that serve clients outside the executive branch, in addition to serving the president him- or herself (Rudalevige 2002). Building political capacity in the "presidential branch," as opposed to the larger executive bureaucracy, is not as reliant on the question of "who the client is" as is the issue of policy centralization. Although it might matter for purposes of analyzing the location of policy making whether an agency serves multiple masters, adding employees with various skills and specializations builds capability for steering policy in the *president's* direction.[20] The number of EOP employees from Kennedy to Obama ranges from 1,514 employees in 1987 to a high of 5,751 in 1974, averaging 2,396.28 over the span of the analysis (Ragsdale 2014: Table 6-1, 349–354). The number of staffers located nearest the president and physically in the White House ranges from 272 in 1967 (late in LBJ's administration) employees to a high of 660 in 1971, early in Nixon's administration, with an average of 401.18 over the span of the analysis (Ragsdale 2014: Table 6-1, 349–354). Although a full accounting of the variation of the growth in staff is outside the scope of this book, suffice it to say that the ebb and flow of employment patterns follows an irregular path. As Ragsdale writes, the patterns tended to follow individual interests of the presidents, who would add or subtract units and therefore employees based on political and policy objectives they sought (Ragsdale 2014).

Although staffing patterns follow an uneven path, they are best under-stood as the sum total of White House reactions to the political environment (for example, Kernell 1989: 234). As noted in the previous section, centralized policy is a matter of degree and includes the EOP. The EOP includes most of what we think of as presidential support staff, responsive primarily to the president's policy goals but sensitive to his or her political interests, and includes such support offices as the White House Office, BOB (Bureau of the Budget)/OMB, the National Security Council, the Council of Economic Advisors, Council of Environmental Quality, the Office of the Drug Czar, and many others. By and large these entities serve a constituency of one: the president. In doing so, they often conflict with other actors in the bureaucracy. Much of this contagion is partitioned along the neutral competence/responsiveness continuum, and the EOP/WHO apparatus, situated close to the president in terms of both ideology and physical space, can be profitably thought of as the "presidential branch" (Hart 1995). They are responsive to the president's political and policy views and are marshaled to move presidential policy in the direction he or she desires.

Analysis of Staff Size

Presidents need political capacity to perform even their most perfunctory duties, and certainly for decision making, formulating, and implementing public policy.[21] Building on the theoretical foundation expounded in this book, this proposition generates the following hypothesis:

H.6.2 *Weakly situated presidents will seek to increase the number of staff advisory personnel in the executive branch.*

This hypothesis needs to be fleshed out in a bit more detail. Put simply, lower-leveraged presidents are acting from a position of relative weakness and can address that weakness by building political capacity in the EOP and its various entities, such as the OMB and WHS. Placing presidential loyalists deep into the executive establishment and responsive to their political and programmatic direction deep into the executive establishment is important for all presidents but particularly for low-leveraged presidents, who are more likely to find themselves engaged in political combat with political contenders such as Congress and, occasionally, with long-established bureaucrats in the executive departments and agencies.[22] Americans are notoriously suspicious of power, so stronger presidents may have an incentive to downplay opportunities to significantly increase executive personnel, thereby avoiding criticism of having contributed to an unpopular aggrandizement of power, a "swelling of the presidency" (Cronin 1973). Presidents are more likely to add political appointees when they need to enhance responsiveness, which was shown in the last section to be traced in part to a president's degree of public leverage.

The model estimated in the following discussion is identical to those in the previous chapter except for a slight theoretical adjustment. Absent from the models are two variables that do not bear on any theoretical linkage to staff size. First, the *Mood* variable is removed from the model because there is no specific reason to assume that the public's view of what should or should not be done in terms of policy will affect a president's decision to increase or decrease capacity. Second, the *War* variable is removed from the analysis. Wartime presidents may well add capacity in other areas of the executive branch and may rely more heavily on White House staff resources (especially the National Security Council), but that is different from adding staff, especially given the symbolic issues that often arise when large amounts of resources are spent on the war effort.[23]

The first important thing to note is that, unlike other analyses in this book, *this analysis should be treated as only suggestive because the impact of the IPL is contingent on which covariates are included.* What is reported in Table 6.3 is the strongest of the models, but the results should be taken with an abundance of caution, whereas the results in the centralization analysis reported earlier in this chapter and those in the previous chapter are on a more solid ground. Nonetheless, the lesson that emerges is clear: whether statistically significant or insignificant, the *IPL coefficients are always stronger and either significant or almost significant, whereas the approval coefficients are not.* The model, though, is much weaker, with an adjusted R^2 of only 0.11.[24]

Proceeding with that caution in mind, I spend some time examining the intricacies of the data to try to uncover patterns that are buried deeply in the ECM analysis. First, the zero- and first-order correlations between

TABLE 6.3
Presidential leverage and executive capacity, 1961–2012.

Variable	Full model	Reduced form	Reduced form with Vietnam/Watergate–era control
Constant	3.37*** (1.01)	3.24*** (0.90)	4.53*** (0.98)
Log EOP size$_{t-1}$	−0.32*** (0.10)	−0.31*** (0.09)	−0.48*** (0.11)
Presidential leverage			
Δ IPL	−0.14 (0.21)		
IPL$_{t-1}$	−0.42** (0.23)	−0.38** (0.19)	−0.30** (0.18)
Political context			
Δ President–Congress polarization	−1.56** (0.72)	−1.57** (0.72)	−0.88 (0.72)
President–Congress polarization$_{t-1}$	−1.85*** (0.54)	−01.75*** (0.53)	−1.73*** (0.49)
Δ Divided government	0.28 (0.21)		
Divided government$_{t-1}$	0.48*** (0.17)	0.46*** (0.16)	0.51*** (0.15)
Δ Democratic president	−0.36** (0.18)	−0.40** (0.17)	0.23* (0.17)
Democratic president$_{t-1}$	0.27** (0.12)	−0.26** (0.12)	0.29*** (0.11)
Budget constraint			
Δ Debt to GDP	−0.02** (0.008)	−0.02** (0.008)	0.01* (0.007)
Debt to GDP$_{t-1}$	−0.008* (0.005)	0.008* (0.005)	
Time			
Δ Year of term	−0.03* (0.02)	0.03* (0.02)	0.009 (0.02)
Year of term$_{t-1}$	0.01 (0.02)		
Vietnam/Watergate dummy			0.26** (0.10)
Adjusted R^2	0.17	0.19	0.29
Standard error of estimate	0.19	0.19	0.18
N	53	53	53

Dependent variable is Δ Log EOP size. Standard errors in parentheses.

*** $p < 0.01$

** $p < 0.05$

* $p < 0.10$ (one-tailed tests)

Source for Executive Capacity: Ragsdale (2014).

the annualized IPL and EOP size are negative and robust (zero-order $r = -0.50$, $p = 0.000$).[25] This suggests that when presidential IPLs are high/low, the number of employees decreases/increases. For the ECM, a series of analyses on measures examining various issues of staff size were run, using the log of all employees in the EOP as the dependent variable. The rationale for using the logged value of EOP size is straightforward, as moving from 1,000 to 1,001 EOP staffers is not likely to be as impactful as moving from 0 to 1.[26] Table 6.3 presents the results of the IPL in the models of the size of the EOP. The first column is a full ECM model, including covariates of various controls for divided government, polarization, budgetary impact, and the time of the president's term; the second includes only the significant variables from the full model; and the third includes the Vietnam/Watergate–era dummy variable.[27] Note also that in Table 6.3, both variables for institutional contagion are included. Unlike the analyses in Chapter 5, diagnostics revealed only mild collinearity problems, but nothing severe; so I include both measures of contagion.[28] For the following analysis, I focus on the reduced form model and how it changes with the addition of the Vietnam/Watergate–era time variable.

Trends in the Control Variables

Though primarily interested in the impact of the IPL on EOP size, I examine the controls first. In the full models, the error correction rate is quite low, indicating that the series returns to equilibrium very slowly. Only about 30 percent of the series equilibrium is restored in a year, with the remaining 70 percent distributed outward in time. In the model accounting for the Vietnam/Watergate–era dummy, the error correction rate is somewhat faster, with nearly 50 percent of the series equilibrium restored in one year because the large spike from LBJ through Ford is controlled.

Capacity diminishes as polarization between the presidency and the median MC grows, though it increases during times of divided government. Democratic presidents decrease the size of the EOP in both the short and long term. Short-term changes in divided government, significant in the reduced form model, achieve some marginal significance in the time-controlled model. One interesting point stands out—where the short-term impact of Democratic presidents was negative in the full and reduced model, the sign shifts to positive once time has been taken into account. Once we control for pre- or post-Vietnam/Watergate levels of EOP size, Democrats in the earlier period (especially Johnson) increased the size of the EOP whereas later Democrats (Carter, Clinton, and Obama) did not. As we might expect, the debt to GDP ratio is slightly negative, suggesting that the EOP is unlikely to grow in periods of budget constraint. However, there is a slight positive relationship in the post-Watergate era. This is consistent with Ragsdale's observation that increases in EOP growth indicate that presidents since Johnson displayed "relatively few attempts . . . to work with less money" (Ragsdale 2014: 313). Finally, presidents are more likely to increase capacity as their terms age, particularly in the pre-Nixon era; as one would expect, presidents were more likely to increase capacity in the era before Ford slashed the budget for the EOP.

Presidential Leverage and Presidential Political Capacity

Turning now to the impact of the IPL in Table 6.3, all three models exhibit a statistically significant negative relationship between leverage and capacity. Presidents with lower leverage increase the size of the EOP, and that increase has a significant long-term effect. As the theory suggests, weaker presidents seek to shore up protection of their political interests by increasing politicized staff in the EOP. This is particularly attractive for low-leveraged presidents because these staffers are outside the direct reach of Congress, are closer in ideology and proximity to presidents, and serve at the president's pleasure.

There is some disagreement in the institutional presidency literature as to the interpretation of such a finding. John Burke argues that, while adding staff responsive to the president's interests, there are costs to such a strategy, and that cost is an excessive politicization that can "limit the opinions among (and thus the quality of advice from) the staff" (Burke 2014: 365). Matthew Dickinson comes to basically the same conclusion and argues that the growth in the presidential branch and the movement away from the "competitive adhocracy" found in FDR's administration has weakened the presidency (Dickinson 1997). But Mayer makes a strong counterargument that the historical record supports the conclusion that

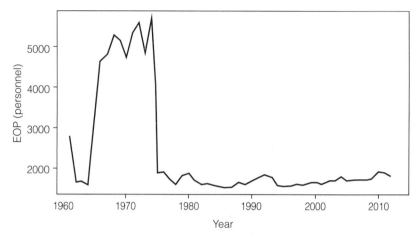

FIGURE 6.1. Total executive staff, Kennedy to Obama I.

Source: Ragsdale 2014: Table 6.1, 351–354.

presidents are not hamstrung by an enlarged staff but in fact are well served by it. He writes, "Presidents have enhanced their control over government activities by expanding the boundaries of White House and Executive Office institutions. The historical evidence simply does not support the position that the presidency has been weakened by the institutionalization of the office" (Mayer 2001: 135).[29] The analysis in this chapter builds on these perspectives by showing that, although all presidents are interested in protecting their political interests, high-leverage presidents either decrease the size of the EOP or leave it alone, subject to minor variation. Thus, the major takeaway from the analysis is that building capacity and politicizing the EOP are driven largely by lower-leveraged presidents.[30] (See Figure 6.1.)

Tracing the Patterns

Given that the impact of the IPL is sensitive to model specification, it is helpful to trace the patterns of how the IPL and capacity-building efforts relate to show that, by and large, variation in staff size is driven by low-leveraged presidents. First, consider the difference in staff size variation between below- and above-average IPL presidents. In the twenty-eight observations where presidents registered a *below*-average IPL, the average size of the executive staff was 2,859, with a standard deviation of 1,630. Those with *above*-average IPL presided over a *much lower* average EOP size of 1,877 and a standard deviation of 846. More telling, when the outlier years of 1966–1974 are removed from the analysis, the pattern remains the same.[31] For presidents with *above*-average IPL, average EOP size was 1,716 with a standard deviation of 263. For those with *below*-average IPL, EOP size averaged 1,778 with a standard deviation of 283. Removing outliers for analytic purposes provides a more conservative estimate of the configuration in the measurement of EOP size and bolsters the conclusion that the variation in increasing staff size is driven by weaker, low-leveraged presidents.

Taking a microlevel view, it is easy to see that the largest increase in the size of the EOP occurred during Johnson's presidency, when he sought to centralize most of the Great Society programs in the White House (Ragsdale 2014: 337; Moe 1985: 253–254). EOP staff size peaked under Nixon because of his efforts to control federal departments from inside the White House (Nathan 1983; Ragsdale 2014: 336). Johnson was primarily responsible for the overall growth of the EOP, and the size remained relatively stable until after Nixon resigned. Responding to Watergate and the perception of the "imperial presidency" (Schlesinger 1973; Rudalevige 2005), President Ford slashed the size of the EOP by two-thirds, and it has not reached or exceeded the 2,000 mark since (Ragsdale 2014).

Consider in even more detail the case of Lyndon Johnson. Assuming the presidency on Kennedy's assassination, LBJ recorded a solid, if average, IPL. Recall that although his approval was high in 1964, the public still held a great deal of trust in government. As Johnson's leverage dropped after his reelection, and as the country grew increasingly mired in Vietnam, LBJ increased his EOP size nearly every year. For example, in 1964, Johnson's EOP registered about 1,542; when his IPL dropped distinctly in 1965 (IPL = 1.05) and 1966 (IPL = 0.87), EOP size increased dramatically. Between 1964 and 1965, EOP size increased 85 percent to nearly 3,000. In the following years, LBJ's leverage continually dropped, though EOP size surged. As his IPL fell from 1.05 to 0.87, the EOP increased another 64 percent; when his IPL dropped again to its lowest point in 1967 (IPL = 0.75), EOP increased another 3 percent to nearly 5,000. The bulk of that growth was located in the White House Office as LBJ sought to run policy and the war from within the walls of 1600 Pennsylvania Avenue (Ragsdale 2014). All in all, LBJ's IPL dropped more than 35 percent between 1964 and 1968, whereas the size of the EOP increased more than 244 percent.

On the other hand, consider the case of Ronald Reagan. Reagan's presidency began with a relatively strong, though slightly below average, IPL of 1.06. As the economy plunged into recession in 1982 and 1983, his IPL dropped into negative territory, and the EOP grew dramatically, as predicted by the leverage framework. Once Reagan's IPL leveled off throughout much of the rest of his presidency, the size of the EOP stayed relatively constant. His IPL remained comparatively high moving into his 1984 reelection campaign, and it rose even more dramatically in 1985 and 1986. Meanwhile, the size of the EOP remained virtually unchanged, hovering in the mid- to lower 1,500s. Only when his IPL dipped in response to Iran-Contra in 1986 and 1987 did the EOP increase, but even then only in the last year of his presidency (from 1,515 in 1987 to 1,645 in 1988).

Other examples are similarly telling. In the wake of his controversial election to the presidency, George W. Bush's IPL was in the lower range through the first eight months of his presidency. The tragedy of September 11 delivered a rally effect to Bush's approval, and his IPL heaved to 1.40 in 2002. But as Bush's IPL took a beating in 2003 and 2004 in response to the drawn-out and expensive war in Iraq, he increased the size of the EOP and its associated expenditures so as to firmly control the war from within the presidential branch (Ragsdale 2014: 313). As his IPL continued to drop toward the end of his presidency, Bush added very modestly to the size of the EOP. On the Democratic side, Presidents Clinton and Obama, who enjoyed robust IPL ratings throughout, did not significantly manipulate the size of the EOP one way or the other.[32] In Obama's case it was not so much a question of the size of the growth of the EOP but rather a shift inside the White House from advisers who were political ideologues to a more pragmatic "outsider" structure (Warshaw et al. 2015).

Again, it is not necessarily the case that there is a direct one-to-one relationship in the series. The strongest model in Table 6.3, which includes the time-sensitive dummy variable, explains less than 30 percent of the variance (Adjusted R^2 = 0.29). The multivariate analysis mirrors the bivariate analysis and comparative descriptive statistics. Weaker presidents (that is, moving toward an IPL of 1.0 [stalemate] or below 1.0 [negative leverage]) are more likely to add EOP staff and thereby increase the politicized presidential branch. Presidents who exhibit higher levels of leverage, well in excess of 1.0 moving up toward 1.2 and greater, are less likely to manipulate the size of the EOP and therefore less likely to increase capacity for responsiveness in the EOP. The major finding from all the analyses presented here is that weaker presidents will increase EOP size, even when we control for the differential effects of pre- and post-Watergate eras. The models are strongest when divided government is included.

But, again, extreme caution should be applied when interpreting the findings. Although results are reasonably strong, they are somewhat contingent on model specification. Consequently, the results should be taken as highly suggestive and not definitive. Weaker presidents are more likely to add staff to the EOP, even after I control for the years before and after Nixon, when trust was at its lowest point. Presidents with higher leverage generally work with the EOP they have, adding to or shrinking the staff, but within far narrower bounds than their low-leveraged colleagues. And, as already noted, no matter what the impact of the IPL, whether it is statistically significant (sometimes, sometimes not), the sign on the coefficient is invariably negative and significant in bivariate and many multivariate analyses. The results are suggestive but to be taken with an appropriate degree of skepticism.[33]

CONCLUSIONS

This chapter links two of the most important developments in the modern presidency, the rise of the public as a source of influence and the development of the institutional presidency.[34] Presidential leverage is systematically related to each and can profitably be interpreted as a "last refuge" for low-leveraged presidents. Specifically, an inverse relationship between leverage and centralization of policy making in the White House was identified. As IPL declines, there is a greater likelihood of centralizing policy making in the White House. Presidents seek responsiveness to their policy proposals, and low-leveraged presidents are more likely to protect the policy content of their proposals by keeping them centralized.

Similarly, this chapter suggests another linkage between the public and institutional presidencies. As IPL increases, presidents are less likely to actively add staff to the EOP, though an abundance of caution needs to be applied when interpreting the findings, given that results are often sensitive to model specification. But surveying several presidential administrations lends support to the idea that weaker presidents are more likely to build political capacity. Higher-leveraged presidents either decrease the size of the political staff or leave it largely unchanged. Finally, results displayed in Table 2, Appendix B, confirm that the IPL is superior to measures of raw presidential approval when explaining variation in presidential activity.

CHAPTER 7

Conclusion

The Place of the President's "Place" in American Politics

THE CONSTITUTION AFFORDS PRESIDENTS a static set of tools they can use to shape the political landscape and the political agenda and when necessary to fend off political competitors. These tools include the veto (including the high bar that Congress must clear to override a veto), presidential powers as commander in chief, and their legislative roles (such as the ability to propose an agenda via the State of the Union address, among others). But other than that, there is little with which to navigate the American state. Presidents have employed administrative strategies derived from the Constitution, meaning they can "go it alone" from time to time using executive orders, signing statements, and other aspects of the administrative presidency. This book has examined how a president's public standing in the American system, conceptualized not in isolation but as embedded in the separation of powers and the public's trust in government, conditions presidential action in a variety of different contexts. The index of presidential leverage (IPL) offers a way to gauge when presidents are more dominant in the public mind than at other times and helps predict what that implies for presidential action.

The explicit argument explored throughout this book has been that although it is important to understand specific support for presidents, for which presidential approval is a proxy, it does not deliver a complete picture of the president's place in the public mind and cannot be fully understood in isolation from an understanding of public attitudes toward government in general. Considering approval in isolation assumes that the other institutions that make up the federal government have no stake in changing public perceptions of those institutions and the people who inhabit them. For public support to be mobilized as political capital, it should be measured relative to public perception of the government within which presidents are embedded. Contextualizing approval within the degree of political trust in the system indicates how much presidents can derive leverage if specific support exceeds systemic support; conversely, they are found wanting if their support declines to the level of diffuse system support or even falls below it. Thus, presidential leverage is a way to think about the place of the presidency in the American system, a system not well designed for presidential leadership.

SOME PROBLEMS WITH APPROVAL AS A MEASURE OF PRESIDENTIAL STRENGTH

Chapters 1 and 2 began with the observation that, whatever else is said about it, presidential approval will take presidents only so far, and therefore they have increasingly moved outside the constitutional framework to find other sources of leverage. Presidents can use political capital when it is present in the form of congressional copartisans, electoral margin, and favorable media coverage (see, for example, Light 1999; Lim 2014). But right or wrong, public approval is often seen as the biggest presidential asset; presidents are strong when they have high approval, and they are weak when it falls below some arbitrary threshold, usually 50 percent. Presumably, presidents do better and have a higher probability of success, however defined, if they are "popular." Anecdotal evidence presented in these chapters illustrates that presidents often operate under the assumption that this is true and that the degree of support they enjoy will pay dividends in a variety of political arenas. Presidents note this in memoirs and interviews, and they interpret approval as a signal to their standing in the public mind.

Although levels of approval may give some insight into their public standing, scholarly work is not so sure about the consequences of those high or low approval ratings. Little consensus exists on how or whether approval works or under what conditions it works. It is not a stretch to surmise that presidents would rather bask in the glow of high approval ratings than not, and surely competing institutions take notice. But it is far from clear that presidents benefit much from, or even shape, high approval.[1] Presidents can move policy and effectively work with Congress, for example, but often only under very specific conditions, and high approval is only one of those conditions (Beckmann 2010; Canes-Wrone 2006).

Presidents may use leverage because the Constitution gives them only limited resources, making them little more than "clerks" (Neustadt 1960). Chapter 3 developed a panoramic view of the American state that traced the nature of public expectations in the political system. Presidents have been both beneficiaries and victims of an institutional inversion that has made the presidency the focal point of the system, although nothing has changed in the Constitution that would upend Congress's place as the predominant institution in the constitutional scheme. For many people, presidents either represent or actually become the face of the American state, although of course they are neither (see Howell 2013; Jones 1994). It is important that presidents find extraconstitutional sources of leverage to cope within the system.

The American state and the separation of powers place myriad impediments in the paths of presidents seeking to put their stamp on the political landscape. This is aggravated by the fact that so many Americans, and even citizens of the world, expect the president to be all things to all people. The "institutional inversion" described in Chapter 3, where presidents have seemingly replaced Congress as the preeminent institution in American politics, has meant that many expect presidents to act on and influence a great many things that are outside the realm of their control but for which they are nonetheless held responsible, such as the economy.[2] The inversion occurred without one word regarding the nature and scope of presidential powers in the Constitution being changed. However, the expansion of governmental responsibilities and the American state have made it imperative for presidents to take the lead. For example, Congress is hamstrung by collective action problems, which is not surprising for an institution comprised of 535 individuals with different constituencies, goals, and temperaments. Where presidents were once able to use and manipulate the media, it is increasingly difficult to do so in the age of social media and constantly developing technology. The interdependent nature of the fractured American political system and the separation of powers necessarily embed presidents in the system. For approval to be truly effective as political capital, it needs to distinguish presidents not just from one another (for example, which president was more popular?) but from the political system itself.

THE INDEX OF PRESIDENTIAL LEVERAGE

The index measures presidential "public place" in the American political system. It is operationalized by measuring a president's approval at a given time and placing it in a context of public attitudes toward the rest of the American political system. The IPL is the ratio of presidential approval to public trust in government. It is conceptualized as part of a president's store of political capital; like other forms of constitutional and statutory capital, it is part of what presidents have and can use in a variety of ways so as to increase the chances of success in the "fractured" and often hostile American state (Ponder 2005a). The IPL begins with the president's public standing, but that standing is contextualized within the broader political system. The operationalization of the variable recognizes that presidents, who are undeniably important and even *the* primary political actor in American politics, exist within the separation of powers. The IPL measures the degree of support they have relative to the system in which they exist.

Chapter 4 describes the development of the IPL, a quantitative index that measures the public place of the presidency in the public mind. Trust is a foundational part of the American state (Easton 1965; Kamarck 2009), so it is appropriate to embed presidential approval in that system. The IPL, which is operationalized as presidential approval relative to trust, identifies the magnitude to which presidents derive political capital from their public standing. Understood this way, the IPL can be used to understand approval as political capital. Raw approval ignores the context and the changing expectations of presidents and leaves us ill prepared to anticipate when presidents will be more and less effective and when they will use one extraconstitutional tool rather than another.

I traced patterns of the IPL both across and within presidents from John F. Kennedy to Barack Obama. Observing variation in the IPL brings the nature of the measure into specific relief. If presidents are not terribly popular (for example, below 50 percent), they can still lay claim to political capital if public trust in government is even lower. Conversely, a president who has robust public approval but serves in a time of high trust in government has little to distinguish him- or herself in the system.

John F. Kennedy enjoyed robust approval throughout his brief term in office, but he served at a time when the public trusted government at consistently high levels. But events such as Lyndon Johnson's and then Richard Nixon's relentless prosecutions of the Vietnam War, the perception of the imperial presidency, and the series of scandals known as Watergate pummeled public trust in government to levels from which it has not yet recovered. This has perhaps advantaged presidents in the post-Watergate era, particularly presidents who enjoy higher levels of approval. Chapter 4 also demonstrated that both trust and the IPL were statistically different in the pre- and post-Watergate eras, though approval was not. In the empirical chapters, it is surprising that only occasionally does parceling time into these two eras significantly and differentially have an impact on presidential action.

EMPIRICAL RESULTS:
THE CONSEQUENCES OF PRESIDENTIAL LEVERAGE

Chapters 5 and 6 provide empirical tests of how the IPL has an impact on various areas of presidential action. It is important to understand that the *analysis does not and is not meant to involve comprehensive coverage of the dependent variables.* Rather, the IPL is subjected to a few aspects of presidential activity to explore its currency as a measure of political capital. Chapter 5 examines the macropolitics of agenda setting and legacy issues. Chapter 6 probes the micropolitics of White House and Executive Office of the President (EOP) decisions in promoting responsiveness to presidential policy making. The broad, directional properties of the statistical results are briefly summarized in Table 7.1. Though the impacts of the IPL were estimated controlling for various contexts (institutional, partisan, war, and budgetary constraints), the focus here is simply on the relationship between the IPL and the dependent variables.[3] I refer readers to the more comprehensive discussion in those chapters, but here I briefly summarize the patterns.

Macropolitics

The upper section of Table 7.1 summarizes the directional findings of Chapter 5, which dealt with macropolitics. Macropolitics considers policy

TABLE 7.1
Summary of empirical results.

	Presidential action (dependent variables in this study)	As the index of presidential leverage (IPL) Increases ...
Macropolitical environment	Proportion of significant laws that originated with the president	Increases
	Unilateral presidential action (executive orders)	Decreases
	State of the Union requests	Decreases
Micropolitical environment	Centralization of policy making in the White House/ EOP	Decreases
	Politicizing the executive office of the president	Decreases (significance sensitive to specification)

output of the political system. I have applied the IPL to three different perspectives. The proportion of important, lasting laws identified by Mayhew that are of presidential (as opposed to congressional) origin is clearly associated with presidents who enjoy greater leverage; as presidential IPL increases, so does the proportion of legacy policies that originated in the White House. Presidential legacies are cemented when presidents have high leverage. For example, President Obama's Affordable Care Act was signed early in 2010, when his IPL was still very strong. It dropped precipitously throughout the remainder of that year, leading in part to the "shellacking" he and his party suffered in the midterm congressional elections. Approval is an integral part of the measure of IPL. But more than any other part of this book, I show that approval in isolation is not significantly related to legacy issues but that the IPL is strongly related and illustrates that public support for presidents needs to be considered in the context of diffuse regime support and is a better, more nuanced illustration of political capital.

Second, unilateral policy making, once seen as an indicator of presidential failure (Neustadt 1960) has more recently been considered as part of a comprehensive strategy to move policy when Congress is resistant (for example, Howell 2003; Mayer 2001; Warber 2006). The results in this book strongly suggest that presidents are more likely to employ unilateral policy making when the IPL is low. Although this finding does not support Neustadt's conclusion that to use "command" authority is to fail, it is curious to note that, as the IPL decreases, use of executive orders increases.[4] Presidents who find themselves beleaguered in the political system are more likely to use unilateral policy strategies. But executive orders tell only part of the story. Future research may examine the relationship, if any, of the IPL to other unilateral tools, such as signing statements, presidential memoranda, policy directives, and so forth.

The final perspective addresses total White House requests in the State of the Union address (SOTU). The SOTU is a president's most prominent public appearance, with the possible exception of crisis situations. The lead-up to the speech lasts for months, so a policy proposal mentioned in the SOTU is of greater interest than a more routine request, has higher visibility, and is thus likely a presidential priority. The analysis in Chapter 5 showed that, as presidents enjoy increased leverage, they tend to put forth less in the SOTU. Although this may seem counterintuitive, consider the rationale. Presidents with stronger IPLs find themselves focusing on fewer, but perhaps larger, issues. Trying to do "everything" almost necessarily leads to policy failure and the consequent post mortems about how the president fell short of achievement. Policy victories lead to increased approval (Cohen 2013); in this age of lower trust, higher-leverage presidents may try to focus their efforts on fewer issues.[5]

This viewpoint gets at least partial validation when the degree to which presidents imprint their legacy onto the American political landscape is examined. Presidential approval measured in isolation and employed as an independent variable in alternate statistical analyses is statistically significant. The variance explained is roughly equivalent to using the IPL as a measure of public support. This is not surprising given that much of the time leading up to the SOTU is rife with media speculation as to the context of the proposals, often with a reference to how much approval the president has or lacks. So even in this hyperpoliticized context of a major presidential speech, the IPL performs about as well as approval and represents the only part of the analysis in which the IPL is not an unambiguously superior measure to employ.

Micropolitics

The lower section of Table 7.1 summarizes the micropolitics of presidential administration, explored in Chapter 6. Recall that Chapter 3 examined the American state (and state theory generally) and the quest for autonomy and capacity. There are many ways to build capacity, such as the addition of presidential support organizations (for example, Hult 2000) and building capacity for responsive competence (for example, Burke 2000; Ponder 2000). Exploring responsiveness in the EOP and centralization of policy making gets at both of these. Decreasing leverage is associated with increasing EOP staff, charged with protecting the president's political interests. Presidents lacking leverage, whether with low approval or higher approval but challenged by high trust in government, are associated with the addition of politicized staff. Similarly, decreasing leverage is associated with increasing centralization. Consistent with the analysis in Ponder (2000), presidents have incentives to protect the nature of the policies that they develop, particularly if they are under stress. Increased responsiveness and centralized policy development are two ways to accomplish this or at least to try. Presidents can develop policies close to the vest, whether in the White House or in the EOP, by protecting policy specifics from being co-opted by interests, Congress, or even bureaucrats in their own executive branch.

However, the tendency for a low IPL to be associated with a "circle the wagons" mentality, increasing the size of the political staff in the EOP and pulling policy making deeper into the White House, can have deleterious effects, not explored here, but that could be developed in future research. For example, reputation effects may be at play. But the danger lies in the possibility of severe backlash to these strategies. Many presidents come to office proclaiming that they will cut the size of the White House staff and/or the EOP. Although this is generally more symbolic than substantive, increasing the staff size and controlling policy making will invite criticism. Additionally, policy centralization is vulnerable to many of the same criticisms because of the perception that the process elbows out the input of valuable perspectives and produces a highly problematic policy that often folds when confronted by information that could have been had in a less cordoned process.

The more presidents tend to centralize or politicize, the higher the likelihood of a narrative that policy making is closed off and does not take advantage of information and, worse, that the president is weak. Examples include the creation of the Department of Education and the first energy program in Carter's administration, both of which suffered from a lack of information when the administration was naïve early on, believing that a comprehensive energy program could be created almost entirely in secret, or when it floundered as it lost political capital. This is further exemplified by the loss of leverage in the case of the Department of Education where President Carter got almost nothing of the broad, comprehensive department he wanted and was able to get only a small, slight department made up almost entirely of the Office of Education surgically removed from the Department of Health, Education and Welfare (see Ponder 2000: Chapters 4 and 5). Bill Clinton's efforts to reform the health care system met the same fate when he was criticized for keeping the policy task force, led by his wife, Hillary Clinton, isolated from others who could have provided information and perspective crucial to getting a better hearing. Although much of the problem percolated up at the end of 1993, when Clinton's leverage was reasonably robust, the proposal died in the crush of events described at the beginning of this book. With Clinton's leverage low and sinking fast, the Senate failed to pass even a watered-down compromise version of the bill. This effort to salvage reputation effects, as well as the consequences of doing so, is a subject for further research.

In sum, low-leveraged presidents are associated with defensive positions (for example, centralization, increased politicization of the EOP, more SOTU requests, more executive orders). High-leveraged presidents are not as associated with them. It is also possible that the relationship is thermostatic; that is, a president who enjoys high leverage is less likely to pursue more because of mood and other factors (see also Erikson, MacKuen, and Stimson 2002; Wood 2009). Nonetheless, anecdotal evidence presented in the chapters supports the conclusion that these actions are driven by low-leveraged presidents.

WHITHER APPROVAL?

Although the book focuses on the IPL as a measure of capital, it is natural to wonder how much purchase political scientists get using the index as opposed to using raw approval as a proxy for that capital. In all of these statistical analyses, approval in isolation either does not explain variation in the dependent variable or it does but at about the same level or more weakly than does leverage. Approval is either marginally significant or not at all. As noted in the previous section, this does not mean that approval is not important; approval is part of the IPL calculation. Rather, it illustrates the importance of contextualizing approval within the system in which presidents are embedded.

A WORD ON THE DOMAIN OF THE THEORETICAL CONSTRUCT: LIMITS OF THEORY AND MEASUREMENT

The analyses presented in this book have identified areas of presidential policy making, embedded in the American state, and where examination of the IPL can move analysis in some different and fruitful directions. It has also helped to identify the domain of the theory and the reach of the measure, what it helps explain and what it does not. For example, in analyses of congressional concurrence with presidents, the IPL had a positive sign but did not approach statistical significance. First-time requests in the State of the Union were similarly unaffected by a president's leverage. This is notable because it lends credence to the idea that presidents seek to build their own brand regardless of their leverage. Neither did approval have an impact. In running preliminary analyses on the content of legislation in the policy agenda, there were some mixed results. Generally, leverage had little impact (but did have some impact on the volume of legislation on which presidents will take a stand). These relationships need to be fleshed out in more detail, but they also suggest that there are places in the American political system and the president's place in that system where approval, whether contextualized as in the IPL or raw numbers, simply does not have an impact.

WHY DOES LESS LEVERAGE SOMETIMES LEAD TO GREATER ACTION?

PROSPECT THEORY AS A RESEARCH AGENDA

Deepening our understanding of the relationship between weakly leveraged presidents and increasing responsiveness, increasing centralization, increasing policy proposals, and, to a lesser extent, executive orders, requires continued theorizing. One fertile area of research in pursuit of this deeper understanding is prospect theory (see Kahnmeman and Tversky 1979, 1984). Prospect theory is a theory of decision making under risk. It holds that individuals are risk averse in the "domain of gains" and risk acceptant in the "domain of losses." In other words, when people are confronted with threats to their well-being, they tend to accept risks in the hope of mitigating or erasing their losses. When faced with "auspicious" prospects, they tend to be (overly) cautious, or risk averse. As Weyland put it, crises can lead to risky behavior, whereas good times induce risk-averse behavior (Weyland 2002: 38–39).[6]

The basic parameters of some of the findings in this book relate to these conditions. When presidential incentives are in play, such as presidents' ability to cope in the system, leave a lasting and positive legacy, or even be reelected, those presidents are more likely to move into protective mode by doing things that are risky to their reputations (for example, centralize policy making in the White House to the detriment of other advisory input or increase the number of responsive appointees in the EOP, although that leaves them vulnerable to criticism of overly politicizing the policy process, and the like.). When presidents have low leverage, they may increase the amount of policy proposals offered. Concerns such as reelection or legacy may be in jeopardy if they continue to appear weak, and they may pursue ill-advised policies or ask for far more than they can ever get from Congress or that can be absorbed by the system. If they hit, then there could be a big payoff in terms of success. But they may very well not get what they want and feed the perception that they are weak and getting weaker. Some theoretical evidence exists to support such a conclusion. Ostrom and Simon's (1985) and to a lesser extent Mueller's (1970) coalitions-of-minorities theses show that, as presidents increase their legislative activity, whether in the form of proposals or issues on which they take a stand, approval tends to decrease. Because I found strong support using the IPL, increasing presidential proposals, especially those in the high-profile arena of the State of the Union, is risky behavior.

Presidents who enjoy high leverage propose less, taking into account that they can focus on big issues, especially early in the term or when leverage shields them in a particular way. High leverage can lead to more. Like approval, though, it must be cultivated. Using the insights of prospect theory can help to uncover patterns and rationale.

ADDITIONAL AVENUES FOR FURTHER RESEARCH

The results presented in this book suggest numerous areas for further research in addition to prospect theory. Archival or interview-based work can be done to gauge the degree to which presidents or their staffs (or Congress, for that matter) pick up on the interplay of approval, trust, and the possibilities for policy making that derive from them. Similarly, research on policy decisions at times of particularly low or high levels of leverage could shed light on public–institutional dynamics from a microperspective.

I have explored how leverage can identify public contexts within which presidents will use executive orders. But researchers can take advantage of the advances in examining other types of unilateral orders, such as directives, signing statements, memoranda, and directives. More can be done with the polarized environment as presidents increasingly exist in a hyperpolarized political setting both within Congress and in terms of approval itself.

This book has presented a measure of the president's approval in the context of trust in the federal government. But there are certainly other ways to contextualize presidential approval, particularly by using different denominators. One way is to look at Congress and its approval ratings or level of trust rather than using trust in government writ large. However, I have consciously calculated presidential leverage with government trust in the denominator because values of trust are almost always higher than looking at just Congress. Thus, it is much more of a "fair fight" to use overall government trust as the denominator. If congressional approval or trust had been used as the contextual part of the IPL, the degree of leverage would likely be far higher. Congressional approval is almost always extremely low (for example, Hibbing and Theiss-Morse 1995). Still, other researchers may find that to be desirable because contagion is often presented in "president versus Congress" terms. For example, although near the end of his term Obama appeared to have robust leverage, he publicly stated that he would act when Congress would not, especially on immigration, the nuclear deal with Iran, overtime pay, and other areas.

WHERE ARE WE NOW?

At the time of this writing, President Obama was in the final months of his administration. Although data limitations preclude analysis of the empirical relationships described in this book through the entirety of his presidency, the IPL itself can be calculated deep into his second term. Figures 7.1a and 7.1b do just that. The bold lines denote Obama's entire term and thus bring current the trends identified in Chapter 4.

Figures 7.1a and 7.1b and Table 7.2 display the trends for approval and trust through virtually all of Obama's two terms.[7] Obama's approval for much of his presidency loitered beneath the 50 percent mark, only reaching or exceeding that mark a few times in his presidency. For example, his approval increased during much of 2016, reaching as high as 55 percent in October.[8] However, it proved difficult to move during most of the eight years he occupied the Oval Office.

The key to understanding Obama's IPL is the very low levels of government trust in general during his two terms. Although the measure of trust calculated does not explicitly include institutions, it is a safe bet to assume that the low levels of esteem with which the public held government, especially Congress, were a major factor contributing to trust's low levels. Time and again, Congress's inability to get much of *anything* done was implicated (Espo 2013; Fox 2013). Much of the conflict in Congress centered not just between Democrats and Republicans but on one Republican faction fighting another Republican faction. Internal disagreements within the Republican caucuses both within and between the chambers

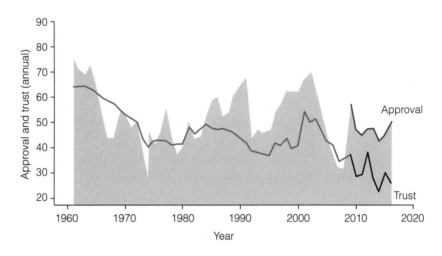

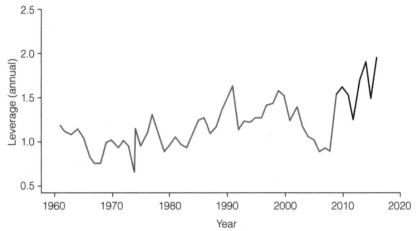

FIGURE 7.1. (a) Obama approval and trust. (b) Obama leverage.

Sources: (a) Approval data are from the American Presidency Project, available at www
.presidency.ucsb.edu/data/popularity.php. Trust data are from public opinion polls and archived
with the Roper Center for Public Opinion, available at http://ropercenter.cornell.edu/. All estimates
were generated using WCALC. See text for details. (b) Calculated by author.

became personal. For example, Texas Republican Senator Ted Cruz held
up business on the Senate floor over a plan to try and fund Obamacare,
going so far as to contribute directly to a government shutdown in October
2013. Most Republicans found this attempt misguided and hurtful to their
party. A spokesman for Republican Majority Leader Mitch McConnell,
no ally of Obama's, said, "It was like a toddler's version of legislating"

TABLE 7.2
Approval, trust, and the index of presidential leverage
in President Obama's second term.

Year	Approval	Trust	Index of presidential leverage
2013	47.41	27.90	1.70
2014	42.84	22.41	1.91
2015	44.79	30.22	1.48
2016*	49.90	25.51	1.96

* *Note*: 2016 is based on estimates through the second quarter. All estimates were generated using WCALC.

Sources: Approval data are from the American Presidency Project, available at www.presidency.ucsb.edu/data/popularity.php. Trust data are from public opinion polls and archived with the Roper Center for Public Opinion, available at http://ropercenter.cornell.edu/.

(Fahrenhold and Zezima 2016). Senator Lindsey Graham, another Republican, saw it as a cynical ploy to launch Ted Cruz as a national figure in advance of a presidential run in 2016: "What he did was stood up for Ted and threw the Republican Party under the bus" (ibid.). There was never any possibility that President Obama would sign any legislation that defunded his signature policy accomplishment, and that stalemate resulted in a government shutdown. Just as the Republican establishment feared, the public largely blamed the Republicans. In a NBC/*Wall Street Journal* poll taken just after the shutdown ended, 53 percent blamed the Republicans against only 31 percent who faulted the president. This coincided with the onset of 2014 and the lowest registered level of public trust in the entire time series covered in this book.

In 2014, to make matters worse, the rise of a Tea Party–inspired Freedom Caucus opposed much of the Republican leadership's agenda and made life so difficult for Speaker John Boehner that he retired from Congress in October 2015, less than a year after House Republicans garnered another sixteen seats, including three previously held by a Democrat. Indeed, the Republicans picked up seventy-seven seats between 2010 and 2014. Many of these successful candidates won while running with rhetoric against the Republican leadership in Congress, pegging them as the old guard and part of the problem, and thus they owed the leadership nothing after their victories, seeing their electoral fortunes as a mandate for change or, barring that, to actively oppose the leadership's efforts to forge compromise with the administration. Much of this disillusionment and disagreement within the party, especially as it tapped into broad support for the power of outsiders to move the country in a different direction, contributed directly to the 2016 nomination of New York real estate magnate and reality television star Donald Trump, against the expressed wishes of many Republican party leaders.

All of this served to help bring down trust in government. To be sure, much of Obama's actions, particularly his use of unilateral authority to try to further his immigration agenda, was seen as cynical power grabs by some of the public. In December, 2014, another NBC/*Wall Street Journal* poll showed that nearly half the public disapproved or leaned toward disapproval of Obama's proposed actions. So surely much of this feeds the decline in trust.

But all of this ultimately redounded to Obama's advantage in the IPL. Even as trust fell, his approval fluctuated within a narrow band, launching his IPL to unprecedented heights. His quarterly IPLs were routinely above 2.0 (see Appendix A). His annual IPLs never achieved those heights, but, as Table 7.2 shows, they came close. However, as noted before, this is a clear example of when a president has leverage in relative terms. Because Obama's approval ratings were lackluster during much of his term, his IPL soared not because of increased approval but rather on account of the declining trust in government. Again, much of that decline is surely due to the seemingly unending escalation of dissension both within Congress and the presidency.

Increasing Polarization: New Terrain for Presidential Leverage?

The Obama administration ushered out at a time when American politics is more polarized at the elite level, particularly *within* Congress as well as *between* Congress and the president, than at any time since the end of the nineteenth century.[9] What does that portend for the future? Though Obama had extraordinarily high presidential leverage, he was thwarted in many corners by an intransigent Congress and a polarized public (at least when it came to presidential approval), and he had a mixed record in the courts. Through the end of his term, nineteen states had rejected billions of dollars available to them through expansion of Medicaid via Obamacare. Therefore, it is not altogether clear what that means for presidential action in an age of polarization.

The preliminary evidence is mixed. Many of the legacy issues of Obama's second term came by means of unilateral powers, such as his attempts on immigration (many of which have been stalled or thwarted in the courts), and his partial opening to Cuba. Congress has refused to lift economic sanctions against Cuba, though increased travel and business opportunities are in the works. When Congress passed a bill to allow victims of the September 11 attacks to sue Saudi Arabia, Obama vetoed the bill in late September 2016 on the grounds that, among other things, individuals would be allowed to conduct part of our foreign policy, and other countries may see the way cleared to haul the U.S. government into court. Obama's veto was soundly overridden, the first veto override of his presidency. However, almost immediately, many in Congress, including Senate Majority Leader McConnell, suffered from buyer's remorse, given what many admitted was the possibility of unintended consequences. McConnell even went so far as to hint that he blamed Obama for the veto override, stating that he thought the president should have reached out sooner and explained to Congress the problems in their own bill (Taylor 2016). The point is that polarization may mitigate some of the effects of leverage identified in this book.

But maybe not. For example, there is little indication in the data that increased polarization is related to presidential leverage. A simple bivariate regression between leverage and lagged polarization is positive, meaning that there may be some slight tendency for polarization to redound in the president's favor, but the relationship falls well short of statistical significance ($b = 0.16$, $p = 0.41$). I also ran a partial regression on some of the data up through 2016, which are not included here because many variables are not available as of yet. But very preliminary analysis indicates that in the area of unilateral powers, for example, the IPL coefficients are of about the same magnitude and in the same direction as the analysis reported earlier. This is consistent with the narrative that emerged from those results: Obama enjoyed high IPLs, and he issued executive orders on a variety of issues, but the number of those orders fell in the "average" range. If he had issued a lot *more* orders, that would have bucked the trend. So in the end, although he did issue some high-profile executive directives, the orders themselves did not seem too much affected one way or the other, a result consistent with the analysis in Chapter 6. Further analyses will be done when all the data are available, but the patterns identified in this book are likely to remain roughly the same, at least as far as the Obama administration is concerned.

But what about future presidents? At this point, it is hard to tell. In the immediate aftermath of the 2016 presidential election, few things are clear. One is that Donald J. Trump has won a majority in the Electoral College, whereas Hillary Clinton bested him in the popular vote by nearly 2.9 million votes. This discrepancy will almost certainly feed the perception of a polarized public, with those supporting Trump touting his legitimacy under the Constitution and Clinton supporters pointing to serious flaws in the manner in which the American system produced a president who earned fewer votes than his opponent for the fifth time in presidential history and the second time in sixteen years. Both candidates were among the most unpopular candidates to ever be nominated by a major party. Like most presidents, Trump will face many daunting challenges on the domestic front as well as foreign policy. Polarization seems to be around to stay for the foreseeable future. Trust in government is also in question. Will it stay low? Or might it find a resurgence? My guess is that it will stay low and largely party driven, but time will tell. Presidential leverage from any source will be an important commodity.

The argument sustained throughout this book is that presidents as the public face of the American state will continue to pursue advantage wherever they can get it, and the public aspect is going to be hard to come by. Trust appears to be destined to remain low and perhaps sink lower regardless of who the president is. Levels of approval are anyone's guess, but they are likely to be as polarized as ever. Presidential approval has a ceiling and, probably, a floor, and this means that polarization is likely to be a marker of American politics for the foreseeable future. What the future of presidential leverage is, and whether individual presidents increasingly resort to constitutional leverage in the face of institutional intransigence, is itself a subject for future study, and contextualizing presidents in the American political state, *as* the state, is worth making the effort. The process of doing so will help to deepen our expanding understanding of the relationships among the presidency, public opinion, and the American state.

Index of Presidential Leverage (IPL) by Quarter, 1961-2016*

Year/quarter	Quarterly IPL
1961 Q 1	1.15
1961 Q 2	1.21
1961 Q 3	1.21
1961 Q 4	1.23
1962 Q 1	1.24
1962 Q 2	1.17
1962 Q 3	1.04
1962 Q 4	1.10
1963 Q 1	1.11
1963 Q 2	1.02
1963 Q 3	0.94
1963 Q 4	1.06
1964 Q 1	1.21
1964 Q 2	1.18
1964 Q 3	1.13
1964 Q 4	1.10
1965 Q 1	1.14
1965 Q 2	1.09
1965 Q 3	1.05
1965 Q 4	1.05
1966 Q 1	0.95
1966 Q 2	0.81
1966 Q 3	0.84
1966 Q 4	0.76
1967 Q 1	0.78
1967 Q 2	0.79
1967 Q 3	0.70
1967 Q 4	0.71
1968 Q 1	0.75
1968 Q 2	0.78
1968 Q 3	0.65
1968 Q 4	0.76
1969 Q 1	1.07
1969 Q 2	1.11
1969 Q 3	1.06
1969 Q 4	1.03
1970 Q 1	1.03
1970 Q 2	1.04
1970 Q 3	1.01

TABLE A.1. (*continued*)

Year/quarter	Quarterly IPL
1970 Q 4	1.01
1971 Q 1	0.94
1971 Q 2	0.82
1971 Q 3	0.88
1971 Q 4	0.93
1972 Q 1	0.98
1972 Q 2	1.09
1972 Q 3	1.15
1972 Q 4	1.22
1973 Q 1	1.29
1973 Q 2	0.98
1973 Q 3	0.75
1973 Q 4	0.65
1974 Q 1	0.62
1974 Q 2	0.66
1974 Q 3	1.18
1974 Q 4	1.14
1975 Q 1	0.87
1975 Q 2	1.03
1975 Q 3	1.04
1975 Q 4	1.01
1976 Q 1	1.11
1976 Q 2	1.09
1976 Q 3	1.11
1976 Q 4	1.22
1977 Q 1	1.61
1977 Q 2	1.46
1977 Q 3	1.42
1977 Q 4	1.27
1978 Q 1	1.09
1978 Q 2	1.01
1978 Q 3	0.96
1978 Q 4	1.23
1979 Q 1	1.05
1979 Q 2	0.80
1979 Q 3	0.77
1979 Q 4	0.78
1980 Q 1	1.29
1980 Q 2	0.94
1980 Q 3	0.85
1980 Q 4	0.78
1981 Q 1	1.32
1981 Q 2	1.41
1981 Q 3	1.22
1981 Q 4	1.10
1982 Q 1	1.01
1982 Q 2	0.94
1982 Q 3	0.87

TABLE A.I. (*continued*)

Year/quarter	Quarterly IPL
1982 Q 4	0.92
1983 Q 1	0.79
1983 Q 2	0.89
1983 Q 3	0.94
1983 Q 4	1.06
1984 Q 1	1.12
1984 Q 2	1.09
1984 Q 3	1.13
1984 Q 4	1.22
1985 Q 1	1.26
1985 Q 2	1.23
1985 Q 3	1.40
1985 Q 4	1.39
1986 Q 1	1.39
1986 Q 2	1.40
1986 Q 3	1.37
1986 Q 4	1.12
1987 Q 1	1.00
1987 Q 2	0.98
1987 Q 3	1.04
1987 Q 4	1.11
1988 Q 1	1.14
1988 Q 2	1.12
1988 Q 3	1.15
1988 Q 4	1.29
1989 Q 1	1.24
1989 Q 2	1.35
1989 Q 3	1.48
1989 Q 4	1.46
1990 Q 1	1.60
1990 Q 2	1.48
1990 Q 3	1.48
1990 Q 4	1.36
1991 Q 1	1.81
1991 Q 2	1.74
1991 Q 3	1.60
1991 Q 4	1.46
1992 Q 1	1.12
1992 Q 2	1.05
1992 Q 3	0.99
1992 Q 4	1.02
1993 Q 1	1.40
1993 Q 2	1.14
1993 Q 3	1.26
1993 Q 4	1.38
1994 Q 1	1.43
1994 Q 2	1.39
1994 Q 3	1.18
1994 Q 4	1.16

TABLE A.I. *(continued)*

Year/quarter	Quarterly IPL
1995 Q 1	1.24
1995 Q 2	1.30
1995 Q 3	1.25
1995 Q 4	1.36
1996 Q 1	1.31
1996 Q 2	1.36
1996 Q 3	1.39
1996 Q 4	1.39
1997 Q 1	1.53
1997 Q 2	1.36
1997 Q 3	1.45
1997 Q 4	1.42
1998 Q 1	1.55
1998 Q 2	1.57
1998 Q 3	1.48
1998 Q 4	1.56
1999 Q 1	1.61
1999 Q 2	1.46
1999 Q 3	1.44
1999 Q 4	1.39
2000 Q 1	1.46
2000 Q 2	1.39
2000 Q 3	1.44
2000 Q 4	1.53
2001 Q 1	1.40
2001 Q 2	1.10
2001 Q 3	0.99
2001 Q 4	1.39
2002 Q 1	1.24
2002 Q 2	1.28
2002 Q 3	1.40
2002 Q 4	1.31
2003 Q 1	1.23
2003 Q 2	1.32
2003 Q 3	1.04
2003 Q 4	1.05
2004 Q 1	1.08
2004 Q 2	1.16
2004 Q 3	1.09
2004 Q 4	0.79
2005 Q 1	0.96
2005 Q 2	0.95
2005 Q 3	0.95
2005 Q 4	1.07
2006 Q 1	1.01
2006 Q 2	1.07
2006 Q 3	1.01
2006 Q 4	1.16
2007 Q 1	0.95

TABLE A.I. (*continued*)

Year/quarter	Quarterly IPL
2007 Q 2	1.03
2007 Q 3	1.28
2007 Q 4	1.25
2008 Q 1	1.03
2008 Q 2	0.71
2008 Q 3	0.65
2008 Q 4	0.92
2009 Q 1	1.27
2009 Q 2	1.65
2009 Q 3	1.23
2009 Q 4	1.57
2010 Q 1	1.85
2010 Q 2	1.83
2010 Q 3	1.59
2010 Q 4	2.10
2011 Q 1	1.97
2011 Q 2	2.02
2011 Q 3	1.40
2011 Q 4	1.76
2012 Q 1	1.61
2012 Q 2	1.23
2012 Q 3	1.23
2012 Q 4	1.23

The observations below were not used in the statistical analyses presented in this book but have been updated through 2016 Q 2.

Year/quarter	Quarterly IPL
2013 Q 1	2.51
2013 Q 2	1.77
2013 Q 3	1.37
2013 Q 4	1.78
2014 Q 1	2.37
2014 Q 2	2.65
2014 Q 3	1.52
2014 Q 4	1.76
2015 Q 1	1.76
2015 Q 2	1.47
2015 Q 3	1.44
2015 Q 4	1.22
2016 Q 1	2.35
2016 Q 2	1.88

Note: Estimates are reported here but not used in the statistical analyses in the empirical chapters. Because of data limitations with many of the control variables employed in the empirical Chapters 4, 5, and 6, those analyses rely on quarterly and annual data through 2012. As of this writing, the IPL has been updated through the second quarter of 2016. See author's website for updates.

Models with Approval and Divided Government

TABLE B.1 INCLUDES THE MODELS using raw approval data as a predictor rather than the IPL. They include the three models in Chapter 5 and the capacity (EOP size) model from Chapter 6. Each model is briefly discussed in the text. Note, though, that for each model the IPL predictor in the main text performs about as well or, in most cases, *better* than the models with presidential approval. The model for legacy issues (significant policies) performed better than the approval models. Most significantly, the lagged IPL coefficients in Table 5.1 were significant across the board at $p < 0.05$, whereas only the differenced approval variable was significant in the polarization model and then just barely at the $p = 0.10$ level. Finally, while the differenced approval variable was significant in the executive orders model, both IPL coefficients were significant in Table 5.2, and the model was significantly stronger in both full models (*Divided Government* and *Polarization*). In the State of the Union messages, the approval model performs slightly better, though not significantly so, with differenced values of leverage and approval both highly significant in both the *Divided Government* and *Polarization* specifications. Thus, on balance, the IPL performs about as well as or better than the approval variables, and this finding adduces evidence for taking presidential leverage into account when trying to understand presidential activity. (See Table B.1.)

In Chapter 6, we encountered an ill-behaved model, and in the text I discussed various modifications wherein the IPL was sometimes a significant predictor of EOP size and sometimes not. I include the model in Table B.2 for illustrative and comparative purposes. Note in this table that the approval measures are never significant, whereas in the results reported in Chapter 6 the lagged values of the IPL were inversely related to EOP size. Still, given the issues involved, this comparison should be noted but, again, considered with caution.

ECM for Chapter 5 analyses using presidential approval:
Divided government and polarization models.

	Significant policies (Divided government)	Significant policies (Polarization)	Orders (Divided government)	Orders (Polarization)	State of the Union requests (Divided government)	State of the Union requests (Polarization)
Constant	−22.97 (37.99)	−15.01 (46.97)	26.19 (23.80)	−1.19 (26.23)	−6.05 (11.6)	−21.50* (14.15)
Y_{t-1}	−0.99*** (0.14)	−0.98*** (0.14)	−0.83*** (0.15)	−0.88*** (0.14)	−0.73*** (0.14)	−0.70*** (0.13)
Δ Approval	−0.55 (0.47)	0.64* (0.49)	−0.40* (0.28)	−0.54** (0.28)	−0.29** (0.14)	−0.35*** (0.15)
$Approval_{t-1}$	0.23 (0.43)	0.23 (0.43)	−0.28 (0.25)	−0.40 (0.24)	0.13 (0.13)	0.04 (0.12)
Δ Mood	1.40** (0.84)	1.53** (0.83)	0.56 (0.51)	0.55 (0.47)	0.33 (0.23)*	0.25 (0.22)
$Mood_{t-1}$	0.78 (0.85)	0.90 (0.83)	1.34*** (0.55)	1.46*** (0.52)	−0.02 (0.28)	0.01 (0.26)
Δ Divided government	−17.59* (11.77)	—	−0.93 (7.18)	—	5.15** (3.52)	—
Divided government$_{t-1}$	−7.00 (9.17)	—	8.94* (5.54)	—	6.22** (2.87)	—
Δ President–Congress-polarization	—	−48.71 (41.31)	—	5.85 (23.57)	—	17.65* (12.98)
President–Congress polarization$_{t-1}$	—	6.71 (40.89)	—	62.25** (23.19)	—	35.30*** (12.94)
Δ Democratic president	−31.00*** (13.98)	−33.60** (18.26)	8.48 (8.52)	12.20 (10.43)	13.03*** (4.18)	15.26*** (5.57)
Democratic president$_{t-1}$	8.44* (9.12)	10.65 (15.50)	21.73*** (6.07)	37.64*** (9.23)	6.46** (2.95)	14.05*** (4.89)
Δ Debt to GDP	0.67 (0.83)	0.80 (0.83)	0.82* (0.52)	0.86** (0.48)	−0.89*** (0.28)	−0.88*** (0.28)
Debt to GDP$_{t-1}$	0.45 (0.50)	0.30 (0.48)	−1.23*** (0.35)	−1.32*** (0.31)	0.19 (0.15)	0.18 (0.15)
Δ War	9.65 (8.19)	9.23 (9.27)	6.01 (5.17)	−1.02 (5.39)	0.99 (2.4)	4.31* (2.77)
War_{t-1}	−6.51 (8.86)	−6.67 (9.98)	9.47** (5.69)	−2.53 (5.95)	4.88** (2.62)	8.99*** (3.01)
Δ Year of term	−6.27*** (1.82)	−6.00*** (2.06)	0.47 (1.15)	−0.99 (1.21)	−1.94*** (0.56)	−2.27*** (0.63)
Year of term$_{t-1}$	−2.43* (1.83)	−2.75* (1.96)	−3.39*** (1.22)	−4.44*** (1.25)	−0.59 (0.59)	−1.09** (0.63)
Adjusted R^2	0.68	0.67	0.43	0.49	0.48	0.49
Standard error of estimate	18.02	18.19	10.99	10.38	5.32	5.24
N	53	53	51	51	52	52

Standard errors in parentheses.

*** $p < 0.01$

** $p < 0.05$

* $p < 0.10$ (one-tailed tests)

TABLE B.2.

ECM model for Chapter 6, Table 6.3 using
presidential approval instead of IPL.

Variable	Full model
Constant	2.11***
	(0.84)
Log EOP size$_{t-1}$	−0.20***
	(0.08)
Δ Approval	0.000
	(0.005)
Approval$_{t-1}$	0.001
	(0.004)
Δ President–Congress polarization	−1.82***
	(0.74)
President–Congress polarization$_{t-1}$	−1.72***
	(0.57)
Δ Divided government	0.38**
	(0.22)
Divided government$_{t-1}$	0.38***
	(0.17)
Δ Democratic president	−0.33**
	(0.19)
Democrat president$_{t-1}$	−0.26**
	(0.13)
Δ Debt to GDP	−0.01
	(0.009)
Debt to GDP$_{t-1}$	0.001
	(0.005)
Δ Year of term	0.04*
	(0.02)
Year of term$_{t-1}$	0.03
	(0.03)
Adjusted R^2	0.10
Standard error of estimate	0.20
N	53

Dependent variable is Δ Log EOP size. Standard errors in
parentheses.
*** $p < 0.01$
** $p < 0.05$
* $p < 0.10$ (one-tailed tests)
Source for Executive Capacity: Ragsdale (2014).

Significant Public Policies Used in Chapter 5, Figure 5.1 and Table 5.1*

TABLE C.1.

Year	President	Policy
1961	Kennedy	Housing Act of 1961
1961	Kennedy	Minimum wage increase
1961	Kennedy	Peace Corps
1961	Kennedy	Arms Control and Disarmament Agency created
1961	Kennedy	Alliance for Progress
1961	Kennedy	Foreign Assistance Act of 1961
1962	Kennedy	Trade Expansion Act of 1962
1962	Kennedy	Manpower Development and Training Act of 1962
1962	Kennedy	Communication Satellite Act 1964
1962	Kennedy	Public welfare amendments
1963	Kennedy	Nuclear Test Ban Treaty ratification
1963	Kennedy	Aid for mentally ill and mentally handicapped
1963	Kennedy	Clean Air Act
1963	Kennedy	Equal Pay Act
1964	Johnson	Civil Rights Act
1964	Johnson	Economic Opportunity Act
1964	Johnson	Tax cut (offered under JFK)
1964	Johnson	Urban Mass Transportation Act
1964	Johnson	Wilderness Act
1964	Johnson	Food Stamp Act
1965	Johnson	Medical Care for the Aged (Medicare and Medicaid)
1965	Johnson	Voting Rights Act
1965	Johnson	Elementary and Secondary Education Act
1965	Johnson	Department of Housing and Urban Development established
1965	Johnson	Highway Beautification Act
1965	Johnson	Immigration reform
1965	Johnson	National Foundation on the Arts and Humanities established

TABLE C.1. (*continued*)

Year	President	Policy
1965	Johnson	Higher Education Act
1965	Johnson	Housing and Urban Development Act
1965	Johnson	Excise Tax Reduction Act
1965	Johnson	Water Quality Act
1965	Johnson	Food and Agriculture Act
1966	Johnson	Department of Transportation established
1966	Johnson	Fair Packaging and Labeling Act
1966	Johnson	Minimum wage increase
1966	Johnson	Demonstration Cities program (Model Cities)
1967	Johnson	Social Security increase
1967	Johnson	Public Broadcasting Act
1968	Johnson	Housing and Urban Development Act of 1968
1968	Johnson	Gun control act
1968	Johnson	Omnibus Crime Control and Safe Streets Act
1968	Johnson	Income tax surcharge
1968	Johnson	National Gas Pipeline Act
1968	Johnson	Truth in Lending Act
1969	Nixon	Coal Mine Safety Act
1969	Nixon	Social Security increase
1969	Nixon	Draft lottery system
1969	Nixon	Nuclear Nonproliferation Treaty Ratified
1970	Nixon	Postal Reorganization Act
1970	Nixon	Water Quality Improvement Act
1970	Nixon	Occupational Safety and Health Act (OSHA)
1970	Nixon	Narcotics Control Act
1970	Nixon	Urban Mass Transportation Assistance Act
1970	Nixon	Unemployment compensation expansion
1971	Nixon	Social Security increase
1971	Nixon	National Cancer Act
1972	Nixon	State and Local Fiscal Assistance Act
1972	Nixon	Anti-Ballistic Missile (ABM) Treaty ratified
1973	Nixon	Agriculture and Consumer Protection Act
1973	Nixon	District of Columbia Home Rule
1973	Nixon	Foreign Assistance Act

TABLE C.1. *(continued)*

Year	President	Policy
1973	Nixon	Aid for development of Health Maintenance Organizations (HMOs)
1974	Nixon	Trade Act
1974	Nixon/Ford	Minimum wage increase
1974	Nixon/Ford	Employment Retirement Income Security Act (ERISA)
1974	Nixon/Ford	Nuclear Regulatory Commission and Energy Research and Development Administration created
1974	Nixon/Ford	National Mass Transportation Assistance Act
1975	Ford	Energy Policy and Conservation Act
1975	Ford	Voting Rights Extension
1975	Ford	New York City bailout
1975	Ford	Tax Reduction Act
1976	Ford	Railroad Vitalization and Regulatory Reform Act
1977	Carter	Social Security increase
1977	Carter	Tax cut
1978	Carter	Comprehensive energy package
1978	Carter	Panama Canal treaties ratified
1978	Carter	Civil Service Act
1978	Carter	Airline deregulation
1979	Carter	Department of Education established
1980	Carter	Trucking deregulation
1980	Carter	Windfall profits tax on oil
1980	Carter	Synthetic fuels program
1980	Carter	Alaska lands preservation
1981	Reagan	Economic Recovery Tax Act
1981	Reagan	Omnibus Budget Reconciliation Act
1983	Reagan	Anticrime package
1985	Reagan	Tax Reform Act
1986	Reagan	Cleanup of toxic waste dumps (expansion of Superfund)
1986	Reagan	Defense Department reorganization
1987	Reagan	Housing and Community Development Act
1988	Reagan	Catastrophic Health Insurance for the Aged
1988	Reagan	Anti–drug abuse act
1988	Reagan	Intermediate-Range Nuclear Force (INF) treaty ratified
1989	Bush 41	Minimum wage increase

TABLE C.1. (*continued*)

Year	President	Policy
1989	Bush 41	Savings and loan bailout
1990	Bush 41	Clean Air Act
1990	Bush 41	Child care package
1991	Bush 41	Persian Gulf Resolution
1991	Bush 41	Surface Transportation Act (ISTEA)
1992	Bush 41	Strategic Arms Reduction Treaty (START) ratified
1992	Bush 41	Economic aid package for former Soviet republics
1993	Clinton	Omnibus Deficit Reduction Act
1993	Clinton	North American Free Trade Agreement (negotiated under Bush 41 but pushed by Clinton)
1993	Clinton	Motor Voter Act
1993	Clinton	National Service Act (AmeriCorps)
1993	Clinton	Reform of college student loan financing
1994	Clinton	Goals 2000
1994	Clinton	Omnibus Crime Act
1994	Clinton	California desert protection
1995	Clinton	Curb on unfunded mandates
1996	Clinton	Telecommunications reform
1996	Clinton	Immigration reform
1997	Clinton	Deal to balance the budget by 2002
1997	Clinton	Overhaul of Food and Drug Administration
1997	Clinton	Adoption of foster children
1998	Clinton	Overhaul of Internal Revenue Service
1998	Clinton	NATO expansion
1998	Clinton	100,000 new schoolteachers
1999	Clinton	Y2K planning
1999	Clinton	Ed-flex program
2000	Clinton	Permanent Normal Trading Relations (PNTR) with China
2001	Bush 43	Bush tax cuts
2001	Bush 43	Use of Force Resolution
2001	Bush 43	USA PATRIOT Act
2001	Bush 43	Airline bailout
2001	Bush 43	Airline security
2001	Bush 43	Emergency spending to respond to 9/11 attack

TABLE C.1. *(continued)*

Year	President	Policy
2001	Bush 43	Education reform
2002	Bush 43	Iraq resolution
2002	Bush 43	Homeland Security Act
2002	Bush 43	Campaign finance reform
2002	Bush 43	Agricultural subsidies
2002	Bush 43	Corporate Responsibility Act
2002	Bush 43	Fast-track trade authority
2002	Bush 43	Terrorism insurance
2003	Bush 43	Tax cut
2003	Bush 43	AIDS funding
2003	Bush 43	$87.5 billion special defense funding
2003	Bush 43	"Healthy Forests"
2004	Bush 43	Disaster relief
2004	Bush 43	Intelligence overhaul in wake of 9/11 Report
2004	Bush 43	AIDS funding
2005	Bush 43	Class Action Fairness Act
2005	Bush 43	Energy Policy Act
2005	Bush 43	Central America Free Trade Agreement
2006	Bush 43	Pension reform
2006	Bush 43	Military Commissions Act
2006	Bush 43	Trade measures
2007	Bush 43	Postal Service reform
2007	Bush 43	India Nuclear Pact
2008	Bush 43	$700 billion bailout for banks
2008	Bush 43	Domestic Surveillance Act
2008	Bush 43	India Nuclear Trade Agreement
2009	Obama	Stimulus (included because it originated in the White House under Bush, but Obama had some input and was largely responsible for pushing the legislation)
2009	Obama	Expansion of National and Community service programs
2010	Obama	Affordable Care Act (Obamacare)
2010	Obama	Student loan overhaul
2010	Obama	New START treaty ratified
2010	Obama	Repeal of "Don't Ask, Don't Tell"
2010	Obama	Bipartisan Tax Deal (included several Republican aims)

TABLE C.1. (*continued*)

Year	President	Policy
2011	Obama	Debt ceiling deal
2011	Obama	Normalization of trade relations
2012	Obama	Fiscal cliff deal (negotiation)
2012	Obama	JOBS Act (Mixed)[†]
2012	Obama	Normalization of trade with Russia

Note: Table consists of the list of significant public policies that were (a) identified by David Mayhew as being important and (b) determined by the author as being developed and proposed by the president and/or executive branch rather than Congress. Simply signing a bill or pushing for passage of a bill developed by Congress does not count for inclusion in these data. See Chapter 5 for details.

[†] See endnotes in Chapter 5 for explanation of coding decisions.

Variables for Centralization
Analysis in Chapter 6

TABLE D.I.

Variable	Description	
Dependent variable: Policy centralization	0 (decentralized) to 3 (fully centralized) with mixed processes in between.	—

Independent variables	Description	Expected direction
Presidential leverage	Ratio of presidential approval to public trust in government (lagged one quarter)	
Negative		
Divided government	0 for unified; 1 for divided	Positive
Democratic president	0 for Republicans; 1 for Democrats	Positive
Congressional compatibility	Poole-Rosenthal distance between president and median member of Congress	Positive
EOP size	Size of Executive Office of the President	Positive
Merit percent	Percentage of civil service under merit service protection	Negative
Crosscutting jurisdictions	Number of agencies affected	Positive
Reorganization	Whether the issue included reorganization	Positive
Complexity	Index 1–3	Negative
Foreign/domestic policy	Index –2 fully domestic to +2 fully foreign	Negative
Budget impact	Dichotomous index, spending impact = 1	Positive
New item	New item = 1	Positive
Presidential priority	Mentioned in the State of the Union	Positive

TABLE D.I. (*continued*)

Independent variables	Description	Expected direction
Salience	Salient issue = 1	Positive
Budget situation	Ratio of budget surplus or deficit to outlays	Negative: Surplus less centralization
Crisis	Crisis legislation	Positive
Month of term	Month as measured from start of the presidency	Agnostic

Source: Most variables adapted from Rudalevige (2002). Leverage, congressional compatibility, and presidential party collected by author.

Notes

CHAPTER ONE

1. The voting data was retrieved on March 18, 2015, from http://clerk.house.gov /evs/1994/roll416.xml.

2. To be sure, Clinton was not the first to experience problems with members of his own party. Writing about another former southern governor who found himself in the White House, Nelson Polsby argued that many of Jimmy Carter's problems of building coalitions among members of his own party were a natural outgrowth of reforms in the presidential nominating system in the early 1970s. Polsby, writing about Carter, could easily have been writing about Clinton when he observed,

> Carter's pathway to the nomination of his party did not entail making peace with the congeries of political organizations that nominated the congressmen and senators with whom he serves. His task was not to assemble a majority, but to come out ahead of the other contestants as frequently as he could . . . The requirements for coalition building (as contrasted with the activities that go into charming the mass media) have been somewhat relaxed.

See Polsby (1978: 105–106). Given that the Republicans have adapted many (but not all) of the same rules as the Democrats, it is likely this observation no longer applies just to the Democrats.

3. Clinton refers to the press conference in his memoir but does not reference his "relevance" quote. He does point out that he agreed with some parts of Newt Gingrich's and the House Republicans' so-called Contract with America, that there were places on which he and the Republicans could compromise, but that he would use the veto if no agreement could be reached. See Clinton (2004: 650).

4. True to his word, Clinton issued vetoes more frequently in the period between the 1994 midterm and the 1996 presidential election. He issued seventeen vetoes in that two-year time frame, nearly half of all the vetoes in his two terms combined. See Ragsdale (2014: Table 9-10, 541).

5. A series of opinion polls attest to this conclusion. For example, a Trust in Government Poll taken in November showed 52 percent felt that Republicans were jockeying for political gain, while 57 percent felt Clinton was standing up for what he believed in. There was plenty of negativity to go around, but in December 49 percent felt more negative toward Clinton because of the shutdown, whereas 62 percent were more negative to congressional Republicans. And a January 7 ABC News/*Washington Post* poll pegged public blame on the Republicans by nearly two to one with 50 percent blaming Republicans, whereas 27 percent blamed the president and 20 percent blamed both. Polls were accessed from the Roper Center database, http://webapps.ropercenter.uconn.edu/, on September 21, 2016.

6. There is good evidence that presidents perceive that the public holds this perception. George Washington argued that the president was the "First man in America" serving as

the "visible point of attachment." Thomas Jefferson remarked in his first inaugural address that only the president "could command a view of the whole ground" (Landy and Milkis 2014: 97).

7. The full text of the interview with Bill Moyers can be found at the American Presidency Project. Retrieved on April 2, 2015 from www.presidency.ucsb.edu/ws/index .php?pid=30161&st=&st1=.

8. See, for example, the Employment Act of 1946, Public Law 79-304.

9. Some of these strategies are akin to the expectations of prospect theory, a point developed in the empirical chapters and the conclusion.

10. In Charles O. Jones's felicitous phrase, presidents must exist in a "separated system" of "competing institutions" (Jones 1994).

11. See Chapter 4.

12. See especially Erikson, MacKuen, and Stimson (2002) and Cohen (1997). For an excellent review, see Druckman and Jacobs (2009).

13. See Cohen (1997).

14. However, there are problems with relying too heavily on public preferences. For example, Druckman and Jacobs survey literature that questions the assumption that the public has well defined and stable preferences on policy alternatives, particularly if those policy proposals are complex or esoteric. On some issues, the public can unquestionably formulate solid and consistent beliefs. But others are more problematic. They summarize, "On salient issues on which the collective public has reached reasoned preferences and maintains them consistently, the potential for responsiveness is real. Without these conditions, responsiveness will be more difficult" (Druckman and Jacobs 2009, 167). Their review as to the problems of defining citizen preferences as "real" is found on pages 165–167.

15. Similar, too, is Charles O. Jones's consideration of "leeway." Jones sees leeway as "essentially an exercise in capitalizing on the conspicuous features of separationism . . . encouraged in post–World War II politics by the frequency of split party government." Leeway is similar to Skowronek's warrants in that they both imply that presidents can use structural and institutional contexts to forge their own paths, perhaps working outside the boundaries of what might be acceptable or predictable (Jones 2000).

CHAPTER TWO

1. Presidents have sought to lead the public even before Jackson, but it was a leadership of a purely partisan nature. Presidents at least as far back as Thomas Jefferson were often linked to newspapers that were overtly partisan or even seen as arms of the administration. See Ellis (2012: 85–87) and Larecy (2002).

2. For a useful summary, see Edwards (2009). For an overview of presidential responsiveness to public sentiment, see Druckman and Jacobs (2009) and Cohen (1997).

3. On this point, see Knight and Wildavsky (1977); Hargrove (1988); and Ponder (2000).

4. Diane Heith, citing Eisinger (2000), writes that presidential attempts to gain quantitative data go back as far as the Hoover administration: "Hoover had his White House staff do . . . a relatively sophisticated content analysis of the editorial pages of newspapers. Without the benefit of polls or statistics, Hoover effectively sampled opinion of the day" (Heith 2004: 2).

5. Although a full review of the literature is not my purpose here, the reader may want to peruse the literature on what we know about approval with specific emphasis on the

"ingredients" of approval; that is, what is approval made of? The literature on presidential approval is voluminous, and attacking it can be daunting. An excellent place to start is Erikson, MacKuen, and Stimson (2002, chapter 2). See also Gronke and Newman (2009).

6. See McCarty, Poole, and Rosenthal (2006). See also the wealth of data in Lewis, Poole, and Rosenthal 2017.

7. See the example of George W. Bush provided by Gary Jacobson (2008). Another feature of the relationship of presidents to public opinion, but outside the scope of this study, is whether presidents can influence opinion through their actions and rhetoric. The record is decidedly mixed. Perhaps the most important and lasting study of manipulating public opinion is by Samuel Kernel (2007). "Going public" is a strategy where presidents appeal over the heads of Congress directly to the people in an effort to persuade the public to support their policies but also to let their member of Congress know so that he or she will cast a legislative vote in support of the president's position. This strategy has been a constant in presidential politics, but research casts doubt on how much the strategy actually works or has ever worked (Edwards 2003). Some studies do show that presidential efforts to shift public opinion are highly contingent on factors specific to the policies themselves (Beckmann 2010; Canes-Wrone 2006; Rottinghaus 2010; and Tedin, Rottinghaus, and Rodgers 2011) and that the nature of the strategy itself has undergone a change of venue of sorts, from going "public" to going "local." But what is beyond dispute is that presidents act as if they can persuade Congress to move closer to their policy preferences.

8. This is the premise of such Hollywood features as *The American President*, where the fictional President Andrew Shepherd's political fortunes on a crime bill were seen to rise and fall with whether his approval ratings were high or decreasing.

9. The literature on presidential success in Congress as partly a function of presidential approval is huge. For some examples, see Bond and Fleisher 1990; Edwards 1989, 2003; Fett 1994; Peterson 1990; Ponder and Moon 2005; and Sullivan 1990. For a review, see Edwards 2009.

10. To use an example from earlier work by Ponder and Moon, why would an extremely conservative representative like Joel Hefley (R-CO), representing an extremely conservative constituency, have cared that President Clinton had high approval ratings nationally as he (Hefley) was deciding whether to vote to impeach the president in 1998? Hefley's district voted heavily against Bill Clinton in 1996, and there is every indication that his constituency would have overwhelmingly favored impeachment. Since members of Congress are directly answerable to their voters, it was not a difficult decision for Hefley to make, and he cast his vote for impeachment even while national pundits wondered why Republicans would vote to impeach a popular president, especially when much of the public, Republican and Democrat alike, opposed impeachment. The answer, we argued, is that constituency-level approval influences MCs to follow their electoral incentives. See Ponder and Moon (2005).

11. See Chapter 3.

12. It is not necessary to adopt the systems framework to apply Easton's critical insights to the presidency.

13. See Erikson, MacKuen, and Stimson (2002, chapter 2) for an excellent analysis of the factors that influence presidential approval.

14. For example, political trust drives support for policies that target underprivileged sectors of society (for example, the poor); if trust is lacking, the political will to address

issues such as race, health care reform, and spending is similarly lacking (Hetherington 2005: chapters 5, 6, and 7; Hetherington and Husser 2012; and Hetherington and Rudolph 2015).

15. On this, see Hetherington (2005).

16. On the presidency and representation of the public, see Wood (2009).

CHAPTER THREE

Portions of this chapter are adapted from Ponder (2005a).

1. See Cooper (2009) for an in-depth analysis of the congressional/presidential inversion.

2. See, for example, Bentley (1908); Truman (1951); Dahl (1961); and Polsby (1980).

3. This is present most notably in the work of March and Olsen (1984; 1989).

4. The literature is voluminous. See, among others, Skowronek (1982); Lowi (1979); Nordlinger (1981); Almond (1988); the critiques by Nordlinger, Lowi, and Fabrini, in the *American Political Science Review* (1988); Carnoy (1984); and Mitchell (1991). On the lack of a "state" in the American system, see Huntington (1981: 34–36).

5. See, among others, Orren and Skowronek (2004).

6. See, for example, Skowronek (1982).

7. Exemplars in this genre include Huber and Shipan (2002) and Johnson (2007).

8. See Galvin (2010) and James (2000).

9. Lewis (2008)

10. See Rockman (1984). This literature has been particularly rich given that the state as a concept encountered difficulty establishing a foothold in analytic treatments of American politics and established the need for extraconstitutional sources of leverage. At the outset of his pathbreaking work on the "new American state," Stephen Skowronek argues that:

> a "sense of the state" pervades contemporary American politics. It is the sense of an organization of coercive power operating beyond our immediate control and intrud-ing into all aspects of our lives . . . (but) it is the absence of a sense of the state that has been the great hallmark of American political culture.

Skowronek observes that the problem for the early American state was couched in its "peculiar" governmental order but that it was successful in ultimately maintaining, even in its early incarnation, an "integrated organization of institutions, procedures, and hu-man talents whose specific purpose was to control the use of coercion within a national territory" (Skowronek 1982: 5).

11. One of the most interesting treatments of the state in terms of its structural prop-erties to reduce transaction costs within a competitive market system is North, *Structure and Change in Economic History*. See in particular chapter 3, "A Neoclassical Theory of the State," pages 20–32.

12. Although the Senate filibuster comes close.

13. Most students of American government will recognize this is in the *Federalist*, particularly Madison's treatments of the philosophical justifications for what I call the fractured nature of the American system, particularly numbers 10 and 51 (Hamilton, Madison, and Jay [1788] 1961).

14. Neustadt (1960: 26).

15. For example, see Neustadt (1960), Skowronek (1993), and Dickinson (1997).

16. I discuss public expectations of the presidency later. For now, see Hargrove (1974); Lowi (1985); Genovese (1995); Huntington 1981; and Edwards (1983, chapter 5).

17. Ornstein, Mann, and Malbin (2010: Table 2.17, 67).

18. For a persuasive account detailing this dynamic, as well as when this might not hold (for example, unpopular presidents), see Lee (2009).

19. For example, Derthick and Quirk (1985) show how a "politics of ideas" can lead to policy change even when the costs of that change are concentrated and its benefits diffuse.

20. See Johnson (2007), Hargrove (1974), Hargrove (1993), and Huber and Shipan (2002).

21. Bert Rockman's (1984) central concern in his treatise on the president and the American state is to explore how leadership can be actualized in a culture that is at best "antistatist" and highly suspicious of government. Huntington's (1981) analysis of the tendency for the American system to work against the capacity of political institutions to meet public expectations comes to the same general conclusion. The challenge for leadership in the face of an ethos of American politics that is suspicious of government and leadership incentivizes presidents to lead from wherever they can. The nature of antigovernment authority in the abstract guarantees presidents will be responsible to their parties and not to the "center" (Wood 2009; compare Erikson, MacKuen, and Stimson 2002).

22. A more extensive treatment of some of these trends is found in Rudalevige (2005).

23. The gap is generic and broadly applicable and has been used to analyze a variety of political situations. One field of inquiry that has benefited from an expansion of this insight is in explaining revolutions generally and political violence specifically. For the seminal work in this area, see Davies (1962). An application to racial urban violence is Miller, Bolce, and Halligan (1977). In much of the study of American politics, the idea of an expectations gap has become commonplace, has been supported on theoretical and empirical grounds, and does not simply afflict the presidency (Kimball and Patterson 1997).

24. Refer to Chapter 4 in this book for a quantitative overview.

25. A journalistic consideration of this general phenomenon, wherein people decry government assistance while taking advantage of it, is Applebaum and Gebeloff (2012).

26. The term comes from one of the presidential roles in Rossiter (1960).

27. For an example of this perspective applied, see Ponder (2000).

28. Cronin and Genovese (2013) detail nine different paradoxes and link them to the expectations gap. See especially their chapters 1 and 2. The general problem of facing conflicting or paradoxical expectations is no longer limited to the presidency. After the Republican takeover of Congress in 2010, the House Appropriations committee, long one of the most coveted assignments on Capitol Hill, suddenly became a political football. Not only did it draw a different kind of legislator focused on budget cutting and deficit reduction, but membership on that committee became a far less desirable commodity. Members simply did not want to be a part of the committee where, if they failed to make substantial cuts, they faced the possibility of being targeted by emergent and seemingly powerful groups such as the Tea Party. On the other hand, if they voted to cut spending on popular programs they could very easily face the wrath of angry constituents who felt the impact of the cuts. See Davidson, Oleszek, and Lee (2012: 175–176).

29. On the administrative presidency, see Nathan (1983). For an excellent and concise overview, see James (2009: 72–76). I examine the relationship between presidential leverage and executive orders, a component of the administrative presidency strategy, in Chapter 5.

30. I provide a theoretical framework for why this is more likely with low-leverage presidents in Chapter 6.

31. Nordlinger (1998: 188). It is not clear how relevant his observations are now, particularly with reference to the rise of the so-called Tea Party movement, which seems to be able to assert its position over that of other, presumably more powerful, Republican

members of Congress. However, consistent with what Nordlinger pointed out long before the Tea Party began to brew, much of this pressure came from a group of freshman Republicans whose politics are very much congruent with the Tea Party, and many of them characterize their own politics as rooted in the Tea Party. See also Mann and Ornstein (2012).

32. See Fisher (2007).

CHAPTER FOUR

1. Stimson (1991). The WCALC program, which is used to extract scores for both trust and approval and described in the text, can be accessed from Stimson's website at http://stimson.web.unc.edu/software/. WCALC uses a recursive algorithm to correct for timing irregularities and produce a smoothed time series. See the website for details. Another application is Wood (2009).

2. See Stimson (1991). For an extensive application, see also Erikson, MacKuen, and Stimson (2002).

3. See the American Presidency Project, an indispensable source to the presidency researcher, last retrieved on September 30, 2016, from www.presidency.ucsb.edu.

4. Technically speaking, such extraction is not necessary for the approval series because Gallup measures them on a regular basis. To keep both approval and trust on a constant metric, I extracted the scores. The correlation between raw approval and extracted approval scores is 0.98.

5. The data from 1961 to 2000 are from Keele (2003), and have been updated through 2012 by the author. The data are extracted using Stimson's WCALC program. See note 7 for the specific questions used to extract the trust series.

6. Many polling organizations also ask questions about other institutions such as the military, organized religion, or higher education. These are found in Ragsdale's Table 5-13 as well.

7. Keele's methodology (and my update) tracks answers to a battery of questions, for example:

1. How much of the time do you think you can trust the government in Washington to do what is right—just about always, most of the time, or only some of the time?
2. How much trust and confidence do you have in our federal government when it comes to handling domestic problems in general?
3. Overall, how much trust and confidence do you have in the federal government to do a good job in carrying out its responsibilities?
4. Would you say you basically trust the federal government in Washington or not?
5. How much trust and confidence do you have in the federal government?
6. You really can't trust the government to do the right thing. Do you agree or disagree with the statement?
7. Would you say the government is pretty much run by a few big interests looking out for themselves or that it is run for the benefit of all the people?
8. Do you think that people in the government waste a lot of money we pay in taxes, waste some of it, or don't waste very much of it?
9. Do you think that quite a few of the people running the government are (1958–1972: a little) crooked, not very many are, or do you think hardly any of them are crooked (1958–1972: at all)?
10. How much confidence do you have in the federal government when it comes to dealing with international problems?

I added this last item to the Keele data. Doing so sets the bar higher for the IPL because it makes it less likely that the president will stand out, given that regardless of predilection much of the public sees international relations as well within the domain of the federal government. Including this item tends to increase the overall measure of trust, making it more difficult for the presidential approval measure to stand apart. Generally, see Keele (2003, chapter 2), for a full description of the application of the Stimson algorithm to the measure of political trust.

8. Readers may wish to consult Appendix A for quarterly data. Because quarterly and annual data are generated using Stimson's WCALC algorithm, I discuss descriptive patterns using the annual series but add observations from the quarterly data where they prove particularly interesting or relevant to the discussion.

9. The zero-order correlation is 0.56, $p < 0.001$.

10. Stimson (2004) argues that trust is essentially approval in disguise. To be sure, trust and approval are likely to move together in similar fashion at pivotal points in time (for example, after the September 11 terrorist attacks). But the correlation of 0.56 leaves nearly 70 percent of the variation explained by other sources. Indeed, George Edwards, surveying a heavily cited study by Bond and Fleisher (1990), which in part correlates Democratic and Republican approval, writes, "The correlation r of .71 between Democratic and Republican approval indicates that although the variables are related, they are conceptually distinct" Edwards (1997: note 2).

11. More precisely, Ford reflects the second half of the third quarter whereas Nixon is the first half.

12. However, when the difference of approval means was calculated on *quarterly* data, the difference *is* significant at the 0.05 level. This is the result of a greater number of observations and slightly greater variance in the quarterly data. Recall, though, that the quarterly data are somewhat less reliable because some readings are estimated on very few polls. Where there is face validity, I will report those observations.

13. Virtually any basic statistics text will provide the interested reader with an overview of measures of dispersion, standard deviations, and Z-scores as they relate to a "normal" distribution. Among the many, good overviews using examples from political science are Pollock (2012: 136–152) and Marchant-Shapiro (2015: 112–120).

14. The range is similar in the quarterly data, though at slightly different times. The high point of 64.2 was realized in the first quarter of 2002, just after the terrorist attacks, and the low was 21.62 in the second quarter of 2010.

15. Because leverage is equal to approval divided by trust, it is not surprising that leverage tracks strongly with each. Given the theoretical justifications, ceteris paribus, leverage increases as trust decreases ($r = -0.35$, $p = 0.01$) and is positively associated with approval ($r = 0.57$, $p = 0.001$).

16. Ragsdale (2014).

17. See also Jones (1994: 152–153).

18. See also Jones (1994: 153). But see Genovese (2001: 152).

19. Recall that because of the way the IPL is measured, anything below 1.0 is "negative territory" given that the president's approval rating lags behind that of trust in government; that is, the public trusts government more than they approve of the president.

20. Jones (1994: 152) has him at five.

21. Polls are Gallup Poll (AIPO), September 1972. Retrieved October 2, 2012 from the iPOLL Databank, the Roper Center for Public Opinion Research, University of Connecticut;

Nixon Poll, February 1973, www.ropercenter.uconn.edu/data_access/ipoll/ipoll.html. As always, presidential approval data are WCALC extracted readings.

22. These numbers translate into a decline of more than 2.5 standard deviations in a very short amount of time. Charles O. Jones argues that policy output in the Nixon/Ford years is often underestimated and that this period saw one of the most productive periods of sustained important legislation in history. This is undoubtedly true, and I will have more to say about this later. Here, suffice it to say that Jones is focusing on how policy and politics coexist in a separated system, and he notes that not all of the output is due to, nor can be attributed to, these presidents, although they may have helped put the policy process in motion and moved big items into the pipeline. See Jones (1994: 156–159).

23. John Zaller shows that the public's perception of Clinton's competence as president trumped their disgust for his relationship with the White House intern Monica Lewinsky. See Zaller (1998).

24. Although there is some dispute about why Bush won the election when the stars were seemingly aligned for Kerry, one theory holds that the Bush-Cheney camp was able to place social issues such as gay marriage on the ballots in pivotal states such as Ohio. This ostensibly brought many conservatives to the polls who otherwise might have stayed home. Once there, many voted for Bush, enough to hand him victories in hotly contested states that he may not have won had it not been for robust conservative turnout on the basis of the hot button culture war issues.

25. In violation of federal law, Libby had leaked the name of CIA agent Valerie Plame to columnist Robert Novak.

26. Some of these include, for example, inaction after locking up the Republican nomination, picking a clearly inexperienced vice presidential candidate in Alaska Governor Sarah Palin, and inexplicably declaring that the "fundamentals of the economy are sound" as some of the nation's largest and most revered financial institutions collapsed and the stock market plunged.

27. CNN (2009).

28. This average approval reading was subject to considerable variation in the quarterly in Appendix A.

29. Only Clinton's 1996 IPL of 1.27 was higher.

CHAPTER FIVE

1. Scholarly attention to big, important policies, however defined, has commanded significant attention. See, for example, Carson, Lynch, and Madonna (2011); Conley (2003); Dodd and Schraufnagel (2012); Erikson, MacKuen, and Stimson (2002); and Mayhew (1991, updated).

2. See Cooper and Brady (1981); Erikson, MacKuen, and Stimson (2002); and Alder and Lapinski (2006).

3. For example, Mueller (1970: 20) offers a "coalitions of minorities" explanation of presidential action, part of which reasons that when presidents offer policy proposals they incrementally alienate various factions of their public support. This result is likely to be cumulative, with public support falling as the number of initiatives increases (see also Ostrom and Simon 1985).

4. Mayhew, n.d.

5. There are three possible exceptions to this rule in the data reported in Appendix C. The first is the ban on congressional insider trading in the Obama administration.

Although Obama did not have a direct hand in developing that legislation, he took a deep interest and specifically called for such legislation in the State of the Union address. Even though the final bill incorporated virtually all of what the president asked for, I did not include it in the final data set. The second is President Obama's role in the fiscal cliff legislation in 2012. Although the bill that was finally signed was bipartisan with significant congressional input, the president played a large role in the negotiations of various provisions, especially the agreement to raise taxes, which was a major part of the process. Finally, there is a question about the JOBS Act, passed into law in 2012. Although it was technically a congressional bill, substantial sections of the bill were originally developed in the Obama administration. Thus, I did include this in the final analysis, though it could be argued the other way. Therefore, unlike the ban on congressional insider trading, I included both of these bills into the final analysis because of the amount of White House involvement in drafting the legislation. Some readers may find these coding decisions controversial. However, if I exclude the fiscal cliff data and the JOBS act and rerun the analysis, the coefficient on the lagged value of leverage is virtually identical to what is reported in Table 5.1, with almost no changes to the significance of other variables save for the coefficients on *War*. In this case, the strength of the model was actually slightly higher than the model reported in the table.

6. It should be noted that a literature has arisen recently that questions the interpretive capacity of many control variables taken together. Some argue that a researcher should interpret the impact of one or a few of the independent variables and not ascribe full meaning to all control variables (for example, Keele and Stevenson 2014). Although I am agnostic on this question, I focus my analysis on the impact (if any) of the IPL on the dependent variables, though I do take note of directional properties of the control variables.

7. I anticipated exploring chamber-specific measures so as to measure the degree to which a strategic president might make differing decisions based on bicameral differences. However, I was forced to construct a measure of the congressional median given the fact that chamber ideology scores correlate quite highly with one another. The inclusion of both distance measures subjected the model to multicollinearity problems and thus created very complicated matters of interpretation. Thus, because removing one of the chamber variables was not consistent with any part of the leverage theory, I opted for the substantively less satisfying but methodologically more appropriate congressional measure, which accounts for both chambers simultaneously. Data on presidential NOMINATE scores can be found at Keith Poole's website (www.voteview.com; retrieved on March 16, 2016) in the legislator files. For an explanation of congressional estimates and their application, see Poole and Rosenthal (1997).

8. In other analyses reported in Appendix B, I control for *Divided Government* (1 = Divided; 0 = Unified). This variable captures a simple institutional relationship that exists when at least one of the chambers of Congress is controlled by the party opposite the president. Generally, this creates enormous collinearity problems when included in a model with *President–Congress Polarization*. Therefore, I leave it out in most cases. There is one case, which I explain later on, where collinearity is not a significant problem, and I will include both measures of institutional contagion in the same model. In nearly all analyses that follow, I controlled for *President–Congress Polarization* to capture the effect of institutional contagion on presidential activity. But collinearity problems usually make it undesirable to include both that variable and the simple *Divided Government* variable in the same analysis. The fact that they are highly collinear makes sense,

of course. It is often (but not always) the case that greater distances between presidents and congressional medians occur during periods of divided government. Ideally, I would like to include both measures in the models whenever I can because I am interested to see if leverage is systematically related to the dependent variables controlling for both the institutional (divided government) and growing ideological distance between president and Congress. For example, when controlling for institutional contagion in the legacy model and using both variables, diagnostics reveal significant collinearity in the divided government and *Congressional Compatibility* variables, with variance inflation factors (VIFs) ranging from nearly 12 in divided government to nearly 40 in the distance. A VIF of 10 or greater is generally considered problematic. Therefore, I ran four separate models (full and reduced form) that include either the *Divided Government* dummy (1 = yes) or the measure on presidential–congressional polarization, namely the absolute value of the distance between the president's DW-NOMINATE score and the median member of Congress, which is termed *President–Congress Polarization*. In the analyses to follow, I include only the *President–Congress Polarization* model. However, the results using only the *Divided Government* variable were virtually identical to the models using *Congressional Compatibility* and can be found in Appendix B.

9. My thanks to Matt Eshbaugh-Soha for providing some of these data.

10. Erikson, MacKuen, and Stimson (2002) measure war as the number of cumulative battle deaths and their impact on public opinion. I estimated models using that measurement strategy but found it to be statistically insignificant in explaining the models estimated in the following pages.

11. This does not include the ordered probit analysis in Chapter 6.

12. Additionally, I estimated an ECM with only the lagged value of the dependent variable and the differenced and lagged values of the IPL as predictors. The results indicate the presence of error correction much more comfortably ($b = -0.89$, $p = 0.000$), and the coefficient on the lagged value of leverage is roughly the same size and in the same direction as that shown in Table 5.1 ($b = 31.14$, $p < 0.03$).

13. A useful overview of the types of unilateral weapons presidents have at their disposal is found in Rudalevige (2014b). See also Rottinghaus and Belco (2017).

14. See Rudalevige (2014a).

15. For a useful analysis of unilateral action from a developmental perspective, see Ellis (2015, chapter 6). A broad overview of the literature and evaluation of empirical claims is Mayer (2009).

16. The public and many pundits were largely wrong when they claimed that Obama had issued more executive orders than other presidents. Simple counts by the American Presidency Project at the University of California–Santa Barbara show that Obama was decidedly moderate in his use of orders. However, his use of unilateral powers when we count memoranda, proclamations, directives, and so forth, were at the upper end of the spectrum. See data in Peters and Wooley 2017, www.presidency.ucsb.edu/.

17. I also estimated a negative binomial count model, and the results are largely the same. In particular, the IPL variable was again negative and statistically significant in models estimating total numbers of executive orders and Warber's policy orders. The results are available from the author.

18. This is virtually identical to a model using *Divided Government* as a proxy for institutional contagion.

19. When models with raw approval scores were estimated, both short-term and long-term approval are negative and statistically significant, again consistent with Mayer (2001). I also estimated the models using Warber's policy data (2006, updated through 2008). The sign on ΔIPL was negative, but, unlike the binomial count model referenced in note 17, it barely missed statistical significance at the 0.10 level ($p = 0.13$). The variables that did realize conventional levels of significance were: *Democratic presidents* (both lagged and differenced), who were positively related to policy orders; the long-term effect of *Debt* was negatively related; and both *War* variables (lagged and differenced) were negatively related.

Additionally, comparing the approval results in Appendix B to the IPL in Table 5.2, we observe a slightly weaker model fit for *approval* (Adjusted $R^2 \approx 0.48$), and the null hypotheses are rejected, albeit with less confidence ($p < 0.10$). Still, the results are unmistakable: although both approval and IPL show a negative relationship to the use of executive orders, the coefficients confirm that *IPL is a stronger predictor than simple approval*.

20. See, among others, Baumgartner and Jones (1993); Cohen (1995, 2012); Edwards and Barrett (2000); Eshbaugh-Soha and Peake (2005); Kingdon (1984); LaRocca (2006); Light (1999); Jones (1994); Peake (2001); and Wood and Peake (1998).

21. This is the case with civil rights and economic policy, but Cohen (1995) reports that public perception of foreign policy stays relatively stable from one year to the next.

22. As I noted earlier, there is considerable doubt as to whether this strategy works anymore or even if it ever did. Still, presidents seem to act as if they believe it does and formulate strategy to do so. When the State of the Union address is over, for example, presidents nearly always leave the day after for a trip out into the country somewhere to push their ideas on the public. Even within the address, they sometimes do so. In his 1992 State of the Union address, President George H. W. Bush touted his economic plan and famously asked the public to "let (Congress) know that they want this action by March 20" (cited in Kernell 2007: 1). Outside the bounds of the State of the Union, presidents have called for direct action in keeping with the tenets of "going public." President Obama even went so far as to ask the public to call their member of Congress and support his approach to the debt ceiling crisis of 2011. "So I'm asking you all to make your voices heard . . . let your member of Congress know. If you believe we can solve this problem through compromise, send that message" (Obama 2011).

23. Although I focus on the high-profile nature of the State of the Union, I also analyzed total legislative requests. Those data do not extend through the entire timeline of the study, ending in 2001. But, as I will note later, the general pattern uncovered in the analysis of the State of the Union is also found in the analysis of all legislative requests. Results available from the author.

24. *Mood* is, however, positive and statistically significant in a model using *Divided Government* as the measure of institutional contagion.

25. These data were collected for Rudalevige 2002, and I owe him thanks for providing me with the raw numbers.

26. This is broadly consistent with Ostrom and Simon (1985), who similarly found an inverse relationship between the size of the agenda and presidential approval.

27. This is also consistent with prospect theory. I return to prospect theory as a potential explanatory framework in the concluding chapter.

28. As a further check on the impact of the IPL, the model was applied to dependent variables that do not extend the full Kennedy to Obama time span. I did so, though, to further explore the impact of leverage on alternative measures of agenda size. First,

Andrew Rudalevige (2000, 2002) has collected a comprehensive list of presidential legislative proposals. Of course, not all of what Congress considers is presidential policy (Peterson 1990). Thus, Rudalevige's data make it possible to distinguish between the comprehensive congressional agenda, those items that the president simply takes a stand on, and what is truly presidential in origin. I examine the total number of legislative requests forwarded from the White House to Congress. Regressing the variables on total agenda size, I find that *Leverage* is once again *negatively* associated with agenda size, along with *Mood* (positive), *Democratic presidents* (positive), with the budget constraint (*Debt/GDP*) barely missing conventional statistical significance.

I also applied the model to the State of the Union calls for action as collected by Hoffman and Howard (2006). Their data differ from actual requests because theirs measure instances when a president mentions that action should be taken, whether by Congress, states, or action on a presidential proposal. The correlation between State of the Union calls for action and total requests is 0.47, $p < 0.05$, leaving a lot of variance to be explained. Consequently, the statistical relationships are very different. Most telling here is that the IPL is positively related to requests for action but is not statistically significant. Neither is raw presidential approval. Interestingly, the only variables related to request for action are a positive sign on the time of term (indicating that although presidents put forth fewer proposals as their term goes on, requests for action increase) and a negative sign on the budget constraint. This suggests an interesting strategic element wherein presidents are less encumbered by their place in the system and continue to generate an agenda by calling on Congress, the bureaucracy, or even states to continue action. Conversely, the State of the Union proposals that passed first through legislative clearance processes in the White House are more directly affected. Further analysis is beyond the scope of this book but could be the subject for future research.

CHAPTER SIX

Portions of this chapter are adapted from Ponder (2012).

1. Its formal title is: "Report of *The President's Committee on Administrative Management in the Government of the United States*" (otherwise known as the Brownlow Report). Cited in Pfiffner and Davidson (2003: 195).

2. See the rest of that book for a careful, thoughtful analysis of the governance structures of the White House. See Hult and Walcott (2004) for their follow-up on the so-called standard model of how presidents structure and use presidential staff. For a particularly insightful analysis of the roots of presidential staff, see Dickinson (1997). The standard history of the development and functions of the "presidential branch" is Hart (1995). The development of the institutional presidency is well illuminated by John Burke (2015, 2000). Excellent descriptive analyses are found in Kumar and Sullivan (2003) and Patterson (2000). For a comprehensive overview, see Warshaw (2013).

3. For a particularly thoughtful discussion of the problem of governance and relations with groups both within and outside the executive branch, as well as a set of recommendations, see Hult (2000).

4. For an extended discussion, see Ponder (2000: 23–29).

5. I deal with the mix of policy and politics extensively in Ponder (2000).

6. As a methodological aside, it is here that the "level of analysis" problem is of particular interest. That is, if America is a weak state, it may be weak in the larger context of consistently pressing its own agenda when it diverges from society. But rhetorically state

actors (that is, leaders) can persuade the polity to accept or at least pay attention to what it is trying to do, though they often have difficulty moving public opinion in a systematic way. Thus, at the subsystem level, the actors of the state (in this case, the president) have autonomy in pressing their agendas qua actors in the political system. To do that, capacities for doing so must be developed.

7. See Villalobos and Vaughn (2009) for an exception.

8. More recently, Jeffrey Cohen suggested linking the public and institutional worlds of the presidency as a way to move presidential studies forward (Cohen 2009a).

9. Much of the following relies heavily on the theoretical framework developed on pages 31–38 of Ponder (2000). Readers are referred there for a full accounting of the theoretical justifications and for further empirical analysis.

10. In *Good Advice* I argue that the youth employment initiative in the Carter administration was a success even though it did not pass in Congress, the reason being that it remained true to the president's stated goals and preferences. The creation of the Department of Education, although it passed in Congress, was classified as a policy failure because the end product had been almost entirely stripped of what the president wanted. See Ponder (2000).

11. See Krehbiel (1991) for an overview of the concept as applied to the American Congress.

12. An issue that naturally arises here is that of presidential compatibility with bureaucratic agencies. Although a full consideration of this topic is outside the scope of the present work, future research could explore the degree to which presidential leverage has an effect on policy-making location. One possible, perhaps counterintuitive, hypothesis could be that high-leverage presidents who are less ideologically compatible with an agency will delegate policy-making authority to those agencies more than will low-leverage presidents, given the considerations addressed earlier. For example, low-leveraged presidents may be less likely to be successful at controlling the political definition of their policies (but highly motivated to do so) unless they centralize, are less credible with the public, and thus be less willing to delegate policy construction to agencies with which they have little in common ideologically. High-leverage presidents can use that leverage to raise salience and be more credible with voters and, perhaps, with Congress and thus more likely to delegate than less compatible presidents. Regardless, this would be one of several exploratory hypotheses but for now is, as noted, well outside the parameters of this study. See Clinton and Lewis (2008) for a systematic effort to measure agency ideology separate from the personnel who staff those agencies.

13. See also Kamarck (2009).

14. Villalobos and Vaughn (2009: 444–445) make basically the same argument in reference to presidential incentives to politicize the bureaucracy.

15. Skowronek (1993) argues that successful presidents protect the meaning of what they are trying to accomplish, fending off opposition attempts to paint them in the most negative light possible. This, it seems to me, is what largely accounts for the failure of Clinton's attempts at health care reform.

16. Rudalevige and Lewis (2005) argue that, although the strategies of centralization and politicization are geared toward the same end (that is, greater responsiveness to presidential programs), they act as substitutes rather than complements.

17. Their study focuses on the Council of Economic Advisors in the EOP.

18. My thanks to Jose Villalobos for providing his updated data.

19. For an early assessment, see Rudalevige (2012). For a particularly nuanced and lucid examination that extends deep into Obama's second term, see Warshaw et al. (2015).

20. Indeed, presidential success and failure is not always determined by whether a presidential policy passes Congress but rather how much a bill's final contents deviate from a president's preferred position (Ponder 2000).

21. See especially Hult (2000).

22. Although this may be more a matter of centralization of policy production, it also means that presidents need to politicize the bureaucracy, especially weakly leveraged presidents. For an extended overview, see Ponder (2000).

23. Removing these variables is anticipated by theoretical concerns. However, it should be noted that when I include the *Mood* and *War* variables, they are *always* statistically insignificant as suggested by the theoretical justification, whereas the *coefficient on the lagged value of the IPL is −0.36 and significant at the 0.10 level (one-tailed)*.

24. See Table 2, Appendix B.

25. Incidentally, the correlation between Rudalevige's measure of EOP size and the total EOP size is 0.66, p = 0.000. The correlation between Rudalevige's measure and IPL is negative as well and statistically significant (zero-order r = −0.30, p = 0.000).

26. However, it is important to note that I ran identical analyses for capacity building in the EOP as a function of presidential leverage and a battery of contextual variables, measuring EOP both as the total number of employees and with OEO and USTR parceled out. Under both operationalization strategies, public presidential leverage was negatively related to EOP size as well, though not statistically significant. I discuss the particulars in the following pages.

27. I performed identical analyses on both the size of the White House and OMB staffs and found that leverage is not systematically related to size of the White House staff in isolation, but the lagged value is marginally significant (IPL$_{t-1}$ = −51.21, p = 0.07, one-tailed), though the full estimated model has an adjusted R^2 = 0.01. Instead, the effects of leverage on capacity seemingly have an impact on the size of the entire EOP staff.

Incidentally, when estimating these models with raw approval, the coefficients are again never close to significant, as the p-values range from 0.32 to 0.72.

28. In the analyses reported in Chapter 5, such was decidedly not the case, and multicollinearity was a major problem. However, multicollinearity is not nearly as large an issue in the model presented in Table 6.3. Variance inflation factors, a common indicator of multicollinearity, registered 9.8 and 10.8 in the divided government variables and 15.0 to 16.9 in the polarization variables. Although these are somewhat problematic, I include them in the model. Recall that the two were parceled out in Chapter 5, given that multicollinearity was a much larger problem, registering VIFs of up to 40.

29. Mayer specifically examined budget and regulatory review.

30. Relatedly, David Lewis shows that as the percent of political appointees in an agency increases relative to careerists, those agencies perform less well on a number of objective criteria (Lewis 2008).

31. These outlier years recorded an average IPL of 0.91, and average EOP size was 5,201.

32. It should be noted that, although Bush and LBJ did increase the size of their respective EOP during wartime, a dummy variable reflecting whether the nation was at war was included in various iterations of the models, and in no instance did it reach conventional levels of statistical significance.

33. As a final check, I examined the impact on specific powerful organizations within the EOP. Recall the impact of the IPL (a) is contingent on the model specified and (b) that *approval*, measured in raw terms, *rarely has an impact on staff size*, whereas the IPL does, but inconsistently. So, in addition to the analysis presented in Table 6.3 and reported here only for purposes of illustration, I undertook a series of empirical analyses that estimated the impact of the IPL and various controls on the size of the WHS and OMB. Results in all estimates are uneven. But a few interesting patterns (or lack thereof) emerge. Specifically, the *Vietnam/Watergate–era* dummy variable is not included in the equations, and models are tested over the entire series; the sign on the ΔIPL variable is *always* negative, indicating an inverse relationship with staff size. This suggests that variation in the size of the staff seems to be driven by low-leveraged presidents, a finding entirely consistent with leverage theory. But, as noted, whether the IPL is statistically significant is sensitive to model specification. Still, the sign is consistently negative, statistically significant or close to significant, and thus worth observing.

Additionally, the coefficients in all models are particularly sensitive to whether President Obama is included. As I demonstrate in Chapters 4 and 7, Obama is often an outlier in terms of his IPL. This seems to have an impact on the measures of staff capacity; it suggests there may be something different about the Obama administration in terms of politicizing his staff, muted by the size of his IPL. It should be noted that the analyses presented in Chapter 5 shows no systematic difference between models that include Obama and those that do not. The differences in the models of staff capacity are likely due to the fact that, though his IPL ranged toward the upper end of the observed spectrum, he did not significantly add to or subtract from the size of the staff, particularly the EOP as a whole. For example, in a model of the WHS that does not include Obama, the ΔIPL is negative and significant ($\beta = -116$, $p = 0.05$, one-tailed test). If we add Obama, neither the long- nor short-term effects of leverage (nor much else) is statistically significant, and the adjusted R^2 plummets to 0.04. However, as I have already demonstrated , the EOP size taken as a whole was significantly related to a series of covariates, including the IPL, regardless of whether Obama is included or not.

34. See Cohen (2009a).

CHAPTER SEVEN

1. See Edwards (2003); Bond and Fleisher (1991); Peterson (1990); and Ponder and Moon (2005).

2. Scholars who examine the state of American politics writ large have come to the conclusion that leadership and politics do not always intertwine, and the public is both hungry for leadership and antagonistic to it. See Cronin and Genovese (2013); Huntington (1981); Lowi (1985); and Rockman (1984).

3. Additional issues had to be dealt with. For example, statistical analyses of most of the dependent variables were hindered by multicollinearity in the control variables that measure institutional contagion (the existence of divided government and the ideological distance between the president and the median member of Congress). Therefore, I ran identical models but used different measures of contagion in each. In most instances, results were identical or largely the same.

4. This is consistent with Mayer's (2001) finding that approval is negatively related to the issuance of executive orders.

5. This inverse relationship between the IPL and agenda size was observed in analyses not fully reported here. Rudalevige's (2002) comprehensive list of the number of policy proposals is negatively related to presidential leverage.

6. Prospect theory has become increasingly used in presidency research. It has been used, for example, to generate insights about presidential decision making (McDermott 19998) and campaign strategies (O'Connell 2011).

7. The marks for 2016 extend through the second quarter and should thus be taken as an approximation for that year.

8. At the time of this writing in October 2016, Obama's approval stood at 53 percent in the Gallup Poll.

9. See various data voteview.com.

Works Cited

Adler, E. Scott, and John S. Lapinski, eds. 2006. *The Macropolitics of Congress*. Princeton, NJ: Princeton University Press.

Almond, Gabriel A. 1988. "Return to the State." *American Political Science Review* 82: 853–874.

American Presidency Project. n.d. Retrieved on September 20, 2016, from www.presidency.ucsb.edu.

Anderson, David M. 2010. "The Age of Leverage." *Issues in Governance Studies* Number 37. Washington, DC: Brookings Institution.

Applebaum, Binyamin and Robert Gebeloff. 2012. "Even Critics of a Safety Net Increasingly Depend on It." *New York Times*, February 11. Retrieved on December 6, 2012, from www.nytimes.com/2012/02/12/us/even-critics-of-safety-net-increasingly-depend-on-it.html?pagewanted=all.

Azari, Julia R. 2014. *Delivering the People's Message: The Changing Politics of the Presidential Mandate*. Ithaca, NY: Cornell University Press

Baum, Matthew A., and Samuel Kernell. 1999. "Has Cable Ended the Golden Age of Presidential Television?" *American Political Science Review* 93 (1): 99–114.

Baumgartner, Frank R., and Bryan D. Jones. 2017. Comparative Policy Agendas Project. Retrieved on May 19, 2017 from www.comparativeagendas.net/.

———. 1993. *Agendas and Instability in American Politics*. Chicago: University of Chicago Press.

Beckmann, Matthew W. 2010. *Pushing the Agenda: Presidential Leadership in U.S.Lawmaking, 1953–2004*. New York: Cambridge University Press.

Bentley, Arthur F. 1908. *The Process of Government*. Chicago: University of Chicago Press.

Berry, Christopher R., Barry C. Burden, and William G. Howell. 2010. "The President and the Distribution of Federal Spending." *American Political Science Review* 104: 783–799.

Bond, Jon R., and Richard Fleisher. 1990. *The President in the Legislative Arena*. Chicago: University of Chicago Press.

Box-Steffensmeier, John R. Freeman, Matthew P. Hitt, and Jon C. W. Pevehouse. 2014. *Time Series Analysis for the Social Sciences*. New York, NY: Cambridge University Press.

Brace, Paul, and Barbara Hinckley. 1992. *Follow the Leader: Opinion Polls and the Modern Presidents*. New York: Basic Books.

Burke, John P. 2014. "The Institutional Presidency." In *The Presidency and the Political System*, 10th edition, edited by Michael Nelson, 349–373. Washington, DC: CQ Press.

———. 2000. *The Institutional Presidency: Organizing and Managing the White House from FDR to Clinton*, 2nd edtion. Baltimore, MD: Johns Hopkins University Press.

Cameron, Charles M. 2000. *Veto Bargaining: Presidents and the Politics of Negative Power*. Cambridge, UK: Cambridge University Press.

Canes-Wrone, Brandice. 2006. *Who Leads Whom? Presidents, Policy, and the Public*. Chicago: University of Chicago Press.

Carnoy, Martin. 1984. *The State and Political Theory*. Princeton, NJ: Princeton University Press.

Carson, Jamie L., Michael S. Lynch, and Anthony J. Madonna. 2011. "Coalition Formation in the House and Senate: Examining the Effect of Institutional Change on Major Legislation" *Journal of Politics* 73 (October): 1225–1238.

Carter, Jimmy. 1982. *Keeping Faith: Memoirs of a President*. New York: Bantam.

Chen, Edwin. 2004. "President Eager to Spend New 'Political Capital'" *Los Angeles Times*, November 5. Retrieved on August 21, 2015, from http://articles.latimes.com/2004/nov/05/nation/na-bush5.

Clinton, Bill. 2004. *My Life*. New York: Knopf.

Clinton, Joshua D., and David E. Lewis. 2008. "Expert Opinion, Agency Characteristics, and Agency Preferences." *Political Analysis* 16(1): 316.

CNN. 2009. "Official Inauguration Crowd Estimate: 1.8 Million," Retrieved on April 2, 2015, from http://politicalticker.blogs.cnn.com/2009/01/22/official-inauguration-crowd-estimate-18-million/. Accessed 2 April 2015.

Cohen, Jeffrey E. 2013. "Everybody Loves a Winner: On the Mutual Causality of Presidential Approval and Success in Congress." *Congress and the Presidency* 40(3): 285307.

———. 2012. *The President's Legislative Policy Agenda, 1789–2002*. New York: Cambridge University Press.

———. 2010. *Going Local: Presidential Leadership in the Post-Broadcast Age*. New York: Cambridge University Press.

———. 2009a. "Alternative Futures: Comment on Terry Moe's 'The Revolution in Presidential Studies.'" *Presidential Studies Quarterly* 39 (December): 725–735.

———. 2009b. "The Presidency and the Mass Media." In *The Oxford Handbook of the American Presidency*, edited by George C. Edwards III and William G. Howell. New York: Oxford University Press.

———. 2008. *The Presidency in the Age of 24 Hour News*. Princeton, NJ: Princeton University Press.

———. 1997. *Presidential Responsiveness and Public Policy Making: The Public and the Policies That Presidents Choose*. Ann Arbor: University of Michigan Press.

———. 1995. "Presidential Rhetoric and the Public Agenda." *American Journal of Political Science* 39: 87–107.

Conley, Patricia Heidotting. 2001. *Presidential Mandates: How Elections Shape the National Agenda*. Chicago: University of Chicago Press.

Conley, Richard. 2011. "The Harbinger of the Unitary Executive? An Analysis of Presidential Signing Statements from Truman to Carter" *Presidential Studies Quarterly* 41:546-569.

———. 2003. *The Presidency, Congress, and Divided Government: A Postwar Assessment*. College Station: Texas A&M University Press.

Cooper, Joseph. 2009. "From Congressional to Presidential Preeminence: Power and Politics in Late Nineteenth-Century America and Today." In *Congress Reconsidered*, 8th edition, edited by Lawrence C. Dodd and Bruce I. Oppenheimer. Washington, DC: CQ Press.

Cooper, Joseph, and David Brady. 1981. "Toward a Diachronic Analysis of Congress." *American Political Science Review* 75:988-1012

Cooper, Phillip J. 2002. *By Order of the President: The Use and Abuse of Executive Direct Action*. Lawrence: University Press of Kansas.

Cornwell, Elmer E. Jr. 1965. *Presidential Leadership of Public Opinion*. Bloomington: Indiana University Press.

Cronin, Thomas E. 1973. "The Swelling of the Presidency." *The Saturday Review*, January 20.

Cronin, Thomas E., and Michael A. Genovese. 2013. *The Paradoxes of the American Presidency*, 4th edition. New York: Oxford University Press.

Dahl, Robert A. 2003. *How Democratic Is the American Constitution?* New Haven, CT: Yale University Press.

———. 1961. *Who Governs?* New Haven, CT: Yale University Press.

Davidson, Roger H., Walter J. Oleszek, and Frances E. Lee. 2012.*Congress and Its Members*, 13th edition. Washington, DC: CQ Press.

Davies, James C. 1962. "Toward a Theory of Revolution." *American Sociological Review* 27 (February): 518.

De Boef , Suzanna. 2001. "Modeling Equilibrium Relationships: Error Correction Models with Strongly Autoregressive Data." *Political Analysis* 9: 78–94.

De Boef, Suzanna, and Luke Keele. 2008. "Taking Time Seriously." *American Journal of Political Science* 52: 184–200.

Derthick, Martha, and Paul J. Quirk. 1985. *The Politics of Deregulation*. Washington, DC: Brookings.

Dickinson, Matthew J. 1997. *Bitter Harvest: FDR, Presidential Power and the Growth of the Presidential Branch*. New York: Cambridge University Press..

Dodd, Lawrence C., and Scott Schraufnagel. 2012. "Congress and the Polarity Paradox: Party Polarization, Member Incivility and Enactment of Landmark Legislation, 1891–1994." *Congress and the Presidency* 39(2): 109–132.

Druckman, James N., and Lawrence R. Jacobs. 2009. "Presidential Responsiveness to Public Opinion." In *The Oxford Handbook of the American Presidency*, edited by George C. Edwards III and William G. Howell. Oxford, UK: Oxford University Press.

Easton, David. 1975. "A Re-assessment of the Concept of Political Support." *British Journal of Political Science* 5: 435–457.

———. 1965. *A Systems Analysis of Political Life*. New York: John Wiley and Sons.

Edwards, George C. III. 2009. "Presidential Approval as a Source of Influence in Congress." In *The Oxford Handbook of the American Presidency*, edited by George C. Edwards III and William G. Howell. Oxford, UK: Oxford University Press.

———. 2003. *On Deaf Ears*. New Haven, CT: Yale University Press.

———. 1997. "Aligning Tests with Theory: Presidential Approval as a Source of Influence in Congress." *Congress & the Presidency* 24: 113–130.

———. 1989. *At the Margins*. New Haven, CT: Yale University Press.

———. 1983. *The Public Presidency: The Pursuit of Popular Support*. New York: St. Martin's Press Palgrave.

Edwards, George C. III, and Andrew Barrett. 2000. "Presidential Agenda Setting in Congress." In *Polarized Politics: Congress and the President in a Partisan Era*, edited by Jon R. Bond and Richard Fleisher. Washington, DC: CQ Press.

Eilperin, Juliet. 2014. "Obama Promises to Use a 'Pen and a Phone' to Push His Agenda." *The Washington Post*, January 14.

Eisinger, Richard M. 2003. *The Evolution of Presidential Polling*. New York: Cambridge University Press.

———. 2000. "Gauging Public Opinion in the Hoover White House: Understanding the Roots of Presidential Polling." *Presidential Studies Quarterly* 30 (December): 643–661.

Ellis, Richard J. 2015. *The Development of the American Presidency*, 2nd edition. New York: Routledge.

Ellis, Richard J. 2012. *The Development of the American Presidency*. New York: Routledge.

Erikson, Robert S., Michael MacKuen, and James Stimson. 2002. *The Macro Polity*. New York: Cambridge University Press.

Eshbaugh-Soha, Matthew. 2006. *The President's Speeches: Beyond Going Public*. Boulder, CO: Lynne Rienner Press.

———. 2005. "The Politics of Presidential Agendas." *Political Research Quarterly* 58: 257–268.

Eshbaugh-Soha, Matthew, and Jeffrey S. Peake. "Presidents and the Economic Agenda" *Political Research Quarterly* 58:127-138

Espo, David. 2013. "Congress: Divided, Discourteous _Taking a Break." Associated Press, August 3.

Evans, Peter, Dietrich Rueschemeyer, and Theda Skocpol. 1985. *Bringing the State Back In*. New York: Cambridge University Press.

Fahrenthold , David A., and Katie Zezima. 2016. "For Ted Cruz, the 2013 Shutdown Was a Defining Moment." *Washington Post*, online, February 16. Retrieved on October 12, 2016, from www.washingtonpost.com/politics/how-cruzs-plan-to-defund -obamacare-failed--and-what-it-achieved/2016/02/16/4e2ce116-c6cb-11e5-8965 -0607e0e265ce_story.html.

Fett, Patrick J. 1994. "Presidential Legislative Priorities and Legislators Voting Decisions: An Exploratory Analysis." *Journal of Politics* 56 (May): 502–512.

Fine, Jeffrey A., and Adam L. Warber. June 2012. "Circumventing Adversity: Executive Orders and Divided Government." *Presidential Studies Quarterly* 42(2): 256–274.

Fisher, Louis. 2007. "Invoking Inherent Powers: A Primer" *Presidential Studies Quarterly* 37: 1–22.

Ford, Gerald R. 1979. *A Time to Heal*. New York: Harper and Row.

Fox, Lauren. 2013. "Do-Nothing Congress Was Way More Productive Than the Current One." *U.S. News and World Report*, December 1. Retrieved on May 19, 2017, from www.usnews .com/news/articles/2013/12/01/do-nothing-congress-was-way-more-productive-than -the-current-one.

Gallup Poll. 2017. "Presidential Job Approval." Retrieved on May 15, 2017, from www .gallup.com/topic/presidential_job_approval.aspx.

Galvin, Daniel J. 2010. *Presidential Party Building: Dwight D. Eisenhower to George W. Bush*. Princeton, NJ: Princeton University Press.

Gass, Nick. 2016. "Americans Split on Obama's Performance ahead of State of the Union." *Politico*. Retrieved on May 18, 2016, from www.politico.com/story/2016/01 /state-of-the-union-2016-poll-obama-performance-217610.

Genovese, Michael A. 2001. *The Power of the American Presidency, 1789–2000*. New York: Oxford University Press.

———. 1995. *The Presidential Dilemma: Leadership in the American System*. New York: Harper Collins.

Gilmour, John B. 1995. *Strategic Disagreement: Stalemate in American Politics*. Pittsburgh, PA: University of Pittsburgh Press.

Greenstein, Fred I. 1966. "The Psychological Functions of the Presidency for Citizens," in Elmer Cornwell Jr., ed., *The American Presidency: Vital Center*. Glenview, IL: Scott, Foresman,

Groeling, Tim. 2010. *When Politicians Attack: Party Cohesion in the Media*. New York: Cambridge University Press.

Gronke, Paul and Brian Newman. 2009. "Public Evaluations of Presidents." In *The Oxford Handbook of the American Presidency*, edited by George C. Edwards and William G. Howell. New York: Oxford University Press.

Grossback, Lawrence, David A. M. Peterson, and James Stimson. 2006. *Mandate Politics*. New York: Cambridge University Press.

Haldeman, H. R. 1994. *The Haldeman Diaries: Inside the Nixon White House*. New York: Putnam.

Hamilton, Alexander, James Madison, and John Jay. [1788] 1961. *The Federalist Papers*. New York: New American Library.

Han, Lori Cox, and Diane Heith. 2013. *Presidents and the American Presidency*. New York: Oxford University Press, 2013.

Hargrove, Erwin C. 1993. "Presidential Personality and Leadership Style," in George C. Edwards III, John H. Kessel, and Bert A. Rockman, eds., *Researching the Presidency: Vital Questions, New Approaches*. Pittsburgh, PA: University of Pittsburgh Press.

———. 1988. *Jimmy Carter as President: Leadership and the Politics of the Public Good*. Baton Rouge: Louisiana State University Press.

———. 1974. *The Power of the Modern Presidency*. New York: Knopf.

Hargrove, Erwin C., and Michael Nelson. 1984. *Presidents, Politics, and Policy*. New York: Knopf.

Harris, John F. 2005. *The Survivor: Bill Clinton in the White House*. New York: Random House.

Hart, John. 1995. *The Presidential Branch: From Washington to Clinton*, 2nd edition. Chatham, NJ: Chatham House.

Heith, Diane J. 2012. "Obama and the Public Presidency: What Got You Here Won't Get You There." In Bert A. Rockman, Andrew Rudalevige, and Colin Campbell, eds., *The Obama Presidency: Appraisals and Prospects*. Washington, DC: Sage/CQ Press.

———. 2004. *Polling to Govern: Public Opinion and Presidential Leadership*. Stanford, CA: Stanford University Press.

———. 2000. "Presidential Polling and the Potential for Leadership." In *Presidential Power: Forging the Presidency for the Twenty-First Century*, edited by Robert Y. Shapiro, Martha Joynt Kumar, and Lawrence R. Jacobs. New York: Columbia University Press, 380–407.

Hetherington, Marc J. 2005. *Why Trust Matters: Declining Political Trust and the Demise of American Liberalism*. Princeton, NJ: Princeton University Press.

Hetherington, Marc J., and Suzanne Globetti. 2005. "The Presidency and Political Trust." In *The Presidency and the Political System*, 8th Edition, edited by Michael Nelson. Washington, DC: CQ Press.

Hetherington, Marc J., and Jason Husser. 2012. "How Trust Matters: The Changing Political Relevance of Political Trust." *American Journal of Political Science* 56 (April): 312–325.

Hetherington, Marc J., and Thomas J. Rudolph. 2015. *Why Washington Won't Work: Polarization, Political Trust, and the Governing Crisis*. Chicago: University of Chicago Press.

Hibbing, John R., and Elizabeth Theiss-Morse. 1995. *Congress as Public Enemy: Public Attitudes toward American Political Institutions*. Cambridge, UK: Cambridge University Press.

Hoffman, Donna R., and Alison D. Howard. 2006. *Addressing the State of the Union: The Evolution and Impact of the President's Big Speech*. Boulder, CO: Lynne Rienner.

Howell, William G. 2013. *Thinking about the Presidency: The Primacy of Power*. Princeton, NJ: Princeton University Press.

———. 2003. *Power without Persuasion: The Politics of Direct Presidential Action*. Princeton, NJ: Princeton University Press.

Huber, John D., and Charles R. Shipan. 2002. *Deliberate Discretion? The Institutional Foundations of Bureaucratic Autonomy*. New York: Cambridge University Press.

Hudak, John. 2014. *Presidential Pork: White House Influence over the Distribution of Federal Funds*. Washington, DC: Brookings.

Hult, Karen M. 2000. "Strengthening Presidential Decision Making Capacity." *Presidential Studies Quarterly* 30: 27–46.

Hult, Karen M., and Charles E. Walcott. 2004. *Empowering the White House: Governance under Nixon, Ford, and Carter*. Lawrence: University of Kansas Press.

Huntington, Samuel. 1981. *American Politics: The Promise of Disharmony*. Cambridge, MA: Harvard University Press.

Jacobs, Lawrence R., and Robert Y. Shapiro. 2000. *Politicians Don't Pander: Political Manipulation and the Loss of Democratic Responsiveness*. Chicago: University of Chicago Press.

Jacobson, Gary. 2008. *A Divider, Not a Uniter: George W. Bush and the American People*. New York: Longman.

James, Scott C. 2009. "Historical Institutionalism, Political Development, and the Presidency." In *The Oxford Handbook of the American Presidency*, edited by George C. Edwards III and William G. Howell. New York: Oxford University Press.

James, Scott C. 2000. *Presidents, Parties, and the State: A Party System Perspective on Democratic Regulatory Choice, 1884–1936*. New York: Cambridge University Press.

Johnson, Kimberley S. 2007. *Governing the American State: Congress and the New Federalism, 1877–1929*. Princeton, NJ: Princeton University Press.

Jones, Charles O. 2000. "Reinventing Leeway: The President and Agenda Certification." *Presidential Studies Quarterly* 30: 6–26.

———. 1994. *The Presidency in a Separated System*. Washington, DC: Brookings.

Kahneman, Daniel, and Amos Tversky. 1984. "Choices, Values, and Frames." *American Psychologist* 39: 341–350.

———. 1979. "Prospect Theory: An Analysis of Decision under Risk" *Econometrica* 47: 263–291.

Kamarck, Elaine C. 2009. "The Evolving American State: The Trust Challenge." *The Forum* 7(4): Article 9.

Keele, Luke. 2007. "Social Capital and the Dynamics of Trust in Government." *American Journal of Political Science* 51(2): 241–255.

———. 2003. *In Whom Do We Trust? The Rational Nature of Trust in Government*. PhD dissertation, University of North Carolina, Chapel Hill.

Keele, Luke, and Randolph Stevenson. 2014. "The Perils of the All Cause Model." Typescript.

Kelley, Christopher S., and Bryan Marshall. 2010. "Going It Alone: The Politics of Signing Statements from Reagan to Bush II." *Social Science Quarterly* 91: 168–187.

Kelly, Nathan, and Christopher Witko. 2012. "Federalism and American Inequality." *Journal of Politics* 74: 414–426.

Kernell, Samuel. 2007. *Going Public: New Strategies of Presidential Leadership*, 4th edition. Washington, DC: CQ Press.

———. 1989. "The Evolution of the White House Staff." In *Can the Government Govern?*, edited by John E. Chubb and Paul E. Peterson. Washington, DC: Brookings.

Kernell, Samuel, and Mathew Baum. 1999. "Has Cable Ended the Golden Age of Presidential Television?" *American Political Science Review.* 93: 99–114.

Kimball, David C., and Samuel C. Patterson. 1997. "Living Up to Expectations: Public Attitudes toward Congress." *Journal of Politics* 59: 701–728.

Kingdon, John W. 1984. *Agendas, Alternatives, and Public Policies.* Boston: Little, Brown.

Knight, Jack, and Aaron Wildavsky. 1977. "Jimmy Carter's Theory of Governing." *The Wilson Quarterly* 1: 49–67.

Koenig, Louis W. 1996. *The Chief Executive*, 6th edition. New York: Harcourt Brace.

Krehbiel, Keith. 1998. *Pivotal Politics: A Theory of U.S. Lawmaking.* Chicago: University of Chicago Press.

———. 1991. *Information and Legislative Organization.* Ann Arbor: University of Michigan Press.

Kriner, Douglas L., and Andrew Reeves. 2015. *The Particularistic President: Executive Branch Politics and Political Inequality.* New York: Cambridge University Press.

Kumar, Martha, and Terry Sullivan, eds. 2003. *The White House World: Transitions, Organization, and Office Operations.* College Station: Texas A&M University Press.

Landy, Marc, and Sidney M. Milkis. 2014. "The Presidency in History: Leading from the Eye of the Storm." In *The Presidency and the Political System*, 10th edition, edited by Michael Nelson. Washington, DC: CQ Press.

Larecy, Mel. 2002. *Presidents and the People: The Partisan Story of Going Public.* College Station: Texas A&M University Press.

Larocca, Roger T. 2006. *The Presidential Agenda: Sources of Executive Influence in Congress.* Columbus: Ohio State University Press.

Lee, Carol E., and Glenn Thrush. 2010. "Barack Obama Vows to Work with GOP after 'Shellacking.'" *Politico* November 4, 2010 (updated). Retrieved on March 18, 2015, from www.politico.com/news/stories/1110/44657.html.

Lee, Frances E. 2009. *Beyond Ideology: Politics, Principles, and Partisanship in the U.S. Senate.* Chicago: University of Chicago Press.

Lewis, David E. 2008. *The Politics of Presidential Appointments.* Princeton, NJ: Princeton University Press.

Lewis, David E., and Terry M. Moe. 2010. "Struggling over Bureaucracy: The Levers of Control." In *The Presidency and the Political System*, 9th ed., edited by Michael Nelson. Washington, DC: CQ Press.

Lewis, Jeffrey, Keith Poole, and Howard Rosenthal. 2017. Voteview.com. University of California at Los Angeles. Retrieved on May 15, 2017, from https://voteview.polisci.ucla.edu/data.

Light, Paul C. 1999. *The President's Agenda: Domestic Policy Choice from Kennedy to Clinton.* Revised 3rd edition. Baltimore, MD: Johns Hopkins University Press.

Lim, Elvin. T. 2014. "The Presidency and the Media: Two Faces of Democracy." In *The Presidency and the Political System*, 10th edition, edited by Michael Nelson. Washington, DC: CQ Press.

Lowi, Theodore J. 1992. "The State in Political Science: How We Become What We Study." *American Political Science Review* 86 (March): 1–7.

———. 1985. *The Personal President: Power Invested, Promise Unfulfilled.* Ithaca, NY: Cornell University Press.

———. 1979. *The End of Liberalism.* New York: W. W. Norton.

Mann, Thomas, and Norman J. Ornstein. 2012. *It's Even Worse Than it Looks.* New York: Basic Books.

March, James G., and Johan P. Olsen. 1989. *Rediscovering Institutions: The Organizational Basis of Politics.* New York: Free Press.

March, James G., and Johan P. Olsen. 1984. "The New Institutionalism: Organizational Factors in Political Life." *American Political Science Review* 78: 734–749.

Marchant-Shapiro, Theresa. 2015. *Statistics for Political Analysis.* Los Angeles, CA: Sage/CQ Press.

Mayer, Kenneth. 2009. "Going Alone: The Presidential Power of Unilateral Action." In *The Oxford Handbook of the American Presidency*, edited by George C. Edwards and William G. Howell. New York: Oxford University Press.

———. 2001. *With the Stroke of a Pen: Executive Orders and Presidential Power.* Princeton, NJ: Princeton University Press.

Mayhew, David R. "Data Sets and Materials." Retrieved on May 15, 2017, from http://campuspress.yale.edu/davidmayhew/datasets- divided-we-govern/.

———. 1991. *Divided We Govern: Party Control, Lawmaking, and Investigations 1946–1990.* New Haven, CT: Yale University Press.

McCarty, Nolan, Keith Poole, and Howard Rosenthal. 2006. *Polarized America: The Dance of Ideology and Unequal Riches.* Cambridge, MA: MIT Press.

McDermott, Rose. 1998. *Risk-Taking in International Politics: Prospect Theory in American Foreign Policy.* Ann Arbor: University of Michigan Press.

Mettler, Suzanne. 2011. *The Submerged State: How Invisible Government Policies Undermine American Democracy.* Chicago, IL: University of Chicago Press.

Microsoft Encarta Dictionary. 2002. New York: St. Martin's Press.

Milkis, Sidney M. and Michael Nelson. 2016. *The American Presidency: Origins and Development*, 7th edition. Washington, DC: CQ Press.

Miller, Abraham H., Louis H. Bolce, and Mark Halligan. 1977. "The J-Curve Theory and the Black Urban Riots: An Empirical Test of Progressive Relative Deprivation Theory." *American Political Science Review* 71 (September): 964–982.

Mitchell, Timothy. 1991. "The Limits of the State: Beyond Statist Approaches and Their Critics." *American Political Science Review* 85 (March): 77–96.

Moe, Terry M. 1989. "The Politics of Bureaucratic Structure. " In *Can the Government Govern?* edited by John E. Chubb and Paul E. Peterson. Washington, DC: Brookings.

———. 1985. "The Politicized Presidency." In *The New Direction in American Politics*, edited by John E. Chubb and Paul E. Peterson. Washington, DC: Brookings.

Mueller, John. 1973. *War, Presidents, and Public Opinion.* New York: John Wiley.

———. 1970. "Presidential Popularity from Truman to Johnson." *American Political Science Review* 64: 18–34.

Nathan, Richard P. 1983. *The Administrative Presidency.* New York: John Wiley.

National Park Service, 2015. "Civil Rights Act of 1963." Retrieved on September 29, 2015, from www.nps.gov/subjects/civilrights/equal-pay-act-1963.htm.

Neustadt, Richard E. 1960. *Presidential Power: The Politics of Leadership*. New York: John Wiley & Sons.

Nixon, Richard M. 1978. *RN: The Memoirs of Richard Nixon*. New York: Simon and Schuster.

Nordlinger, Eric A. 1981. *On the Autonomy of the Democratic State*. Cambridge, MA: Harvard University Press.

Nordlinger, Eric A., Theodore J. Lowi, and Sergio Fabbrini. 1988. "The Return to the State: Critiques. *American Political Science Review*. 82: 875–901.

Norpoth, Helmut. 2001. "Divided Government and Economic Voting." *Journal of Politics* 63 (May): 414–435.

North, Douglass C. 1981. *Structure and Change in Economic History*. New York: W. W. Norton.

Nye, Joseph S. Jr., Philip D. Zelikow, and David C. King, eds. 1997. *Why People Don't Trust Government*. Cambridge, MA: Harvard University Press.

Obama, Barack. 2011. "Address by the President to the Nation." July 25. Available at www.Whitehouse.gov.

O'Connell, David. 2011. "Situational Gamblers: Prospect Theory and the Commonalities of Presidential Campaign Management." *Presidential Studies Quarterly* 41 (March): 64–92.

Ornstein, Norman J., Thomas E. Mann, and Michael Malbin. 2010. *Vital Statistics on Congress*. Washington, DC: CQ Press.

Orren, Karen and Stephen Skowronek. 2004. *The Search for American Political Development*. New York: Cambridge University Press.

Ostrom, Charles W. Jr., and Dennis M. Simon. 1985. "Promise and Performance: A Dynamic Model of Presidential Popularity." *American Political Science Review* 79: 334–358.

Patterson, Bradley. 2000. *The White House Staff: Inside the West Wing and Beyond*. Washington, DC: Brookings.

Peake, Jeffrey S. 2001. "Presidential Agenda Setting in Foreign Policy." *Political Research Quarterly* 54: 69–86.

Peters, Gerhard, and John T. Wooley. 2017. The American Presidency Project. Retrieved on May 15, 2017, from www.presidency.ucsb.edu.

Peterson, Mark A. 1990. *Legislating Together: The White House and Capitol Hill from Eisenhower to Reagan*. Cambridge, MA: Harvard University Press.

Pew Research Center. 2002. "Unusually High Interest in Bush's State of the Union." Retrieved on May 18, 2016, from www.people-press.org/2002/01/17/unusually-high-interest-in-bushs-state-of-the-union/.

Pfiffner, James P., and Roger H. Davidson. 2003. *Understanding the Presidency*, 3rd edition. New York: Longman.

Pollock, Philip H. III. 2012. *The Essentials of Political Analysis*, 4th edition. Los Angeles, CA: Sage/CQ Press.

Polsby, Nelson W. 1980. *Community Power and Political Theory*. New Haven, CT: Yale University Press.

———. 1978. "Coalition and Faction in American Politics: An Institutional View." In *Emerging Coalitions in American Politics*, edited by Seymour M. Lipset. San Francisco, CA: Institute for Contemporary Studies.

Ponder, Daniel E. 2012. "Presidential Leverage and the Politics of Policy Formulation." *Presidential Studies Quarterly* 42 (June): 300–323.

———. 2005a. "Presidential Leadership in a Fractured State: Capacity, Autonomy, and the American State." *International Journal of Public Administration* 28: 531–546.

———. 2005b. "Presidential Leverage and the Presidential Agenda, 1967–1994." In *In the Public Domain: Presidents and the Challenges of Public Leadership*, edited by Lori Cox Han and Diane J. Heith. Albany: State University of New York Press.

———. 2000. *Good Advice: Information and Policy Making n the White House*. College Station: Texas A&M University Press.

Ponder, Daniel E., and C. David Moon. 2005. "A Tale of Three Variables: Exploring Alternative Measures of Presidential Approval on Congressional Voting." *Congress and the Presidency* 32 (Autumn): 157–169.

Poole, Keith, and Howard Rosenthal. 1997. *Congress: A Political-Economic History of Roll Call Voting*. New York: Oxford University Press.

President's Committee on Administrative Management. 1937. *Report with Special Studies: Administrative Management in the Government of the United States*. Washington, DC: Government Printing Office.

Quirk, Paul J. 2009. "Politicians Do Pander: Mass Opinion, Polarization, and Law Making." *The Forum* 7(4): Article 10.

Ragsdale, Lynn. 2014. *Vital Statistics on the American Presidency*, 4th edition. Washington, DC: CQ/Sage.

Roberts, Joel. 2007. "Poll: Bush Approval Rating at New Low" CBS News. Available at www.cbsnews.com/news/poll-bush-approval-rating-at-new-low/.

Rockman, Bert A. 1984. *The Leadership Question: The Presidency and the American System*. New York: Praeger.

Roper Center for Public Opinion. n.d. Retrieved on May 17, 2017, from http://ropercenter.cornell.edu/.

Rose, Richard. 1991. *The Postmodern President*. 2nd edition. Chatham, NJ: Chatham House.

Rossiter, Clinton. 1960. *The American Presidency*. New York: Harcourt Brace.

Rottinghaus, Brandon. 2010. *The Provisional Pulpit: Modern Presidential Leadership of Public Opinion*. College Station: Texas A&M University Press.

Rottinghaus, Brandon, and Michelle Belco. 2017. *The Dual Executive: Presidential Unilateral Power in a Separated and Shared Power System*. Stanford, CA: Stanford University Press.

RT. 2015. "Obama Approval Ratings See Boost before 2015 State of the Union Address." Retrieved on May 18, 2016, from www.rt.com/usa/224143-obama-approval-rating-sotu/.

Rudalevige, Andrew. 2014a. "Five Points to Ponder on the Immigration Directives." *Washington Post*, November 25. Retrieved on June 15, 2015, from www.washingtonpost.com/blogs/monkey-cage/wp/2014/11/25/five-points-to-ponder-on-the-immigration-directives/.

———. 2014b. "The Presidency and Unilateral Power: A Taxonomy." In *The Presidency and the Political System*. 9th edition edited by Michael Nelson. Washington, DC: CQ Press.

———. 2012. "Rivals, or a Team? Staffing and Issue Management in the Obama Administration." In *The Obama Presidency: Appraisals and Prospects*, edited by Bert A. Rockman, Andrew Rudalevige, and Colin Campbell. Washington, DC: Sage/CQ Press.

———. 2005. *The New Imperial Presidency*. Ann Arbor: University of Michigan Press.

———. 2002. *Managing the President's Program*. Princeton, NJ: Princeton University Press.

———. 2000. "Managing the President's Program: Centralization and Legislative Policy Formulation, 1949–96." PhD dissertation, Harvard University.

Rudalevige, Andrew, and David E. Lewis. 2005. "Parsing the Politicized Presidency: Centralization, Politicization, and Presidential Strategies for Bureaucratic Control." Paper presented at Annual Meeting of the American Political Science Association, Washington, DC.

Schattschneider, E. E. 1942. *Party Government.* New York: Farrar and Rinehart.

Schlesinger, Arthur M. Jr. 2007. *Journals: 1952–2000.* New York: Penguin.

———. 1974. *The Imperial Presidency.* Boston: Houghton Mifflin.

Schlesinger, Arthur M. Jr. 1973. *The Imperial Presidency.* New York: Knopf.

Simon, Dennis M. 2009. "Public Expectations of the President." In *The Oxford Handbook of the American Presidency,* edited by George C. Edwards and William G. Howell. New York: Oxford University Press.

Simon, Herbert. 1947. *Administrative Behavior.* New York: Macmillan.

Skowronek, Stephen. 1993. *The Politics Presidents Make: Leadership from John Adams to George Bush.* Cambridge, MA: Harvard University Press.

———. 1982. *Building a New American State: The Expansion of National Administrative Capacities, 1877–1920.* New York: Cambridge University Press.

Sorenson, Theodore. 1965. *Kennedy.* New York: HarperCollins.

Stimson, James A. n.d. "James Stimson's Site." Retrieved in 2015 from http://stimson .web.unc.edu/software.

———. 2004. *Tides of Consent: How Public Opinion Shapes American Politics.* New York: Cambridge University Press.

———. 1991. *Public Opinion in America: Moods, Cycles, and Swings.* Boulder, CO: Westview Press.

Stimson, James A., Michael B. MacKuen, and Robert S. Erikson. 1995. "Dynamic Representation." *American Political Science Review* 89: 543–565.

Sullivan, Andy. 2011. "Public Strongly Opposes Debt Ceiling Increase" Reuters/ Ipsos, January 12. Retrieved on May 15, 2017, from www.reuters.com/article /us-usa-poll-spending-idUSTRE70B38620110112.

Sullivan, Terry. 1990. "Bargaining with the President: A Simple Game and New Evidence." *American Political Science Review,* 84: 1167–1196.

Sundquist, James. 1981. *The Decline and Resurgence of Congress.* Washington, DC: Brookings.

Taylor, Andrew. 2016. "McConnell: Obama Was Too Slow to Warn about 'Potential Consequences' of 9/11 Victims Bill." *Associated Press,* September 29.

Tedin, Kent, Brandon Rottinghaus, and Harrell Rodgers. 2011. "When the President Goes Public: The Consequences of Communication Mode for Opinion Change across Issue Types and Groups." *Political Research Quarterly* 64 (3): 506–519.

Truman, David B. 1951. *The Governmental Process. Political Interests and Public Opinion.* New York: Knopf.

Villalobos, José D. 2013. "Agency Input as a Policy Making Tool: Analyzing the Influence of Agency Input on Presidential Policy Success in Congress." *Administration & Society* 45(7): 837–874.

———. 2008. "Presidential-Bureaucratic Management and Policy Making Success in Congress." PhD dissertation, Texas A&M University.

Villalobos, Jose, and Justin Vaughn. 2009. "Presidential Staffing and Public Opinion: How Public Opinion Influences Politicization." *Administration & Society* 41 (July): 449–469.

Walcott, Charles, and Karen M. Hult. 1995. *Governing the White House: From Hoover through LBJ*. Lawrence: University Press of Kansas.

Warber, Adam L. 2006. *Executive Orders in the Modern Presidency: Legislating from the Oval Office*. Boulder, CO: Lynne Rienner Press.

Warshaw, Shirley A. 2013. *Guide to the White House Staff*. Los Angeles, CA: Sage Reference, CQ Press.

Warshaw, Shirley A., with Jacqueline Beckwith, Rachel Haskins, and William Essigs. 2015. "The Struggle to Govern in the Obama White House: How Internal Clashes Led to Dysfunction." Paper presented at the annual meeting of the American Political Science Association, San Francisco.

Waterman, Richard W., 1989. *Presidential Influence and the Administrative State*. Knoxville: University of Tennessee Press.

Waterman, Richard W., Carol L. Silva, and Hank Jenkins-Smith. 2014. *The Presidential Expectations Gap: Public Attitudes Concerning the Presidency*. Ann Arbor: University of Michigan Press.

Weatherford, M. Stephen. 1984. "Economic 'Stagflation' and Public Support for the Political System." *British Journal of Political Science* 14: 187–205.

Weber, Max, Hans Gerth, and C. Wright Mills. 1958. *From Max Weber: Essays in Sociology*. New York: Oxford University Press.

Webster's New World Dictionary. 1982. New York: Simon and Schuster.

Weko, Thomas. 1995. *The Politicizing Presidency*. Lawrence: University Press of Kansas.

Weyland, Kurt. 2002. *The Politics of Market Reform in Fragile Democracies*. Princeton, NJ: Princeton University Press.

Whittington, Keith. 2009. "Constitutional Constraints in Politics." In *The Supreme Court and the Idea of Constitutionalism*, edited by Steven Kautz. Philadelphia: University of Pennsylvania Press.

Wood, B. Dan. 2009. *The Myth of Presidential Representation*. Princeton, NJ: Princeton University Press.

Wood, B. Dan, and Jeffrey S. Peake. 1998. "The Dynamics of Foreign Policy Agenda Setting." *American Political Science Review* 92: 173–184.

Wood, B. Dan, and Clayton Webb. 2011. "Explaining Presidential Saber Rattling." Paper presented to the faculty at Vanderbilt University.

Zaller, John. 1998. "Monica Lewinsky's Contribution to Political Science." *PS: Political Science and Politics* 31: 182–189.

Zarefsky, David. 1994. "'Public Sentiment Is Everything: Lincoln's View of Political Persuasion." *Journal of the Abraham Lincoln Association* 15 (Summer): 23–40. Retrieved on January 17, 2014, from http://quod.lib.umich.edu/j/jala/2629860.0015.204/--public-sentiment-is-everything-lincolns-view-of-political?rgn=main;view=fulltext#note_6.

Index

Note: Page numbers followed by *f*, *n*, or *t* refer to figures, endnotes, and tables, respectively.

measurement of, 31; presidential leverage as measure of, 15; unilateral actions of, 19–20

Taft, William Howard, 45

Tea Party, 87, 88, 107, 163, 191*n*28, 191*n*31

Trump, Donald, 164, 166

Trust in government: in Bush 41 administration, 57, 78, 79*f*; in Bush 43 administration, 57, 74, 82, 83*f*, 84, 87, 119; in Carter administration, 57, 74, 75*f*; chronological measure of, 56*f*; in Clinton administration, 4, 74, 80–82, 81*f*; defining, 54, 192*n*7; diffuse support equivalent to, 28–29; economy as factor in, 16, 29, 66; factors in, 16; in Ford administration, 72*f*, 73; in Johnson administration, 66–68, 67*f*, 153; in Kennedy administration, 57, 65*f*, 66, 153; lack of, as obstacle to governance, 191*n*21; low points in, 28, 87, 163; media linked to declining, 11; in Nixon administration, 57, 69, 70*f*, 71, 153; in Obama administration, 1, 57, 74, 86–88, 86*f*, 161, 162*f*, 163*t*, 164; persistence of low, 45, 57, 166; post-Watergate, 58–59, 59*t*; presidential approval in relation to, 1–2, 5–7, 12–16, 25–32, 52, 56, 87, 89–90, 149–50, 193*n*10; pre-Watergate, 58–59, 59*t*; public ignorance of government role as factor in, 45–46; public policy affected by, 189*n*14; in Reagan administration, 57, 77*f*. *See also* Index of presidential leverage

Unilateral actions and authority: occasions for using, 9, 49–50; presidential leverage and, 108–13, 154–55; prevalence of, 108; research recommendations regarding, 160; of strong vs. weak presidents, 19–20, 38, 108–9, 113, 155

Unitary executive theory, 45

United States. *See* State

U.S. Congress: approval ratings of, 160–61; ideological compatibility of presidents with, 98–99, 103, 106–7, 111, 117; inversion of governmental dominance by, 8–10, 18–19, 25–26, 33, 41–43, 151; leverage wielded by, 27; presidents' relations with, 39–40, 47–48, 137

U.S. Constitution: on administration of government, 122–23; inversion of institutional power delineated in, 8, 18–19, 25–26, 33, 41–43, 151; presidential powers deriving from, 3, 5, 149, 151; as source of presidential leverage, 8–10

U.S. Department of Education, 157, 199*n*10

U.S. Supreme Court: and *Bush v. Gore*, 82; and governmental structure, 40; and presidential power, 8, 10; public policy role of, 92

U.S. Trade Representative, 138

Van Buren, Martin, 78

Veto power, 3–4, 8–9, 71, 165

Vietnam War, 10–11, 22, 28, 45, 56, 67–68, 71, 118, 153

War, presidential actions affected by, 100–101, 111, 118

War Powers Resolution, 74

Warrants, 95, 128

Warrants, for political power, 16–17, 95, 128, 188*n*15

Washington, George, 187*n*6

Watergate scandal, 11, 22, 28, 45, 56–57, 69–71, 153

Wave elections, 80, 84

WCALC algorithm, 53–54

Weak presidents: agenda setting by, 115–16, 159–60; centralization of policy making by, 20; IPL scores as indication of, 62; measurement of, 30–31; presidential leverage as